Willard W. Cochrane has been direct agricultural economics in the United Department of Agriculture and economic advisor to the Secretary of Agriculture (1961-1964). During the 1960 presidential campaign, he was agricultural advisor to John F. Kennedy. In 1964 he returned to teaching as professor of agricultural economics, and is now Dean, Office of International Programs, University of Minnesota. Professor Cochrane is the Author of **Farm Prices— Myth and Reality** and co-author of **Economics of American Agriculture,** 2nd edition, and **Economics of Consumption.**

University of
Minnesota Press

The City Man's Guide
to the Farm Problem
Willard W. Cochrane

McGraw-Hill Book Company
New York Toronto London Sydney

To my sons
PETE, STEVE, JAMIE, *and* TIM
*who come from a long line of farmers but
are destined to be city men*

Preface

THIS book is for the interested layman who wants to make sense out of the farm problem. It is directed toward the city man for a number of reasons. He has the political power and the budget incentive to resolve the farm problem in some way, but he typically doesn't know modern agriculture, doesn't understand the basic problems of modern farming, and cannot understand why farmers need special consideration or help from the government. This book is therefore aimed at the city man, who can and probably will take corrective action with respect to the farm problem some day in the not too distant future, but whose knowledge and understanding of the problems and issues are woefully weak.

In a sense a thesis runs through this book. Simply stated it is this: Farmers stand hopelessly divided and badly confused before their problem; their political power is dissipated and their understanding is muddied. The city man too is confused, but he does have the political power, and one of these days he is going to use it. The purpose of this book is to give the city man a basis for understanding farm policy issues before he and his representatives in Congress start throwing their weight around.

This is not a book *for* farmers or *against* farmers. It is a book *about* farmers and their very difficult problems in the complex of modern agriculture. The book is directed toward the city man, but I hope it will help some farmers ponder their problems more realistically than they have in the past. Although farmers are closer to the farm problem than the city man, the average farmer's understanding of the economic fix he is in is no better and possibly worse than the city man's. It is possibly worse, because the farmer has great difficulty untangling his hopes and dreams from the hard economics of the situation in which he finds himself.

Since the purpose of this book is to provide a basis of understanding, we cannot turn immediately to the fun of farm politics or the excitement of policy solutions. To understand the farm problem and the policy issues involved we must first understand the organization of the total agricultural complex, the structure of the farm plant, the behavior of farmers, and even the behavior of consumers toward food and fiber products. For the problems and difficult policy issues in farming do not stem from misdeeds and evil men, they stem from the organization of agriculture, the unique structure of farming, and the behavior patterns of farmers and consumers. Before one can talk sense about farm policy issues, one must understand the nature of modern agriculture and its farming component.

Much of this book will therefore be concerned with describing and analyzing the farm economy. This could be a dull business, but it need not be, because modern agriculture is an exciting place, and it is the responsibility of the author to see that the discussion of it is also exciting. This book is therefore nontechnical, making little use of the paraphernalia of the economist. This does not mean that the coverage is superficial; on the contrary, I have attempted to write a profound book dealing with the farm problem — but a book written in nontechnical lingo.

For the reader looking for a more technical treatment of farm policy, or something more in the nature of a textbook, two new books merit consideration: *Government and Agriculture* by Professor Dale E. Hathaway and *American Farm Policy* by Professor Don Paarlberg. My earlier book *Farm Prices: Myth and Reality* might also be mentioned in this connection.

The analytical story set down in this book obviously is influenced by and in a sense grows out of my experience as Economic Adviser to the Secretary of Agriculture in the Kennedy administration. But this is not a book that tells all about the Department of Agriculture during the Kennedy administration, nor is it a personal history of my experiences. It is a discussion and analysis of the farm problem in terms of the facts of the situation, the economics of the situation, and the politics of the situation.

One final point: I, like all before me, have been plagued by constant revisions in agricultural data and statistics out of the United States Department of Agriculture. In this connection, Oskar Morgenstern tells the following story about Geoffrey Moore, an early agricultural economist:

Geoffrey Moore, in his excellent article on the "Accuracy of Government Statistics," has used the study of revisions of agricultural statistics in his analysis of errors. He cites an example of a case in agricultural production in which a preliminary estimate of the potato crop was radically changed by revisions. He exhibits Department of Agriculture estimates for the census years 1919 and 1924. In 1919 the preliminary estimate for that year's crop was 358 million bushels. In 1920 this was revised to about 356 million, and in 1921, after the census figures were published, the potato crop was stated to be 323 million bushels. The Census figure was 290 million bushels, and subsequently the 1919 crop was estimated by Agriculture to be about 298 million bushels. The 1924 crop estimates underwent similar changes; Agriculture stated the crop to be over 450 million bushels, Census then published a figure close to 350 million bushels, and subsequently Agriculture revised its estimate for 1924 to about 380 million bushels.[1]

In the use of data, I have tried in all cases to use the latest and most firm estimates of the USDA. And, although in many cases the figures in the volume will be revised before it reaches final publication, I believe that most of the figures are *representative* of the true situation. But where the figures undergo significant change, critics please remember the experience of Geoffrey Moore.

[1] *On the Accuracy of Economic Observations,* 2nd ed., Princeton University Press, 1963, p. 208.

Acknowledgments

TO SORT OUT all the different ideas and strands of thought that have found their way into this book, and acknowledge the person or persons that first presented the idea or developed the thought would be an impossible task. This book attempts a synthesis of farm economics and farm policy for the informed layman, and to the extent that it is successful, the ideas and works of many men are fused into a harmonious whole. All of my teachers and all of my colleagues over the past thirty years contributed to the writing of this book. Where, however, the text relies directly on the work of one man or group that fact is noted in the text or in a footnote.

Many of my former colleagues in the United States Department of Agriculture did, however, assist in the preparation of this volume by providing data and estimates and by reviewing and criticizing the manuscript. Those to whom thanks are due for helping directly include John A. Schnittker, Nathan M. Koffsky, M. L. Upchurch, K. E. Ogren, Lee M. Day, John H. Southern, Patrick E. O'Donnell, Robert L. Tontz, the late Robert H. Masucci, the late John M. Brewster, C. Kyle Randall, William H. Waldorf, Geraldine Cummins, and Isla B. Marsden.

Special thanks are due my wife, Mary, who read the entire manuscript and helped make it a bit more readable, and to Mrs. Kay Perry who typed the many versions of the manuscript.

All charts used in the text are based upon drawings obtained from the United States Department of Agriculture. The charts and photographs obtained from the United States Department of Agriculture and photographs provided by the International Harvester Company, Deere

Acknowledgments

and Company, Massey-Ferguson, Inc., and Minneapolis-Moline, Inc., improve, I believe, both the appearance of the book and the presentation of its ideas.

Lastly, the favorable intellectual and work setting that is to be found at the University of Minnesota contributed importantly to the writing of this book.

WILLARD W. COCHRANE

University of Minnesota
June 1965

Table of Contents

PART I. THE SETTING

1

The Shape of Modern Agriculture

MODERN agriculture is a complex of many activities. It reaches into the nonfarm sector for supplies; it stretches across the lands of rural America; it re-enters the nonfarm economy with marketing, processing, and distribution activities; it grows and develops on research and education; it is dependent upon government services at many levels; and it is changing so rapidly that most people, including those intimately involved with it, do not know where it begins and where it ends. But it was not always thus.

In 1800, the farmer and his family produced most of the capital resources employed on the farm. The farmer combined those meager capital resources with land and family labor to produce raw food and fiber products. These products were most often processed and consumed on the farm or, sometimes, sold directly to town dwellers. These various activities, all, or practically all, undertaken by the farmer, were described as agriculture. Thus farming and agriculture were one and the same thing in 1800.

But during the nineteenth century, and particularly in the latter half of it, production and marketing functions began to peel off the farming operation. Farm machinery and implements became more productive and more complicated, and had to be produced by specialized producers — in factories. Farmers began to seek improved seeds and varieties of livestock from other specialized producers. Thus more and more farmers began to purchase capital inputs from nonfarm sources.

At the same time the farmer began shedding processing and marketing functions. Milling and weaving moved off the farm; and as transportation facilities improved livestock and grain products started moving long distances — from the Middle West to the eastern seaboard and down the Mississippi to the Gulf.

By the beginning of the twentieth century most farmers in the United States had ceased fabricating machines, implements and other capital items, and ceased processing and marketing their own raw products. They bought their capital inputs and sold their raw products at the farm gate. Farming had become a business with a single function: the combining of labor and capital with an extensive use of land, under essentially uncontrolled physical environmental conditions, to turn out a raw product.

The typical farm no longer performed several functions integrated sequentially through time under one management; it now performed one function in the web of economic activity. For many years there remained one important exception to the above general conception: farmers continued to produce grain and livestock on the same farm. Grain was first produced and second used to produce livestock in a two-step sequence. But with this one important exception farming became just one major function or step in the over-all agricultural complex.

The trends of the nineteenth century have continued and intensified in the twentieth. New and wondrous machines for tilling the soil, planting, and harvesting have been developed. And to machines have been added many new capital inputs including hybrid seed, chemical fertilizer, chemical weed and pest killers, and special feeding rations. All these the modern farmer must buy from nonfarm sources if he is to be efficient and productive and survive.

Similarly, the marketing system has deepened and widened to include gigantic and complex processing and handling facilities, new food products, new packaging and dispensing methods, and new and luxurious retail outlets. In this sea of production and marketing functions the farming operation, or enterprise, remains, but only as a part, and not a major part, of the total agricultural complex.

Farming and Agriculture Defined. In the preceding discussion and throughout this book the terms farming and agriculture are used to denote specific but different concepts. "Agriculture" is used to describe all activities in the production and distribution of food and fiber products. "Farming" describes those productive activities that make extensive use of land and take place under essentially uncontrolled physical environmental conditions. It should be recognized, however, that the whole thrust of technological development is to bring under control the many environmental conditions impinging on farming. When this happens in the distant future farming will cease to exist in the historic sense. But for the present and the foreseeable future the farming operation still takes place over wide reaches of land under uncontrolled weather and biological conditions.

The focus of this book is on farmers and their problems. But to understand farmers and their problems, we must gain an appreciation of where farmers and their farming operations fit into modern agriculture. Farmers perform an indispensable function in the national economy; they produce the raw food and fiber products. But others perform indispensable functions too; tractors can't move without gasoline, and wheat produced in Kansas must be milled into flour and transported to New York before New Yorkers can eat it as bread. Our problem then is to get a picture of the total process of producing and distributing food and fiber products and the place of farming in that process. We turn now to the delineation of such a picture.

THE MODERN AGRICULTURAL COMPLEX

The modern agricultural complex is made up of four major sectors or components. They are (1) a nonfarm supply sector which produces and distributes producer goods and services for farmers; (2) the farming operation itself, which combines land, labor, and management, and many and varied capital resources to turn out raw food and fiber products; (3) the marketing system which transports, stores, processes, packages, and ultimately distributes a finished product to consumers; and (4) a set of services provided by government which includes research, extension and education, regulatory activities, and financial and income support and assistance to farmers.

The Nonfarm Supply Sector. The nonfarm supply sector has become big business. Here we find the great machinery companies and their farflung distributive systems; the great chemical companies and their varied products including weed killers, insecticides, and pesticides; and the great fertilizer and feed companies with their everpresent distributive systems. Alongside these private companies we also find large-scale farmers' supply cooperatives which have competed successfully with the private firms in supplying fuel, feed, fertilizer, and seed to farmers.

The Shape of Modern Agriculture

There is a lot of little business in this nonfarm supply sector too, particularly in the area of services. Modern farming requires a constant supply of the services provided by bankers, lawyers, veterinarians, electricians, and mechanics — services usually supplied by relatively small local firms. In sum, the typical commercial farm in the 1960's is highly dependent upon the nonfarm economy for production goods and services; from 50 to 60 per cent of the total annual production expenditures of the national farm plant in the early 1960's were made to acquire producer goods and services from the nonfarm sector.

Perhaps a better picture of the magnitude of the nonfarm supply sector may be gained from looking at the dollar value of purchases by farmers of off-farm inputs. Total purchases by farmers of some of the more important categories for 1963 are as shown in the accompanying tabulation.[1]

Seed	$ 564,000,000
Fertilizer and lime	1,741,000,000
Fuel; repairs and other operating costs of capital items	4,011,000,000
Miscellaneous: pesticides, electricity, veterinary services, insurance premiums, blacksmithing and hardware supplies, and containers and binding materials	3,120,000,000
Buildings and machinery	4,849,000,000

These items alone total $14.3 billion, and the list does not include feed purchased from nonfarm feed producers and many locally acquired services. We conclude that purchases of producer goods and services by farmers from nonfarm suppliers ran over $15 billion in 1963.

Another way of visualizing the magnitude of this nonfarm supply sector is in terms of employment. About 1.1 million people are employed in industries producing and distributing goods and commodities used by farmers, and this estimate does not include the many people providing services to farmers. But regardless of the measure used to gauge the size of the nonfarm supply sector, it turns out to be very big. Further, production on modern farms would grind to a halt, and very quickly, if these goods and services were shut off or even seriously reduced. Modern farming is based on tires, fuel, chemicals, steel, and complex technological processes.

The Farm Plant. The national farm plant in 1963 was composed of

---

[1] An excellent source of information on all aspects of farm income and expenditure is the yearly July issue of the *Farm Income Situation,* Economic Research Service, USDA.

3,573,000 farms. The total number of workers on these farms, including farm operators, family members, and hired laborers, was 6,518,000. This plant and labor force produced farm products in that year that were marketed for $36.9 billion. To this we add government payments to farmers of $1.7 billion and nonmoney income of $3.1 billion in the form of food and housing, to arrive at a national gross farm income of $41.7 billion. In other words, the farm sector generated a gross income of $41.7 billion in 1963 from the production and sale of raw products, from the undertaking of certain activities for government, and from the production and home use of food, fuel, and housing services.

On the basis of the above data the average farm in the United States in 1963 had a gross income of $11,682 and a net income of $3,504. The average annual income per farm worker in 1963 was $2,375 (compared with a factory worker's average annual wage of $5,168). It is sometimes argued that the above national averages are meaningless because they include many small farms. The logic of that argument, of course, depends upon what the averages are used for. Here we are trying to describe the farm income situation in one figure, and it is a fact that there were a lot of small, low-income farms in the early 1960's. It is thus appropriate that the average reflect those many low-income farms.

The above data provide a brief description of the over-all magnitudes of the farming sector. Much more could be written in the way of description, and much more in the way of analysis. And it will be written in later pages, for the focus of this book is on farmers and their farming operations. But for the present we have established only the over-all magnitudes.

The Marketing System. The marketing, processing, and distribution sector of the agricultural complex is more than three times the size of the farm sector, measured in value terms. Limiting our discussion to food products alone, for the moment, and to that part of food production consumed domestically (for which data are available), domestic consumers in 1963 spent $66.4 billion on food products. Of this total, farm producers received $21.4 billion and all agencies of marketing and distribution received $45.0 billion.

Why is the food marketing bill so high? Many have studied this question, but no one has yet provided an answer completely satisfactory to all concerned. A Presidential Commission is investigating the problem as this book goes to press; perhaps it will provide some satisfactory answers. Certainly one point has been established by numerous studies: food marketing costs are not high because of exorbitant profits in the system. Profit rates in food distribution and processing are among the lowest in the whole nonfarm economy.

Probably the answer is to be found in the fact that consumers demand and stand ready to pay for a large number of services associated with and built into their food products. The typical American consumer is no longer satisfied with a scaly apple in November: he wants a luscious red apple the year around; he no longer is willing to peel or squeeze an orange: he wants easy-to-pour orange juice; he is no longer willing to tolerate an egg of dubious color and smell: he wants beautiful fresh eggs every day. To provide these and many more similar services the marketing and distribution system must assemble a standardized raw product from a large number of producers, transport the product under controlled conditions, store the product under controlled conditions, usually process the product, package it in attractive containers, distribute it to many retail food markets, and finally move it off a shelf into some consumer's food basket — and all this possibly two thousand miles away and two months after the raw product left the farm.

The marketing bill for nonfood products of domestic farm origin is also sizable. In 1963 consumers spent $103 billion on food and nonfood products (textile, tobacco, and leather products, and alcoholic beverages) that originated on American farms. Of this total expenditure, the marketing system received, or took, $73.5 billion, all farmers received $23.8 billion, and government collected $6.2 billion in excise taxes. The breakdown of the marketing bill for 1963 is shown, in billions of dollars, in the accompanying tabulation.[2]

Food	$45.0
Nonfood	
Textile products	13.8
Alcoholic beverages	8.7
Tobacco products	3.1
Leather products	2.9
Total	$73.5

Marketing is an expensive process. Approximately 8.4 million man years of labor were required to market those food and nonfood products that originated on American farms and were sold to domestic civilian consumers in 1963. If the handling of products moving into export and

[2] For greater detail see *Marketing and Transportation Situation*, Economic Research Service, USDA, August 1964, and more recent issues.

those originating from imports is included, total full-time employment in marketing increases to between 9 and 10 million man years. It takes a lot of people, paid reasonably high wages, and tremendous investments in storage, transport, processing, wholesaling, and retailing facilities to perform all the marketing functions peeled off the farming operation and added by enterprising marketers over the past hundred years.

The tail is now wagging the dog. This is so partly because it has outgrown the dog; but other forces are at work. The growth of the food chains and their emphasis on merchandising an attractive product of standard quality have put new pressures on the farmer. Raw-product buyers are no longer interested in just any product that is offered to them; they want a raw product that satisfies certain physical specifications so that the final product at retail is of uniform quality day in and day out. Raw-product buyers therefore now seek sources of supply that are certain and adequate and that meet their product specifications. This puts more pressure on farmers to produce a product that fits the requirements of the market. Any old product won't do; the farmer must now tailor his productive operation and schedule closely to the needs and demands of the big buyers.

Government Services. The government services sector of the modern agricultural complex really had its origin in the Morrill Act of 1862, which created the land-grant system of agricultural and mechanical arts colleges. Next came the Hatch Act of 1885, which provided federal funds for each state to carry out research in the agricultural sciences; this act brought into being the system of agricultural experiment stations. The passage of the Smith-Lever Act in 1914 brought into being the Agricultural Extension Service, with the purpose of carrying information, technology, and know-how directly to the farmer's door. With the creation of the Extension Service, the structure of the modern agricultural college was established to do three major kinds of work: resident instruction, research, and extension teaching. Out of this has developed a vast research and educational mechanism which has played a major role in the development of the rest of the agricultural complex.

To the work of the agricultural college in this area of research and extension must be added the continuing contribution of the United States Department of Agriculture, which has a large program of basic research, applied research, and public service in crop and livestock production, marketing and distribution, product utilization, economics and statistics, and forestry. This program rivals and possibly exceeds in scope the work of the combined agricultural colleges.

The federal Land Bank system was created in 1916 to provide long-term credit to farmers. Since then a whole series of credit agencies has been established by federal action to assist farmers. Emergency credit and mortgage acts were passed in 1921 and 1933 to assist and relieve farmers at those critical times. An intermediate or production credit system was established in 1923. A system of supervised credit for low-production, poor-risk farmers was established in the 1930's; this type of credit is currently extended by the Farmers Home Administration. A whole structure of government-initiated or government-administered credit services now answers the special credit problems of farmers: land, production, cooperatives, low-production farms, rural electric facilities, and special feed and seed loans.

Along with credit in the early part of this century came many regulatory activities. Some, such as the Food and Drug Act of 1906, were designed primarily to protect the consumer. But many more were established to protect farmers from sharp and unfair practices in the marketing of their produce; two important laws of this kind were the Packers and Stockyards Act and the Futures Trading Act, both passed in 1921. Since then both the federal and state governments have added a large number of regulatory activities, including the inspection of meat, poultry, and milk, and the establishment and maintenance of grades and standards of many agricultural commodities.

The last, the largest (measured in dollars and cents), and certainly the most controversial service provided by government to farmers is price and income support. This activity had its origin in the Great Depression and has become an integral part of the agricultural complex. Price stability and income support are provided farmers, directly or indirectly, in all of the major agricultural commodities.

Without question, government price and income support programs are currently holding farm incomes far above what they would be without such programs. The consensus among agricultural economists is that over-all net farm income would fall by 50 per cent within a few years, if all present commodity price and income support programs were eliminated. There is no consensus, and there is much debate, however, over what farmers' income position would in the 1960's be if there had never been any support programs.

Also without question, government support programs have eliminated much of the price instability in agricultural commodities, and thus eliminated much of the financial riskiness inherent in farming for centuries. This has made production planning in farming easier, more rational, and less of a gamble, and has contributed to the flow of capital into farming and the adoption on farms of new and improved technologies.

Governmental price and income support has provided farmers with assistance and service, but the programs are costly, the long-run income results debatable, and the whole policy subject to intense controversy. The future of this kind of service is in doubt, as it has been from its very beginning. The principal purpose of this book is to analyze the policy questions bearing on this service, and, if possible, to make a contribution to their resolution.

It is impossible to estimate precisely the value, or cost, of this government services sector, but some order of magnitude is discernible. The cost of farm price and income support and the disposition of surplus products in the middle 1960's was running close to $6 billion a year. In 1963, total expenditures for education, research, and extension for both federal and state governments ran close to a billion dollars. Expenditures for all regulatory activities by both federal and state governments probably ran well under a billion. Net additions to farm debt (both real estate and nonreal estate) by governmental and quasi-governmental lending agencies ran close to $500 million in 1962. The total value, or cost, of the government services sector in the early 1960's would thus be $8 to $8.5 billion.

The Total Value of Activities in the Agricultural Complex. The dollar value of all activities in the four sectors of the agricultural complex ran between $120 and $125 billion annually in the early 1960's; this is close, as it should be, to a USDA estimate of $125 billion for the total dollar value of the final goods and services produced by the combined resources and efforts of the agricultural complex. This means that the total agricultural complex accounts for about a fifth of the Gross National Product of the United States. Viewed in this way, agriculture continues to be a large and vital segment of the national economy. But the farming

11

sector of the agricultural complex accounts for only about 4 per cent of the Gross National Product.

In thinking and talking about farmers and agriculture it is important that we know exactly what it is we are thinking and talking about. If it is what we have defined as the modern agricultural complex, then we have under consideration a vast network of activities that originates in the nonfarm economy with the supply of producer goods and services, moves to the farming operation itself and then back into the nonfarm economy in the marketing and distribution function. And at all levels government service is involved. This complex constitutes a major segment of the total national economy.

But if it is farming, as defined here, that we are considering, then we are dealing with a set of production activities on the land which remain highly important to the consumer but account for a relatively small part of total national economic activity.

It would be a mistake to regard this agricultural complex as a finished thing. It has been in rapid transition for a hundred years, and it shows every promise of continuing to grow, change, and develop at a rapid pace during the next several decades. Certainly more automatic handling machinery, irrigation equipment, and fertilizers are going to be used on the farm of the future. This means that the nonfarm supply sector is going to expand its production activities to supply these producer goods to farmers. And certainly the consumer is going to demand and get more processing and service built into his food products, possibly demand even new kinds and forms of food products. All of this means more activity in the marketing and distribution sector.

In the farm sector it seems likely that more functions will be peeled off the traditional farming operation and transferred to factories and specialized production units. Broiler and egg production points the way. Twenty years ago eggs were most often produced by farm flocks and fryers were young cockerels from farm flocks that didn't lay eggs. Now both broilers and eggs are produced in specialized producing units (we still don't have a name for these units) that are really factories, and where both products are produced under the most advanced technology and the most rigorous controlled conditions with respect to breeding stock, feed, sanitation, and so on. Broilers are now raised under controlled conditions more rigorous than those in most manufacturing processes.

The same development is currently going on in cattle feeding; more and more cattle are being finished in specialized feed lots. To some degree dairying, too, is undergoing the same change. Only the pig at the moment seems immune to these developments. It may well happen over the next several decades that feed grains will be produced on farms, and feeder cattle and pigs will be produced on different farms (baby chicks both for broilers and egg production are no longer produced on farms), and then both young animals and feed will move to highly automated factories with rigorously controlled production processes.

In the not too distant future we may have livestock product factories that are no more like farming than a peach canning factory is today. This change has already happened in broilers, it is well on its way in eggs, it is happening in beef, it is starting in dairying, and it could easily happen in hogs. If and when that day comes, the farming sector will have shrunk absolutely, and the processing sector will have expanded greatly — or perhaps we shall be discussing a fifth sector in the agricultural complex in 2000, the livestock factory sector.

THE NATIONAL FARM PLANT

We have described briefly above the structure and the magnitude of the modern agricultural complex, sketching the farm sector in terms of national averages and aggregates. Now we want to delve within the national averages and aggregates and see the national farm plant close up.

We first observe that a large number of farms are still in business — to repeat, 3,573,000 operating farms in the United States in 1963. These farms come in all shapes, sizes, financial conditions, and levels of productivity. A quick glance at the statistics might suggest that there is simply a large number of assorted farms in the United States, but it is possible to bring order out of the statistics (see Table 1). A relatively few highly productive farms produce more than 50 per cent of the total farm product, and about 1.5 million farms produce over 90 per cent of the total product. At the other end of the scale, almost 2 million low-production, part-time and retirement farms produce less than 10 per cent of the total farm product.

In somewhat more precise terms 1,587,000 farms in 1963, each with gross sales over $5,000, produced 91 per cent of the total product from farming; in percentage terms 44 per cent of all farms produced 91 per

The Shape of Modern Agriculture

Table 1. Number of Farms by Major Economic Classes, U.S., 1963

Economic Class	Number of Farms		Percentage of Sales of Farm Products
	Total	Percentage of Total	
*Full-Time Farms**			
Annual sales			
$20,000 and over	384,000	10.7%	54.5%
$10,000–$19,999	594,000	16.6	23.6
$5,000–$9,999	609,000	17.0	12.6
$2,500–$4,999	463,000	13.0	4.8
$50–$2,499	202,000	5.7	.8
Other Farms			
Part-time	903,000	25.3	2.3
Retirement and abnormal	418,000	11.7	1.4
Total	3,573,000	100.0	100.0

Source: Economic Research Service, USDA.

*Farms on which the principal occupation of the operator is farming, though he often has some off-farm employment.

cent of the total product. This group of farms constitutes the real commercial farm plant of the United States; these are the farms that really turn out the product.

There were 665,000 full-time farms (the principal occupation of the operator was farming) in 1963 that grossed less than $5,000. These farms were 19 per cent of the total number of farms and produced 5.6 per cent of the total product from farming. These are the low-production farms of modern agriculture and make up its hard-core poverty sector.

Table 1 shows 1,321,000 other farms according to USDA definitions. These are part-time, retirement, and abnormal farms, and really should not be considered a part of the national farm plant. In the first place, they are almost nonproductive; in 1963 they made up 37 per cent of the total number, yet produced less than 4 per cent of the total product of farming. In the second place, in 1963 the average part-time farm had a net income from farming of only $189, and a net income from off-farm sources of $4,380. The operators of these farms have for all practical purposes left farming; they are living in the farmhouse, milking a cow or two, raising a few chickens or pigs — and working in the city. And the retired farmers are retired, not farming, except again for a cow or two and a few chickens or pigs. Most of the discussion and analysis that follows will therefore exclude these two "other farm" groups. In this view, the national farm plant includes not 3,573,000 farms, but only

14

2,252,000. And in this latter grouping, we can say that 1,587,000 farms really turn out the product.[3]

It is of interest to observe what has happened to the number of farms in recent years and what is likely to happen in future years. The total number declined importantly between 1949 and 1963; the number of full-time farms, where the principal occupation of the operator is farming, declined from 3,365,000 to 2,252,000 over the period 1949–63, or just about 80,000 farms a year (Table 2).

Table 2. Number of Farms by Major Economic Classes, U.S., 1949, 1963, and Projected 1970

Economic Class	Number of Farms		
	1949	1963	1970
*Full-Time Farms**			
Annual sales			
$20,000 and over	155,000	384,000	522,000
$10,000–$19,999	342,000	594,000	529,000
$5,000–$9,999	739,000	609,000	450,000
$2,500–$4,999	944,000	463,000	117,000
$50–$2,499	1,185,000	202,000	50,000
Subtotal	3,365,000	2,252,000	1,668,000
Other Farms			
Part-time	1,585,000	903,000	792,000
Retirement and abnormal	772,000	418,000	408,000
Total	5,722,000	3,573,000	2,868,000

Source: Economic Research Service, USDA.
*Farms on which the principal occupation of the operator is farming, though he often has some off-farm employment.

But within the aggregate of full-time farms, two divergent trends are evident. The number of farms grossing more than $10,000 a year increased between 1949 and 1963, while the number of farms grossing less than $10,000 a year decreased. The reason for the first trend was that farms got larger during this period, and few of the larger farms went out of business; the reason for the second was that many small farms failed, though some grew larger and moved up to a larger economic class.

Recent trends in farm numbers are expected to continue into the future. Experts in the USDA project a decline in number of full-time farms through 1970 at a rate of slightly over 80,000 a year. The number

[3] Additional information about size of incomes by economic class and sources of income for 1949, 1963, and 1970 (projected) can be gleaned from Appendix Tables 1, 2, and 3.

of farms grossing less than $10,000 will fall precipitously over the period 1963–70; the number of farms grossing between $10,000 and $19,999 is likely to decline modestly; and the number of farms grossing over $20,-000 will increase sharply. The explanation for these divergent trends is the same as in the previous case; on the average, farms are going to continue to get larger and thus move into higher income categories: almost exclusively, it will be small farms that will go out of business.

The national farm plant is changing. The number of farms is declining significantly. The size of farms measured in volume of product produced is increasing significantly. The number of farm workers is declining irregularly but persistently — about 270,000 a year. And even the total number of acres cropped has declined since 1949.

Although the national farm plant has been contracting for a long time in terms of the above indicators, the total output from this plant has increased greatly. During the period 1949–63 total output increased 29 per cent. This was not done by magic, but by better management, improved technology, and heavy investments of capital. The how and why of these developments will be the subject of much analysis in this volume; for the moment let us simply note them as a part of the dramatic changes taking place in the national farm plant.

The national farm plant is highly specialized in the production of different crops and livestock products. Once farm management specialists preached diversification of production on each farm to avoid the risk of heavy losses because of a poor crop or a low price in one commodity. But with the modern drive to increase production efficiency — to increase output per unit of input — and with government programs to support and stabilize prices, farmers have tended to specialize more and more in one or two crops or one livestock enterprise. Each crop and livestock product now tends to be produced where it has the greatest comparative advantage — that is, farmers in a given area specialize in those crops that yield the greatest income for that area.

Feed grains are produced on the rich, black soils of the Middle West; wheat is produced on the Great Plains; beef cattle are produced in the Rocky Mountain region and then fattened in locations accessible to feed supplies; dairy cattle are found on the pasture lands of the Lake States; and cotton is produced in the long hot growing season of the South. This specialized production pattern may be seen in Figure 1, which shows the major types of farming in the forty-eight adjacent states.

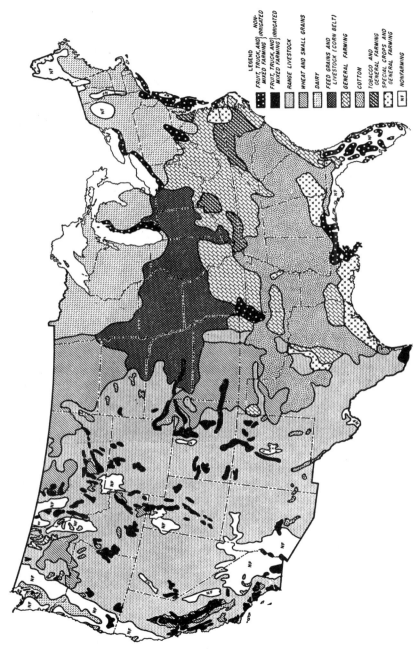

Figure 1. Major types of farming areas in the adjacent forty-eight United States

The Shape of Modern Agriculture

The size, investment, and returns of typical farms in these different types of farming areas may be seen in Table 3. A look at Table 3 brings out several points: (1) the size of farm varies greatly by type of farm; (2) investment per farm tends to be high in all types; (3) returns to the farm operator tend to be low, even negative in some types. And there is nothing unusual about 1963; it was an average to better-than-average year for farmers.

THE TWO WORLDS OF FARMING

A study of the data in Table 1 suggests two very different farming worlds: the world of highly productive, commercial farmers, and the world of poor, low-production farmers. Some 978,000 farms fall into the highly productive world: each grosses over $10,000 a year; the net income per farm averages over $5,000 a year; and as a group they produce about 78 per cent of the total farm product. As we shall see, these farms have income problems, but not production problems. It is on these farms that the technological revolution roars forward, and on these farms that yields and production increase yearly. These are the farms that have pushed total farm output ahead of food and fiber requirements, and made farm surpluses synonymous with American agriculture.

At the other extreme are the 665,000 low-production farms, those where the operators and their families live in poverty; each grosses less than $5,000 per year; the net income per farm averages less than $1,700 a year; and the group produces only about 6 per cent of the total farm product. Many of the families on these farms live in abject poverty; certainly this is true of the 200,000 families living on farms grossing less than $2,499 per year.

A brief look at Table 2 makes it clear that the number of low-production poverty farms has declined greatly since 1949; and we expect that decline to continue through 1970. A few such farm families may have improved their economic lot and moved into the commercial world, but not many. Most of the decline represents a movement out of farming by the families, through death, by outright migration, or via the part-time farming route.

Most of the farm operators living in poverty are old and poorly educated, with woefully inadequate productive resources. Provided their living and employment needs are met in some way, it is neither bad policy nor a national shame for them to leave farming, for their chances

Table 3. Size, Investment, and Returns by Type of Farm, United States, 1963

Type of Farm* and Location	Size of Farm in No. of Units	Total Farm Capital, 1/1/63	Gross Farm Income†	Return per Hour to Operator and Family Labor
Dairy, Central Northeast	32.2 cows	$ 43,400	$ 14,475	$0.42
Dairy, western Wisconsin	23.8 cows	37,410	10,267	0.64
Hog and beef fattening, Corn Belt	153 c. acres†	98,920	31,024	–.54
Cash grain, Corn Belt.............	246 c. acres	137,020	24,581	2.18
Cotton, southern Piedmont	101 c. acres	30,750	7,153	0.44
Cotton (nonirrigated), Texas High Plains	445 c. acres	84,950	19,584	2.70
Cotton-specialty crops (irrigated), San Joaquin Valley, Calif.	329 c. acres	305,450	112,987	§
Tobacco, North Carolina Coastal Plain	47 c. acres	27,640	12,581	1.70
Spring wheat, small grain, livestock, Northern Plains	588 c. acres	57,540	12,384	1.49
Winter wheat, sorghum, Southern Plains	684 c. acres	125,910	16,632	–.50
Cattle ranches, Intermountain region	149.5 cows	95,550	17,460	1.15

Source: *Farm Cost and Returns Commercial Farms by Type, Size and Location,* Agricultural Information Bulletin No. 230, Economic Research Service, USDA, June 1964, p. 4.
*All except cotton farms in California are family-operated.
†Includes both income from farming and government payments.
‡c = cropland.
§Not applicable.

of becoming successful farm operators are nil. But it *is* a shame if these people are crowded off the land with no place to go.

To this point no mention has been made of the economic class $5,000–$9,999. There are 609,000 farmers in this class; it is the largest single full-time class. The farms in this group are not, on the average, large enough to fall in the truly commercial group but neither are these farm families living in poverty. *This group is in transition.* Some of its members are making a go of their operations and are on their way to higher income. Others are falling by the wayside. Some are young farmers getting started, others are middle-aged men who have worked hard for ten or twenty years, but lack the managerial skill to compete in the modern business world. All depend upon their farms for their principal income, but none had sufficient resources as of 1963 to earn a good living for their family at current farm prices.

In many ways, this group's heartache is the greatest. These families expect and hope to continue farming, and to earn decent incomes by doing so. Some will, but most will not. The number of farms in this class declines importantly in the projection from 1963 to 1970 in Table 2. And not many of those farms are going to move up into the next class, for the next class too will be losing numbers between 1963 and 1970. Most of those in the $5,000–$9,999 class as of 1963 will still be in that class in 1970 or will have left farming. This hurts. Hence it is not surprising to find many such farmers joining radical farm organizations with direct action programs.

These, then, are the two worlds of farming in the 1960's: a highly productive, commercial world, and a low-production, poverty world, with a transition zone in between. The characteristics of the two worlds are different, their problems are different. A useful analysis of one has no meaning for the other. The solutions for each are different. An effective solution for one has no meaning for the other. In this book the two worlds of farming will therefore be treated separately. The commercial world and its problems and issues will be treated in Part II, the world of poverty in Part III.

FAMILY FARMS AND FARMERS

No discussion purporting to describe the shape of modern agriculture, no matter how brief, would be complete unless it dealt with the fact and issue of the *family* farms, a topic that is a joy to farm politicians and to successful family farmers. The family farm type of production organization has been and remains the dominant form of organization in the United States. Thus it is not surprising to find farm politicians singing its praises to family farmers who are or aspire to be successful family farmers.

The important questions are these: Is it an efficient form of productive organization? Is it here to stay? The answer to the first question is that it can be and often is. The answer to the second is that it is a durable institution but there are clouds in the horizon. But before elaborating these answers, we should perhaps be clear about what a family farm is and is not.

In Jefferson's day and in his thinking a family farm was an organization managed by a farmer who assumed the business risks, and who, with his family, did most of the farm labor, and who was a freeholder (owned his own farm). With the emphasis on enlarging farms in recent years the renting of additional acres or whole farms by family operations has become established practice. But with this exception the Jeffersonian concept of a family farm has changed very little. The definition of a family farm commonly used in the USDA these days is as follows: a family farm is a business in which the operator and family manage the operations, assume the financial risk, and provide most of the labor. Since the average farm family can provide about 1.5 man years of labor, the above definition is made operational by assuming that any farm operated by a family is a family farm if it hires less than 1.5 man years of labor. If it hires more than 1.5 man years of labor it becomes a larger-than-family farm.

To the above concept we need to add one further idea: the concept of adequacy. All the farms considered above in the poverty group were family farms, but all were clearly inadequate in productive resources. In appraising the family farm as a productive unit some standard of adequate size is required: a farm must have gross sales of at least $10,000 a year to use efficiently a modern line of machinery and provide a decent living for the family. The operational concept of an adequate family farm thus turns out to be one where the family operates the farm, hires less than 1.5 man years of labor, and has gross sales of at least $10,000 a year.

All the evidence we have from production economics studies indicates that the family farm, once it reaches a size where a full line of machinery can be used efficiently, is as efficient in physical productivity as a farm twice its size or ten times its size. Stated differently, the average costs of producing a unit of product fall rapidly until an adequate-sized family farm is reached, but unit costs of production hold almost constant for farms of larger size, including large-scale corporate farms. It is true that large-scale farms have certain bargaining advantages in borrowing money and purchasing supplies, and they also have certain marketing advantages where buyers seek large quantities of a standardized product. But in sheer production efficiency, an adequate-sized family farm is as efficient as any large-scale unit yet devised in the United States.

As for the staying power of family farms, it is true that most of the farms that have gone out of business in the past twenty years have been family farms. But this is not *because* they were family farms; rather it is because they were small and inefficient, with inadequate production resources. It happens that practically all farms in the United States, except a few very large farms and a few freaks, are organized on the family farm pattern — and the small inefficient ones among these that lack financing, cannot use a full line of machinery, or are poorly managed have gone out of business in large numbers. This would have happened to these units, however, regardless of their form of business organization. In the world of modern technology they had become anachronisms, and they had to go.

On the other hand, the number of adequate-sized family farms has actually increased in recent years, from 334,000 in 1949 to 650,000 in 1959. All evidence points to a continuation of this trend in the decade of the 1960's. In other words, the kind of farm that is managed and operated by a family, that uses mostly family labor, and that is large enough to make full use of modern machinery is actually increasing in number. The size of this farm, whether measured in acres or in investment, is growing year by year; but it remains a family farm by the above generally accepted definition.

At the same time the number of larger-than-family farms has been declining slightly. In 1949 there were 150,000 such farms, in 1959 this number had declined to 144,000. This trend too is continuing in the 1960's.

For all the difficulties and ills that beset farming and farmers, we can see some bright spots ahead. As Table 2 shows, most of the very small, low-producing farms will be gone by 1970. The 1960's will be rough, but the terrible poverty sore in the farm sector of agriculture will be largely eradicated by 1970. Without effective anti-poverty programs, however, this sore may simply be transferred to the nonfarm sector. At the same time the number of viable, efficient family farms is increasing. We can look forward by 1970 to a structure of farms more compatible with modern business methods and modern technological practices than anything we have had in agriculture since before the Great Depression of the 1930's.

2

𝄽

A Dynamic Farm Economy

THE national economy has not grown at a sustained rate over the past century, but over the whole period it has developed spectacularly. In the context of this developing national economy, we have already observed the emergence in the agricultural complex of the nonfarm supply sector, the marketing and distribution sector, and the government services sector. From the discussion in the opening chapter, it might be inferred that the farming sector was static or slow-growing, but this is not true. The farm economy has undergone change and growth over the past hundred years rivaling if not exceeding that of the rest of the economy. Certainly from 1945 to 1965 its change and growth have exceeded change and growth in the nonfarm economy; for example, since 1947 worker productivity in farming has increased more than twice as fast as that in nonfarming.

THE LONG VIEW: THE PAST CENTURY

Farming was an expanding industry in the traditional sense from 1870 to 1910; both the number of people employed and the number of acres cropped increased during this time. This was the period when the West was finally won; the period of the homesteader, the covered wagon, and the walking plow; the period of the Seventh Cavalry, the end of the buffalo and the fighting Plains Indians; this was a period of terrible hardship and frequent failure as the first settlers learned to farm the arid plains.

In one decade, the 1870's, the farm working force increased by two million and the number of acres cropped increased by 50 per cent. (See Table 4, where the story of the development of the farm economy un-

Table 4. Changes in Farm Employment, Crop Area, Farm Output, Output per Worker, and Total Population, 1870–1960, with Projections for 1970

Year	Farm Employment		Change in Cropland Used for Crops†	Change† in Farm Output‡	Change in Output per Worker†	Total Population	
	Number (millions)*	Change†				Number (millions)§	Change†
1870	8.0	..	..	..	..	39.9	..
1880	10.1	26%	52%	55%	23%	50.3	26%
1890	11.7	16	30	19	3	63.1	25
1900	12.8	10	29	30	18	76.1	21
1910	13.6	6	4	4	–2	92.4	21
1920	13.4	–1	11	12	13	106.5	15
1930	12.5	–7	4	13	22	123.1	16
1940	11.0	–12	–4	11	26	132.1	7
1950	9.9	–10	3	25	39	151.7	15
1960	7.1	–28	–7	21	68	180.7	17
1970**	5.5	–23	4	20	54	211.4	17

*1870 to 1900 based on data from the United States Bureau of the Census. Population Series P-9, No. 11. From 1910 to 1960 the figures are from *Average Annual Farm Employment*, Agricultural Marketing Service, USDA. Projections for 1970 based on trends in the 1950–60 decade.

†Percentage of change from preceding decade.

‡Three-year averages centered on the year indicated except for the 1970 projection. Estimates for 1870–1900 made by the Agricultural Adjustment Research Branch, Farm Production Economics Division, Agricultural Research Service, USDA. 1870–1960 figures are from *Changes in Farm Production and Efficiency*. Projection for 1970 based on projection compiled by the Economic Research Service, USDA.

§Reports of the Bureau of the Census. Projection for 1970, Bureau of the Census.

**Assumes 1962–63 farm programs in existence through 1970.

folds.) Expansion in the national farm plant was almost as great in the 1880's and 1890's as in the 1870's. But the rate of expansion declined to a walk in the first decade of the twentieth century. The western frontier closed down between 1910 and 1920; the West was won and settled. In terms of employment the farm economy ceased to expand by 1910.

The 1870's was a time of deep farm depression. The homesteader not only battled an inhospitable physical environment — Indians, drought, and grasshoppers — he also battled low and falling farm prices. His economic situation improved a little during the 1880's, and then took a turn for the worse again in the 1890's. The reasons are clear from Table 4. Total farm output increased by 55 per cent in the 1870's, but total population (one good measure of the size and growth of the domestic market) increased only 26 per cent. The excess production of the 1870's had either to be exported or to be used or wasted in uneconomic ways domestically. Exports of grain to England and Western Europe did increase during this period, but not enough to create a strong demand for the burgeoning supplies of North America. Food and fiber supplies pressed hard against market demand during the period of the 1870's and drove farm prices down to disastrous levels.

The rate of increase in farm output slowed during the 1880's and ran behind the rate of population expansion, so the economic situation in the farm economy improved. But farm output shot ahead of population growth in the 1890's and once again the farm depression deepened. The history of farm depression and prosperity in the United States can almost be read directly from the two columns in Table 4 showing the percentage of change in farm output and the percentage of change in total population.

The farm economy crossed a great divide during 1910–20. Farm employment increased in every decade up until that one and thereafter declined. The cropland of the national farm plant expanded every decade up to 1910–20 and thereafter fluctuated from decade to decade. Farm output increased, but at a declining rate, from 1870 to 1910, and thereafter increased at an increasing rate. Output per worker jumped around unpredictably before 1910; after that it skyrocketed.

Something fundamental to or about farming in the United States changed between 1910 and 1920. Before then the national farm plant grew and developed by territorial expansion and an increased number of farmers. After 1920 it continued to grow, but in a new way: it grew through capital formation, the adoption of new and improved practices and technology, and improved management. In this scheme of development the farm plant requires and uses fewer workers, and, generally speaking, fewer acres. New and improved capital goods and new technological practices are substituted for labor and land, and unit costs of production are reduced in the process. This is the modern form of agricultural development.

The new age of farming that thus began to take shape between 1910 and 1920 was firmly established in the 1920's. The traditional approach to farming — son learning from father and farming as his father and grandfather had before him — had crumbled slowly during the nineteenth century, and was shattered completely during the 1920's by the gasoline engine, the tractor. The traditional approach could never return because the new age of farming is based on modern technology and changes with changes in technology. The modern commercial farmer changes his farming methods every year, as new techniques are developed and offered to him. He expects, on the average, to increase his yields per acre and the total product of his farm every year, not by magic and not by luck, but by adopting new, improved producer goods and practices. And this he and his fellow commercial farmers have done.

Total farm output increased about 12 per cent in each of the three decades following 1910, increased 25 per cent in the 1940's, and increased 21 per cent under the wraps of government controls (however weak) during the 1950's. In this long period of farm output expansion, from 1910 to 1960, employment in farming was cut almost in half.

The first decade of the twentieth century opened the golden age of American agriculture: farm prices were good and so were farm incomes. The reason is not difficult to find. Total farm output, as the result of capital starvation following thirty years of farm depression and a slowed rate of settlement, increased only 4 per cent between 1900 and 1910. After thirty years of rapid output expansion, based on extensive growth, the farm plant stood almost still for a decade, while population increased 21 per cent. The supply-demand relationship had done an about-face; population was now pressing on food supplies and the obvious happened: farm prices increased almost 40 per cent between 1900 and 1910. With population continuing to run ahead of farm output expansion, and with the further impetus of World War I, farm prices and incomes soared during 1910–20. Farmers had twenty prosperous years during which demand ran far ahead of supplies and pushed farm prices to dazzling heights. It was a golden age, an age farmers have tried to recapture through the parity price formula, but without success.

The twentieth century has not always been kind to farmers. After World War I, farm prices fell sharply, but a favorable relation between population and output kept them from tumbling into the subbasement during the 1920's. That decade was not a happy one because so many farmers paid the price — business failure — for the land speculation of the preceding decade. But conditions could and did get much worse. The relation between population and farm output became decidedly unfavorable to farmers during the unhappy 1930's: population growth increased only 7 per cent and farm output 11. The consequence once again was tumbling farm prices and badly depressed farm incomes. Farmers who farmed through the 1930's do not worry about the "freedom to farm." Only one thing gnaws at their innards: the possibility of another farm depression like that of the 1930's.

In the 1940's farm output continued to outrace population, but once again we were at war. During World War II and in the great hunger that followed, we converted the food needs of the world into an effective demand for American farm commodities. And this worldwide demand generated by war and its aftermath once again drove farm prices to high levels.

But the situation in the 1950's reverted to that of the 1930's: farm output increased 21 per cent, population only 17 per cent. With food supplies again pressing on population, and no hot war to counteract this force, a strong downward pressure was exerted on farm prices. The decade of the 1950's was one of chronic downward pressure on prices, chronic surpluses, and chronic misunderstanding of the farm economy.

The basic situation in the 1960's almost repeats that of the preceding decade. New technologies continue to pour forth, farmers adopt them in an effort to become more efficient, and total output increases. Assuming a continuance of the production control programs in effect in 1962–63, total farm output is projected to increase 20 per cent in the 1960's, exceeding the expected population growth and continuing the downward pressure on prices of the 1950's. One possible difference should be noted, however; operating under rather strong incentives to restrict production, farmers are increasing output by about as much in

A Dynamic Farm Economy

the 1960's as in the 1950's. The production potential of the farm plant has gotten out of hand.

THE ROAR OF THE PAST TEN YEARS AND THE CRISIS OF THE NEXT TEN

The ten-year period 1954–63 was a momentous one for American farms and farmers. The full force of the technological revolution was brought to bear on the farm economy. The farm population declined from 19 to 13 million; farm employment declined from 8.6 to 6.5 million. The number of farms fell from 4.8 to 3.6 million. Concurrently, total farm output increased by 20 per cent, and over-all farm efficiency by 20 per cent. This is the greatest gain in productive efficiency of any ten-year period in the history of American farming. A small, dwindling, and highly productive labor force, in association with modern machinery and other technologies, is increasing total farm output more every year than the increase in total requirements, thereby keeping agriculture in a state of chronic surplus.

The surplus of food and fiber products should force farm prices down to levels where that surplus would disappear — to levels 20 to 30 per cent below the 1963 level. But farm prices generally have not fallen because they have been supported in the major commodities by the government. These programs, which have supported the incomes of most commercial farmers and maintained the financial position of the larger and more efficient farmers reasonably well, have of course contributed to the continuing surplus. The larger and more efficient commercial farmers are jamming the new and improved capital and methods into practice and increasing output. And the solvent condition of the larger and more efficient commercial farmers makes financing new and improved capital and methods possible and even necessary. The pressure of supplies on population is thus maintained.

The chronic surplus has been managed in three ways. First, the rate of output expansion was held down to the record of the ten preceding years by a system of loose, weak controls, first under the Eisenhower administration and later under the Kennedy-Johnson administration. In other words, farm output was held in check and kept from soaring well above the increase of 20 per cent of the preceding ten years by a set of not very tough mandatory production controls, a large Soil Bank program, and voluntary commodity programs. Second, supplies in ex-

29

cess of what the commercial market will absorb at support price levels moved into government stocks; such stocks — principally of wheat, feed grains, and cotton — built up to a level of almost eight billion dollars' worth by December 1959; since then the level has been somewhat reduced. Third, a food aid program for the developing nations (Food for Peace) has since 1955 moved a billion to two billion dollars' worth of food and fiber products overseas annually to the developing nations. This major surplus-disposal program has kept government-owned stocks from becoming an unbearable load.

These three management devices have made the farm price support program work and have kept the surplus from getting out of hand. But almost everyone is unhappy with the results of the government programs of price and income support and the complementary devices of supply management. Farmers feel strongly that their incomes are too low; they feel that there is something wrong when the average farm worker earns less than half what an average factory worker earns. And we recall that hourly returns to the operator and family labor in 1963 were very low for most types of farms and sometimes negative (Table 3). But both farmers who are dissatisfied with the present level of farm incomes, and writers who argue that returns to the large, efficient commercial farms are really not very bad and price and income support programs should therefore be eliminated, should recognize that *the present level of farm income rests squarely on the operation of major programs of price and income support,* and that farm incomes would be at least 50 per cent lower for many years to come if these programs were eliminated.

On the other hand, the city man and his spokesmen are highly critical of programs that annually cost between $4 and $6 billion. No one can deny that these programs are expensive. But more important, both the farmer and the city man should recognize that it is becoming more difficult to make these programs work even tolerably well, because the productive potential of the national farm plant is increasing. The roar of the past ten years thus grows louder.

All the trends of the past ten years associated with the technological revolution in farming can be expected to continue and intensify during the next ten. The number of persons living and working on farms will continue to decline at a rapid pace. It is probable that farm employment will be below 5 million and possibly edging 4 million by 1973. The number of full-time farms will be less than 1.5 million, but the average farm will be much larger and much more productive. And the production potential of the national farm plant will be pressing against the existing production controls with a greater force than it did in 1963. In other words, the problem of holding the rate of farm output expansion within reasonable and tolerable bounds will be much greater in 1973 than it was in 1963.

This means that, at the existing level of price support and with existing management devices, the government cost of farm price and income support programs must rise, either through enlarged incentive payments to take more land out of production, or through a larger takeover of surplus commodities and their storage and disposal. Or it means that the level of price support and hence the general level of farm prices must fall to where the rate of farm output expansion is slowed down and the cost of the price and income support programs is reduced. Such a reduction in the farm price level cannot be small; it must be large enough to impair the financial position of the commercial farmers and thus restrict their capacity to invest in new, improved capital goods and methods. This is the long-run wringer at work that no one associated with agriculture wishes to contemplate, but which could become a necessity.

Barring war or severe drought, a crisis in American farm policy is likely during the next ten years. The increasing production potential of the farm plant, with its implications for the government budget and the farm price level, is forcing the issue. The stakes in the present farm policy game are becoming so big that sometime in the near future the body politic will have to reassess the situation and decide how and under what conditions it wants to continue the game.

Is it willing to protect and support incomes in the farm sector and help feed the hungry millions in the developing countries at a government cost that begins at something like $6 billion and runs up from there? Or does it demand that the domestic farm economy be deflated in price level, income, and production potential, with all the pain and heartache that such a deflation process will entail, as well as reducing the volume of food aid to the developing countries? This is the choice that confronts the body politic now, and that will reach crisis proportions during the next ten years.

A Dynamic Farm Economy

No matter how the farm policy crisis of the 1960's is resolved, the farm economy is going to continue to change, develop, and become more productive. This is the case because modern farming is built on scientific research, technological development, adoption by farmers of new, improved producer goods and practices, and increased know-how. A change in farm price and income policy could speed up the development process or slow it down, but it won't stop it, because scientific research is going to continue in the universities and government; private firms in the nonfarm supply sector will continue to develop new, improved producer goods; the Extension Service, magazines, and the distributive organizations of private firms will continue to operate; and the educational and management level of farm workers will continue to rise.

We can expect the national farm plant to undergo wondrous and exciting changes grounded on these developments in the next thirty or forty years. Let us therefore consider probable and possible developments, first in the scientific world and then in the farm plant up to the year 2000.

The Scientific Base.[1] First we shall consider what may happen in the next ten years.

Adequate water will be our biggest challenge. Nuclear explosives may be used to create reservoirs above and below ground, to get at previously untapped water underground, and to blast out great navigation and irrigation channels that will carry water long distances from its source.

Improved water management will increase production in dry-land farming areas without irrigation. Much farm land will be leveled and contoured to make maximum use of water as well as of tillage machinery. Great advances will be made in water harvesting — saving water from one part of the land to use on another. To provide water for livestock, ground covers of asphalt, plastic, and synthetic rubber will increase the runoff into tanks, ponds, or large collapsible rubber bags. One-way chemicals may be found that will control the movement of moisture, allowing it to go down into the ground or into a reservoir but not be lost to the atmosphere by evaporation.

---

[1] This section (pp. 32–39) is adapted from material provided by the Agricultural Research Service, USDA.

New materials have brought us to the threshold of many engineering developments that will reduce the cost of labor as well as decrease the waste of water. Easily moved porcelainized metal units that can be assembled in many ways, like an erector set, may replace much concrete. Synthetic rubber tubes a yard across will carry irrigation water in many canal beds. Storage facilities will deepen and exposed surfaces will become smaller as we try to bury our water reserves underground or otherwise shield them from the thirsty rays of the sun.

Radar and other electronic techniques will be perfected to measure the precipitation, distribution, and rate of travel of water in streams and across watersheds. Automated irrigation may be close at hand, through the use of radio signals or refinements of the principle of the ancient waterclock, which measured time by the fall or flow of water. Infrared photography may bring prescription irrigation: aerial photographs will indicate the surface temperature — and therefore the moisture content — of soils and crops, to show precisely when, where, and how much water is needed.

The natural fertility of our soils will not be so important as in the past. Soils will be given uniform, desirable properties — physical, chemical, and biological — by man. *Farmers may have their soils custom rebuilt with the particular properties that their operations need.*

The use of fertilizers will continue to grow; new fertilizers will release their nutrients as needed by plants but will resist loss of them through leaching and in other ways.

The shapes of our crops will change. They will be altered not only to make possible the mechanization of their production but also to allow them to use water efficiently. We shall grow some plants to uniform heights to aid in harvesting by machine and to reduce evaporation. Conversely, in more humid areas we may plant them in hedges to open up fields to air and sun.

Crop quality, plant height, rate of growth, and date of maturity will be much more controllable than they are today. Plants will be put through their paces not only by breeding methods but increasingly by the use of biological, chemical, and physical aids. Hormones and plant growth regulators will speed growth, narrowing the time from planting to harvest; will alter and control the quality of their fiber and other characteristics; and will lengthen their storage life. For example, it has been found that when growth is retarded with chemicals, the plants also become more tolerant to such adverse conditions as salt, drying, or low temperatures. When the physiological changes involved are known, this fact may be put to use.

One of the most significant developments of recent years was the discovery of a plant pigment named phytochrome, which, by its reaction to light, controls the growth of plants from germination to fruiting. Woody plants such as nuts and fruits may be made to flower and fruit promptly, without spending years in a juvenile stage of growth. Such speed-up techniques could advance breeding research immeasurably.

While making better use of the crops we have, we shall also develop new ones. Plant explorers of the USDA are now searching in other countries for crops that will produce some of the industrial oils, pulps, and gums we now import.

Research in human nutrition will continue to affect farm production as it has in the past. Public concern over the effects of obesity on health and the nutritional implications of fatty acids in our food, as yet undetermined, have affected the meat and dairy industry and caused changes in such products as margarine. Recently, nutritionists have again recommended reducing our caloric intake to fit today's energy needs. This may mean more emphasis on fruits and vegetables, lean meat, and low-fat milk.

Protein-calorie malnutrition in young children, perhaps the most important nutrition problem in the world today, results not only from too little food, especially protein, but also from a poor balance of amino acids in the proteins eaten; wheat, for example, is low in lysine. Basic research on the way living cells make and use acids may some day make it possible to change the protein content of cereals. Eventually scientists may be able to increase wheat's lysine content by altering the genetic messages carried by the molecules of nucleic acids.

Protection against insects and other pests will create a paradoxical problem: The public will expect greater freedom from insects in foods, homes, and public facilities — higher standards of cleanliness and greater security from annoyance. Growers, too, will be unwilling to sacrifice any of their potential productivity to pests. On the other hand, people will demand that this high level of pest control be maintained without danger to beneficial forms of life or any other hazard to man and his environment.

These paradoxical demands will require a more concerted and varied approach to pest control than has yet been used. Existing pesticides will be improved and new ones will be developed that offer wider margins of safety without really sacrificing efficiency. More and more, growers will integrate physical, chemical, and biological methods of control, and will often conduct organized, community-wide efforts against pests. Because each pest may require very specific weapons, control may become more costly.

The most lasting benefits will come from understanding the physiology and behavior of insects. Scientists can then concentrate their efforts on ways to govern that behavior — behavior in relation to light and darkness, to temperature, to reproduction, to food supplies, and to plant or animal hosts. Obviously, such approaches will require exhaustive research on each insect. However, of the ten thousand different kinds of destructive insects in the country, only a few hundred can be classed as major pests. To make the greatest impact, scientists will concentrate on these, taking the most damaging ones first.

Pest control by introducing a sterile population has already been applied to rid vast areas of the United States of a destructive livestock pest, the screwworm. Large numbers of screwworm flies are reared in the laboratory, sterilized by atomic radiation, and released to mate with the wild population. Since eggs produced from such matings do not hatch, reproduction eventually ceases. The next decade may see sterility — artificially induced by radiation, chemicals, or other means — successfully employed to help eliminate or control several pests — tropical fruit flies, the codling moth, the boll weevil, the pink bollworm, and the tobacco hornworm. The sterility principle may also prove useful against some higher animals that plague our crops, forests, and livestock.

Laboratory animals free from specific germs and viruses are already available for research. In the next decade, many of the more advanced livestock farms may raise pigs and possibly calves and lambs free of all or most diseases, meaning that many young will be taken from their mothers by Caesarean section and raised under sterile conditions, thus breaking the disease cycle. Intensive campaigns now in progress may, within the next decade, eradicate such animal diseases as cattle brucellosis and hog cholera from this country.

The efficiency of animal production will increase materially because of controlled breeding, improvements in animal nutrition, and more mechanization in many livestock operations. Livestock will be bred to provide tenderer and tastier steaks, chops, and other popular meats. The use of artificial insemination will be extended to the breeding of most farm animals. By means of hormones, the times when animals come into heat and are bred will be controlled, so that "spring" lamb, for example, will become a year-round meat.

Germ plasm from superior females will be fertilized with sperm from superior males and the ova transplanted into females of ordinary stock. The offspring will therefore be products of two superior animals.

More meat animals will be fattened in relative confinement, with automatic feeding, air conditioning, and other environmental controls that will promote rapid gains in weight, less disease, and improved efficiency in the use of feed by animals. This can greatly increase productivity, because about three fourths of the important variations in livestock traits are environmental, not genetic, in origin. The control of light in windowless poultry houses may make it possible to breed hens adjusted to a "day" shorter than twenty-four hours, with a consequent stepping up in the number of eggs they can produce a month.

More specialized equipment, including aircraft, will be designed for applying chemicals to control the fertility and other physical conditions of the soil and to fight the natural enemies of plants and animals.

These are some of the advances that we may expect from research in the next ten years. Now let's try to look further ahead into the last part of this century.

Research has already greatly extended the senses of man. Delicate instruments explore a whole physical world of sounds, electromagnetic impulses, colors, odors, and flavors to which we are largely oblivious, but which may completely control other living things. For example, USDA scientists have designed a microcalorimeter that can measure temperatures to one-millionth of a degree: it can measure the minute amount of heat given off when a protein molecule in a cell of a seed ruptures.

The computer has freed the scientist of much routine labor in calculation. In the future, high-speed computing will free even more of his time for broader research. Research teams all over the nation may have access to a central computer through communications lines running from their own laboratories. Three-way conversations involving a computer and scientists working, perhaps in different countries, on different aspects of the same problem may not be too far in the future.

A Dynamic Farm Economy

By the year 2000, farmers should be less at the mercy of the weather. Information from weather satellites will increase the accuracy of long-range weather forecasting. The satellites will warn of tornadoes, hurricanes, and typhoons in the making, so that they can be prepared for, and perhaps diverted or dissipated.

Desalting water and modifying the weather by seeding clouds are intriguing possibilities for increasing water supplies. Desalting is at present uneconomical for agriculture, and weather modification unreliable, but both may well become practical by the end of the century. Before even slight weather modification becomes feasible, however, research must be done on the changes in the relations among plants, soil, and water that such modification would bring about.

If we succeed in reducing evapotranspiration greatly through surface treatment of water, soil, and plants, and if vast areas are so treated, we must be able to predict the effect on the other elements associated with the hydrologic cycle. We must, for example, estimate the rise in temperature that would result when quantities of solar energy are not used up in evapotranspiration.

The need for water for living, recreation, and industry may curtail its agricultural usage in much of the West. As population increases and shifts westward to create this need, we may use the tremendous potential for agricultural production offered by the wet lands of the Gulf States and the southern coastal plains. We could reshape, drain, and otherwise customize much of this land, with tools we already have, at less cost than we could extend irrigation in the West.

Atomic energy has begun to free us from the limitations imposed by chemical and hydraulic energy in the past; its potential appears relatively unlimited. It might be used to desalt water economically. Rural cooperatives are exploring the practicality of using atomic power at two electrical plants. As such power becomes cheaper and more efficient, its use for farm electrification will certainly increase.

Farmers will put electricity to work much more extensively for such things as true automation (that is, mechanized production processes, automatically controlled), and electronic, environmental, and quality control. Electrical energy, like chemicals, can modify the life processes and responses of farm animals, plants, insects, bacteria, and viruses. We may find that masers or lasers, for example, can control insects or other agricultural pests. Foresters may use concentrated light beams — lasers

— and sonic vibration to cut wood. Wave lengths of the entire electromagnetic spectrum can be used in ways limited only by the creative imagination of biologists and engineers.

Exploration of cells, genes, enzymes, seed proteins, and viruses will reveal more of the secrets of life itself. Because of such basic research, plant breeders may use a virus that acts as a carrier to incorporate genes from other species into crops. Scientists may learn how plants form carbohydrates through photosynthesis and how to duplicate the process. When this happens, feed supplies for livestock, and perhaps some food for direct human consumption, will be produced in factories rather than through plants on the land. Revolutionary as such breakthroughs would be, suburbanites will be more gratified if a lawn grass is developed that grows only an inch high. As our control over life processes increases, we might do just that.

By 2000, virus-free plant stocks will be as available as certified seeds are today. We shall learn how to manipulate the teeming life beneath the ground to control soil-borne diseases — perhaps by altering the balance of the soil's microscopic flora and fauna. The science of nematology, now in its infancy, will give us better control over the long-lived nematodes that sap the health of plants and animals. Disease-fighting chemicals may be made to move through plants systemically to prevent infection from pathogens. Diseases and genetic abnormalities will be induced to cripple insects and other pests.

As we learn more about the parasites and diseases of livestock, the gap between veterinary and human medicine will narrow. Both sciences will benefit from new discoveries about blood antigens and reproduction, and about the viruses, disease resistance, and environmental reactions of both plants and animals.

What part, for example, do viruses play in upsetting a turkey's genetic code to trigger parthenogenesis — the production of offspring by an unfertilized female? If we can learn the role of viruses here, we may be able to better understand and treat cancer of animals and man.

Experimental veterinary therapeutics, long neglected, will be one of the major fields of publicly supported research. Before the turn of the century, cures will be found for such diseases as tick fever of cattle and coccidiosis of poultry.

Thus far, scientists have been largely content to improve the breeds of livestock that immigrants brought from their European farms. Perhaps some species of wild game may be either improved or crossed with domestic animals to develop new sources of meat, milk, fur, or fleece. The musk ox and the reindeer may be bred to become valuable domestic animals in Alaska.

Physiological research will make it possible to treat male germ plasm to control the sex of farm animals, and to predict whether eggs will develop into male or female birds. Fertilized ova may be removed from females and developed in artificial media outside the parent, permitting valuable breeding stock to produce many times the number of offspring they could by natural methods.

Tomorrow's research will continue to reshape agriculture and the farming sector within it probably more drastically than it has in the past. It will augment men's basic understanding of the world of living things, and its benefits will spread far beyond our shores to help banish hunger from the world. But it will also bring with it stresses and strains in business and social organization in the farm economy — stresses and strains that will be exceedingly difficult for farm people to live and work through.

The Farm Plant. No man can really know what the farm plant will look like thirty or forty years hence. But certain well-established trends and principles of development provide some guides that we shall use here to construct a picture of farming in the United States in 2000.

First, the number of farms is going to decline for many years to come. USDA experts foresee that the number of full-time farms will be down to 1,668,000 by 1970 (Table 2). By 2000, this number could easily be cut in half. Concurrently, as we have said, the size of farms is going to increase; size as measured by acres may not continue to increase over this long period, but size as measured by investment and volume of output will expand greatly. If the size in acres does not go on expanding, and investment continues to increase, then, assuming a constant price level, we must envision farms where the investment in machinery, equipment, and other producer goods has increased very greatly. The typical farm, as of 2000, will be a huge conglomerate of machines, equipment, and technical processes, mostly operated automatically and watched over by a few skilled workers; the farm of 2000 may be comparable to the fuel-cracking plant of today — miles of pipe, technical production processes, tanks, and gauges, with a few skilled workers supervising the whole operation.

A Dynamic Farm Economy

The above complementary trends — decline in the number of farms and increase in the size of farms — are projected to 2000 not because I have a ruler that won't bend, but because of the nature of technological development in farming. Farms get larger and decline in number as machines and technical processes are developed which permit one man to produce more, reduce his unit costs, and hence improve his income position. This is exactly what has been happening — and what seems likely to continue to happen into the indefinite future.

Take the farm tractor, for example; tractors are becoming more powerful, move faster, and do more things. Every time a farmer buys a new model he can farm more acres and do more operations; he therefore seeks more acres to farm and adds productive operations. In this way the average farm grows in size and the number of farms in a given area declines. Automatic feeding has a similar effect in livestock production; it permits one man to turn out more product and, if properly designed and managed, it reduces unit costs of production. In this case, the size of the farm grows in investment and volume of production, if not in acreage.

Technological advance is what dictates expansion in the size of farms. Technological advance makes the arm of the average farm worker longer and stronger, and dictates that the size of farm, measured in acres or in investment or both, should grow if that longer and stronger arm is to be used efficiently.

Another and related aspect of technological advance in farming is the bringing under control of the varied and often hostile physical environment. It will be recalled that much of the scientific work discussed in the previous section was concerned with such control — control of diseases, temperature, water usage, and so on. We must expect that farm production which took place under almost completely uncontrolled conditions in 1900, and which in the 1960's is rapidly moving under controlled conditions, will by 2000 take place under almost completely controlled conditions.

Livestock production and fattening by 2000 is likely to occur almost entirely in "factories" with controlled breeding, controlled light and temperature, controlled feeding, complete mechanization and automation, and perhaps completely sterile conditions. Such a controlled operation is the way to produce livestock products that are best in terms of taste and quality, with animals that are efficient in rate of gain in weight.

A Dynamic Farm Economy

This situation, which has arrived in the production of broilers, will become general by 2000, but at a more advanced state of technology.

Crops in 2000 will still be grown on the land — but not just any piece of land. Cropland will be carefully graded and contoured to permit a rigorous control of the use of water. Nutrients in the soil will be tailored to the specific needs of each crop. The soil will be treated to control weeds, harmful organisms, and plant diseases. The plants themselves will be improved to give higher yields and to have other desired characteristics such as a short growing period, a stalk that lends itself to mechanical harvesting, and nutrients in the seed or fruit that are in demand.

The weather may be controlled somewhat, and certainly it will be better understood and therefore "controlled" through the use of water and the development of desired characteristics in plants. Crop production will be highly mechanized, and possibly automated with respect to preparing the land, planting the crop, and harvesting it. The crop farm in 2000 may, from a distance, look like a crop farm in the 1960's: crops will be growing in the fields, but there the similarity will stop. The investment per acre in machinery and equipment, production supplies, and technical processes will be many times that of the 1960's. And the yields per acre, under these controlled conditions, will be double or triple those of the 1960's. Science and management will have taken over farming, and out of this combination will emerge production units that stagger the imagination.

The practical policy question immediately comes to mind: how will the family farm organization fare in this brave new world? The answer probably turns on the nature of our policy with respect to family farms. If a positive policy to maintain the family farm is formulated and sustained, then the family farm can probably survive. But with no policy, the family farm concept is likely to disappear. The problem is not one of physical organization or production efficiency; it seems likely that farms can be organized to make use of the most advanced technology and to require no more labor than could be supplied by an average family plus one hired man.

The real problem is a different one. Financing a highly efficient farm production unit in 2000, which could require the investment of several millions of dollars, by an average farmer using traditional financing methods is out of the question. If the idea of the family farm is to survive

41

A Dynamic Farm Economy

among the technological developments presented here, new and creative means of financing will need to be developed to enable a family to put together a two-million- or a five-million-dollar production unit and still hold onto entrepreneurial and managerial control of the organization. A way must be found for a well-trained, skillful farm operator to get control, not of $30,000, but of $3,000,000 to get started in farming.

If a way is not found, the money to finance these farms of the year 2000 is likely to come from commercial nonfarm sources: insurance companies, feed companies, processors, and retail organizations. And operational control invariably follows financial control. We could thus in 2000 have family farms in form but not in spirit — farms organized into productive units that are supervised and operated by a family with the help of one or two workers, but managed by and with their financial risks assumed by a nonfarm organization.

The form of farm business organization in the wild, exciting future appears to be in doubt. The outcome could be determined by policies yet to be developed for financing family farms. But one thing seems certain, the production unit in farming in the year 2000 is going to require a large total investment, its production will be mainly automated and rigorously controlled, and it will need highly skilled and competent management. The farm of 2000 will be as different from the farm of 1900 as a space rocket is from a BB gun.

PART II. THE COMMERCIAL FARM ECONOMY

3

ꝑ

The Engine of Farm Production

WE HAVE read the record of farm output expansion: since 1940 it has soared. And we have seen that this record of output expansion did not occur in the traditional way by increasing the land under the plow and adding workers; it came about through investment in new and better capital goods and the adoption of new and better practices. In this scheme of development total resources — inputs — employed in farming have increased only slightly; in fact, the total productive resources in farming have not increased at all since the early 1940's (Figure 2). Farmers have produced a larger and larger total output with the same volume of resource inputs, measured in constant dollars.

Economists have had a hard time understanding and grasping the implications of this process of development. Before 1950 most of them failed to comprehend what was going on in farming. For a century and a half before then they had worked out a logic, often using farm examples,[1] based on *static models* or *stationary states* in which technological advance is assumed away, and in which output expands in an industry as total resources move into that industry in response to relative high product prices, and output contracts as resources flow out in response to low prices. Thus when farm output expanded markedly in the 1940's and 1950's, economists assumed that this was brought about by an increased application of inputs in farming, which in turn had been caused by high farm prices.

The facts are that farm prices were high in the 1940's, but they were

[1] Alfred Marshall, *Principles of Economics*, 8th ed., Macmillan and Company, 1920, Book V, Chapters II, III.

not in the 1950's, and there was no significant increase in the resources employed in farming in either decade. What really happened went something like this: Farmers replaced worn out tractors with new tractors that were speedier, pulled heavier loads, and did more things faster. They developed a skilled labor force that could understand and operate more complicated and more productive technological processes, but they employed fewer workers. They put together a new production package — improved tillage practices, more fertilizer, more plants to the acre, and improved plant varieties — that greatly increased yields.

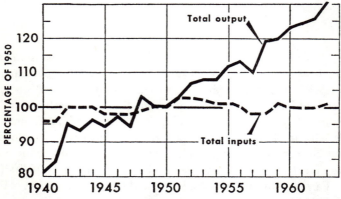

Figure 2. Farm output and inputs (1963 data preliminary)

The engine of modern farm production is farm technological advance. It took most economists a long time to grasp this changed state of affairs, but they have it now. The problem now is for laymen, and particularly farmers themselves, to grasp the implications of this technological upheaval.

Technology Defined. A brief digression on the meaning of technology and farm technological advance is in order here. Technology is a way of achieving some practical purpose: using a bow and arrow to kill game is an example of technology; using a high-powered rifle to kill game is a new and improved technology. The rifle is new in that it came after the bow and arrow; it is improved because it is a surer, more effective way of killing game. Technology often involves tools and machines but it need not; it might involve a new plant-breeding, sanitation, or fertilizing practice. It is a way of achieving some practical purpose. The way may be simple or it may be complex, but it is a way of doing something.

Farm adoption of a new technology is putting a new way of doing something to work on the farm. It will be an advance if it increases the efficiency of the resources employed in production — if it increases the output of the product per unit of inputs.[2] This means that a farm technological advance reduces the cost of producing a unit of product on the farm; a farm technological advance is thus a new way of producing a product that reduces the per unit cost of that product.

SUPPORT FOR THE ENGINE:

EDUCATION, RESEARCH, AND EXTENSION

Farmers adopt new technologies, but for the most part they do not develop them. In the total process of technological advance farmers should come in for their share of the glory: they assume the risk of applying the technology, they take the financial risk, and they must have the technical and management skills necessary to operate successfully the new practice or contraption. But the new technology, the magic, usually comes from somewhere else.

Sometimes it comes directly from the governmental services sector. Sometimes it comes directly from the nonfarm supply sector. But more often it has had a complicated, tortuous, and perhaps even accidental history in both of these sectors, and possibly a history also of some basic research outside the agricultural complex. We shall now want to take a look at the educational, research, and extension or informational efforts that support farm technological advance.

In 1862, when the United States Department of Agriculture and the land-grant college system came into being by congressional action, there were in existence basic sciences — physics, chemistry, physiology, and medicine. There was also an agriculture, or farm economy, just beginning to break the bonds of tradition wherein farm practices were handed down without change from father to son. In between there were a few agricultural societies experimenting with seeds and plants from foreign lands, and a few mechanics and tinkerers, such as Cyrus Mc-Cormick, who developed the first successful grain harvesting machine over the period 1835–55. But there was no real agricultural science or

[2] In economic parlance, farm technological advance shifts the production function to a higher level.

sciences. Such fields as are now commonplace — agronomy, soil chemistry, plant pathology, and animal husbandry — based on scientific methods and experimentation, simply did not exist in 1862.

There was thus the question — What should these new institutions do? The new USDA could continue to collect and disseminate seeds as its predecessor agencies had done, but in time it would need a stronger reason for being than that. What then should the new agricultural colleges do? The practical answer was — teach good farming practices to farm youth. But what was there to teach? Farm youth already knew the accepted practices; they had learned those from their fathers. And there existed no body of good practices based upon scientific work in agriculture to teach. The other answer was to teach the basic sciences (chemistry and physics), literature, and philosophy. But how was this to help farm youth become better farmers?

The struggle between the proponents of these differing views continued for twenty or thirty years inside and outside the colleges, with the private church-affiliated college groups sniping from one side and farmers' support running from total indifference to making fun of those impractical professors. As Professor James Bonnen has said, "It is difficult to read the early history of the USDA or that of the LGC's [land-grant colleges] without wondering how any of these institutions survived." [3]

But they did. And slowly both the USDA and the land-grant colleges began to approach agriculture scientifically. How the forces of scientific education and research for agriculture won the battle and built the base for scientific agriculture in this period between the warring forces of vocationalism on the one hand and pure science and philosophy on the other is not at all clear. But at least in the colleges, Professor Bonnen believes that the warring forces "helped each other more than they knew. . . . The vocational outlook was necessary if the institutions were to obtain the support of their potential constituents; the application of science to vocation was necessary before the system could develop a product of genuine value to any constituent." [4] This was a period of institution building, and it was slow because there was no blueprint to guide the building process.

In any event both the USDA and the land-grant colleges survived,

[3] "Some Observations on the Organizational Nature of a Great Technological Payoff," *Journal of Farm Economics*, December 1962, p. 1280.
[4] *Ibid.*, p. 1282.

expanded, and, by 1890, were ready to make their mark. The years from 1890 to 1920 can be described as the time when the agricultural sciences developed and became mature disciplines. By the middle 1890's the successful agricultural college had professorships in horticulture, entomology, agricultural chemistry, botany, agronomy, dairy husbandry, and animal husbandry. In the USDA "Tama Jim" Wilson, Secretary of Agriculture from 1897 to 1913, reorganized the department to bring science to farming. The many independent offices, divisions, and sections of the department were consolidated into the bureaus of Plant Industry, Animal Industry, Soils, Statistics, Entomology, Biological Survey, and Forestry. Each bureau reported directly to the secretary. With his department organized into bureaus corresponding to the scientific disciplines and reporting directly to him, Tama Jim pushed the development of sciences in and for agriculture hard, very hard.

The result of this expanded and professional work was a great accumulation of knowledge about the chemical and physical properties of the soil, and the growth processes, the genetics, and the diseases of plants and animals, where almost none had existed a quarter or a half century before. From this basic scientific knowledge about the subject matter of agriculture recommendations for improving farming practices could now flow. Plant breeding on a controlled basis to improve strains and varieties could take place, information about plant nutrients could be given to farmers, and the control of plant and animal diseases could move out of the witch-doctor stage.

In short, by the time the United States entered World War I, the agricultural sciences had come of age. There was much solid material to teach college students, and much information to extend to farmers. By 1914, farmers were being advised on the basis of scientific knowledge what to feed, how to fertilize, what improved seeds to use, and how to rotate their crops. Technology at the farm level was on the move. It had taken fifty years to put it on the move — twenty-five years of fumbling and twenty-five years more of scientific achievement. But the time had come to stop laughing at "those impractical fellers up at the state university."

The Extension Service came into being in 1914, and by 1918 some 2,435 counties in the United States had agricultural agents. The Extension Service came along at the right time. There were a great number of relatively simple but important new technologies to take to the farmer such as vaccination to control certain diseases in livestock (hog cholera, for example), disease-resistant strains of various small grains, and animal feeding practices. All this one well-trained college graduate could do. The county extension agent thus became a very important man in American agriculture in the 1920's; he was the man who carried the new technologies to the farmers.

In the 1930's the county agent was pressed into the service of the old Agricultural Adjustment Administration (AAA) and became something of a local administrator, and this happened again during World War II; he helped ration fuel, tires, and machinery during the latter period. By the end of World War II the level and sophistication of farm technology was becoming too complex for one man to handle in all its varied aspects. The county extension agent and his assistants (some counties having three or four assistants) remain key men in local farming affairs since World War II, but the day of the generalist who extends technical information to farmers is past. In the 1950's and 1960's the disseminators of new and improved production practices were most often specialists — perhaps Extension Service specialists, but more often salesmen, or representatives, of private firms from the nonfarm supply sector.

We must go back and pick up the research and developmental threads of our story. Between 1930 and 1960, the agricultural colleges became part of great state universities in which the whole spectrum of science and technology had expanded greatly. In the expansion of science after World War II research has not increased as rapidly in the agricultural sciences as it has in medicine or physics, but the agricultural sciences have continued to grow, and they have benefited greatly from general research in medicine, genetics, physics, chemistry, and botany. The typical agricultural college in a state university is a large research complex with a research budget running up to five or six million dollars a year, standing between the basic sciences on one side and a newer, modern phenomenon on the other.

That phenomenon is the establishment of first-rate research departments in the private firms of the nonfarm supply sector. The big machinery, seed, feed, chemical and pharmaceutical companies, as well as the food-processing firms, all maintain their own research departments, where the emphasis is, of course, on development — the development of specific technologies that meet the production needs of farmers and can therefore be sold to them.

The Engine of Farm Production

The total American agricultural research complex in the United States is rounded out by the work of the USDA. Though, relatively, research in the agricultural sciences does not now have the pre-eminent role in the USDA that it did in 1910, it has grown absolutely, and had an annual budget running well over $200 million in the middle 1960's. This is a big operation; not so big as many farm groups with technical problems think it should be, but nonetheless big. The total complex — state agricultural colleges, USDA, and private research establishments — provides a substantial and growing scientific and technical base for agriculture and farming; the total expenditure for research in the three areas was $730 million in 1963–64.

As the research complex of agricultural sciences and technological developments deepened and widened over the thirty years between 1930 and 1960, a rough division of labor also began to appear. All sorts of exceptions exist, but the agricultural colleges and the USDA tend to concentrate on the more basic research and the training of agricultural scientists, while the private firms tend to concentrate on research designed to produce specific technologies for farmers' use. An agricultural college is more likely to do the basic genetic and breeding work on a plant leading to a hybrid with certain desired characteristics, whereas the private firm is more likely to do research on that hybrid leading to a plant variety particularly adapted to a specific area with unique growing conditions.

The USDA and the agricultural colleges tend to concentrate on research problems of general applicability, and the product of their research flows into the public domain for all to use. Private firms, on the other hand, tend to concentrate on developing specific technologies to meet specific production problems; their research findings are usually secret, and the product of their research is usually sold under a brand name.

Sometimes most or all of the basic research is done by private companies, as in the case of some of the chemical pesticides, and sometimes both the basic research and the development are done by a college or by the USDA, as was the case in the control measures for combating the screwworm in cattle. It would therefore be wrong to try to compartmentalize agricultural research too rigidly, but it is not wrong to present a picture of a vast complex of science, technological development, and extension work in the broadest sense that is continuously bringing forward and carrying to the farm gate many and varied new and improved technologies.

In a rough flow scheme there are first the basic sciences, chemistry, physics, and biology, that make certain important physical relations known; next are the agricultural sciences that adapt knowledge from the basic sciences to build bodies of knowledge in the agricultural fields; next is the developmental research that converts the knowledge from the agricultural sciences into specific problem-solving knowledge; next is the production of specific technologies for adoption and use on the farm — machines, vaccines, hybrid seeds, mixed-feed formulas; finally, there is a variety of means for extending this technology to the farmer — extension specialists, salesmen, company servicemen, farm magazines, advertising and professional men.

This is a vast network as of the 1960's. Unplanned, it is woven together by the free movement of public information and the ever-present price system. It is part private and part public. It was a century in the building, and it is working marvelously well. It supports the process of farm technological advance by regularly bringing forth techniques and practices that advance the productivity of farming across the nation. It makes the farm economy run.

Simultaneously with the spectacular achievements in the agricultural sciences and technology, the technical and management skills of commercial farm operators have steadily improved, not dramatically, but steadily. The typical commercial farm operator of the 1960's was not a college graduate; some of the older operators were not even high school graduates. But most of the younger or middle-aged operators were high school graduates, and most had good vocational training in agriculture in their high schools or as a part of the 4H programs of the Extension Service.

The upgrading of labor skills in farming has been an indirect process. The agricultural colleges have trained the high school vocational agricultural teachers and the youth workers in the Extension Service, and these teachers and youth workers have trained the farm youth. The young man starting in farming in the 1960's had several years of vocational agricultural training in high school and took part in several technical production projects in 4H. High school provides the basic literacy that anyone must have to work and live in this modern world; vocational training assists the young farmer in several ways: he learns that his father's way of farming is not the only way; he learns the most advanced practices and technologies at the time and how to operate and manage them; and, probably most important, he acquires an attitude toward farming — that it is a developing industry and that he must grow, adapt, and change with it if he is to be a business success.

Many farmers do not understand the social and economic implications of the technological revolution. But the young to middle-aged farmers understand machines, plants, and animals in the technical sense — they can handle, repair, produce, and manage them. Farm technological advance finds a friendly and competent reception among such operators and their families.

HOW THE ENGINE WORKS

Now we shall consider farm technological advance — our engine — at the research, development, and farm levels, and we shall review and analyze the process by using a hypothetical example. In Chapter 2 we noted that electric energy can modify the life process. Let us now consider this example: A scientist working on a basic problem in a state university theorizes that a plant treated in a particular way by electrical energy during its growth will develop certain desirable mutations and produce twice as much fruit in succeeding generations. For the moment, this is a hypothesis put forth by a scientist in a research paper.

Now a geneticist in the United States Department of Agriculture picks up the idea and begins to experiment with it. He discovers that the mutations do occur, but unpredictably. He then enlists the aid of a plant breeder and they continue to develop plant sports, breeding those sports that have the desired characteristic — that produce twice as much fruit. They continue until they get a plant that will breed true: that is, the seed from the mutated plant will consistently yield the characteristics of the parent plant. These men in turn write a paper, and their results become common knowledge among plant breeders.

The research and experimental phases are past, but much developmental work remains to be done. The new variety may yield twice as much as the original variety, but it may not be resistant to certain plant diseases, and the plant stalk may be too weak for the weight of the head, hence not stand up well for mechanical harvesting.

Here a private seed-producing firm may enter the picture, and start cross-breeding the new variety with other varieties to develop a disease-resistant variety with a strong short stalk. After three or four years, the firm may come up with a variety ready to be put on the market — one that yields only a third more than the original variety, but which is disease-resistant and has a strong stalk.

Between the writing of the original paper and the offering of the new variety by the private seed firm, ten or twenty years may have elapsed. At each stage, researchers will have been lured up blind alleys and some research teams will have failed and given up. But with many researchers involved, free access to research experiences and results, and a generous expenditure of money, breakthroughs occur. It is impossible to say when or where a breakthrough will take place, but they do happen, and after a course of events somewhat like that described above.

Will the farmer adopt this new variety when the seed company's salesman comes around? In the first year most will not adopt it, but a few will. The innovator — the man constantly on the lookout for new production practices that will lower his costs per bushel and who has the technological background to read and understand the literature about the new variety — will adopt it if he believes its potential is good. Assuming that the variety proves out under practical conditions, the output per unit of productive resources will have increased on the innovator's farm. His costs of producing a bushel will have gone down and, assuming prices unchanged, his net return will have increased. The innovator is thus rewarded for his superior business and technological judgment and skill.

The next year more farmers will adopt the new variety; the news about the higher yields will have got around. The neighbors of the innovator will have seen the increased yields, the county agent will have held meetings to discuss the new variety, and the salesman will have told everyone who would listen. In a few years the variety will be widely adopted, and *total* production on each farm and in the producing area will increase significantly.

The process of adoption in such a case is fairly simple. The cost of adoption would be low; the price of this improved variety would be very little more than that of previous improved varieties that had gone through a comparable development process. Production practices in the field would be little different. The only question at issue was whether the new variety increased the output by a third. Once this was established under practical growing conditions, the new variety's widespread adoption would be assured.

But the case is not always so simple. The new technology may require a major capital investment, or a major reorganization of the farm operations. And the question is often asked — If farming is unprofitable, why does any farmer adopt new practices? Or, if everyone adopts the new practice, total output expands, and the product price falls — Why does any farmer adopt the practice in the first place?

To fully understand the process of farm technological advance and thus answer such questions, we must first look at the economic structure of farming. Farming is an atomistic industry: each producer is so small compared with the total output of the industry that each has no perceptible influence on output or upon the price of his product.

In other words, *the farmer is a price taker.* But though he cannot influence the price at which he sells, he can on his individual farm do something about his production practices and organization, and influence his own costs of production. Thus, with price given to him — a price made in the world market, in Washington, or in heaven — which he individually cannot influence, he can, if he can get his unit costs down, improve his economic position. He can reduce his losses or improve his profits as the case may be. And he can get his unit costs of production down by the adoption of a new technology that increases his output per unit of resources employed.

This he does if the new technique is available and if he is an astute business manager. This he does whether he is losing money at the time or making money, for in either case the adoption of the new technology improves his own economic situation. This is why new and improved technologies are adopted, whether economic conditions are good, bad, or indifferent. Each farmer sees the new technology as a solution to his problem; it is a way of getting his costs down. There is always an incentive for the farmer to adopt a new and improved technology.

This generalization is equally true throughout the whole of the adoption process. The early innovator sees the opportunity to increase his profits and he succeeds, because he makes the adoption and reduces his costs before price declines. His neighbors, and the average farmers of the community, adopt the practice to reap the rewards achieved by the innovator, but when many farmers have adopted it, total output increases and a downward pressure on prices is created. Whether the price actually declines and wipes out the income gains of the average farmer depends upon the existence or nonexistence of a farm price support program.

With no program, the price of the product must fall, and some or all of the gain is wiped out. If prices are supported, the gains of the technological advance are held by the average farmer. Where price falls in the free market, the laggard must adopt or be crushed in the price-cost squeeze. And after the price has fallen through the aggregate effect of increased total output, *all* farmers — innovator, average, and laggard — must hold to the practice in order to keep their costs of production from rising again and thereby reducing their net return per unit of product.

In another context I have called this the agricultural treadmill.[5] Under free market conditions, it certainly is a treadmill: farmers are simply the instruments of technological advance through which cost and price reductions are passed along to the consumer. Technological advance with price support is something else again. Here some or all the benefits of technological advance are held by Mr. Average Farmer as well as by the early bird. But there are implications even here, some good, some bad, that need analysis, which will be provided in Chapters 4 and 7 of this volume. The point to be made here is that farm technological advance works at all times to expand farm output through the ubiquitous incentive of reducing costs and thereby, in an atomistic situation, of increasing net returns. Technological advance is the engine of the modern farm economy.

FARM TECHNOLOGICAL ADVANCE ILLUSTRATED

Perhaps a major analysis of farm technological advance in the United States would disclose which parts of that advance have contributed most to increased production, which next most, and so on. But lacking such an analysis, it would be misleading to try to rank in order of importance the different aspects of farm technology. All have been important, and many technological practices complement one another. For example, the rapid increase in corn yields in the 1950's and 1960's was not the result of improved varieties alone; it was the result of combining improved varieties, improved water control, increased fertilizer applications, and more plants to the acre. Such a package of practices is often required to achieve a significant jump in production.

[5] *Farm Prices: Myth and Reality*, University of Minnesota Press, 1958, Chapter 5.

The Engine of Farm Production

But some technological developments have been more spectacular than others: the farm tractor, which released some fifty-five million acres over a quarter century from the production of crops for animal power to the production of products for human consumption, is one such; hybrid corn is another.[6] It is also true that two such spectacular developments as the tractor and hybrid corn do not lend themselves equally well to pictorial illustration. It is easy to show the development of farm power and mechanization through pictures, but plant breeding, seeds, and growing plants are difficult to show graphically.

To illustrate the dramatic development in farm technology during the past half century a series of photographs (between pp. 66 and 67) shows the old and the new in farm power and mechanization. This aspect of farm technological advance is not shown because it is necessarily most important, but because it has been spectacular and because it lends itself to presentation in pictures. So see what man has wrought on farms over the past fifty years.

[6] For a good case study of this development see Zvi Griliches, "Hybrid Corn: An Exploration in the Economics of Technological Change," *Econometrica*, October 1957.

4

♠

The Technological Payoff

THE technological payoff in farm production is here; it has been here for about two decades, and it promises to become more valuable and more certain in the years to come. We have already seen the increases in total farm output of recent decades (Table 4). Total farm output increased 20 per cent during the 1950's; and over the slightly longer period 1950–63, it increased 28 per cent.

The steady upward march of farm output in recent years may be seen in the accompanying tabulation. The index of farm output stands

1940	70	1952	92
1941	73	1953	93
1942	82	1954	93
1943	80	1955	96
1944	83	1956	97
1945	81	1957	95
1946	84	1958	102
1947	81	1959	103
1948	88	1960	106
1949	87	1961	107
1950	86	1962	108
1951	89	1963	112

at 70 in 1940, and moves up persistently at an average rate of 1.8 points per year through 1963. Two points should be kept in mind in appraising this record. First, total output slips backward in a few years, owing to weather and pests which research and technological development are striving mightily to bring under control. Second, the increases in total output from 1958 to 1963 took place in spite of strong measures to control production; between 50 and 60 million acres were annually diverted from production and kept idle by government programs in 1961,

1962, and 1963. But total farm output pushed forward: this is the technological payoff.[1]

The simplest and probably best understood measure of farm production efficiency is *yield per acre*. Here the data are both interesting and startling. Let us look first at that great commodity corn on which the modern livestock industry is built. Corn yields in bushels per acre from 1870 to 1940 are shown in the accompanying tabulation. Yields behaved

1870	29.3
1880	27.3
1890	22.1
1900	28.1
1910	27.9
1920	29.9
1930	20.5
1940	28.9

in these decades as they had during the preceding two centuries; they fluctuated with weather, but showed no noticeable improvement. During the late 1930's and early 1940's, however, a package of new technologies including hybrid varieties, more plants to the acre, and much heavier applications of fertilizer was adopted by American farmers, and the picture changed thereafter; yields in bushels per acre shot up as follows:

1950	38.2
1960	54.5
1963	67.3

Corn yields per acre increased more during the twenty-three-year period from 1940 than they had from the dawn of history to 1940. And the potential for increasing the use of fertilizer is such that a national yield figure of 100 bushels per acre should be possible by 1975.

Similar phenomena have been taking place in other major crops — wheat and cotton (see Table 5). The yield per acre of cotton rose importantly during the 1930's, but the wheat yield did not. During the 1940's, all three crops showed important increases in yield and in the 1950's yields soared in all three crops. Wheat yields are subject to greater instability than the other two crops, because it is grown mainly

---

[1] For those who want more details about farm production and measures of efficiency than the following, an excellent source is *Changes in Farm Production and Efficiency: A Summary Report*, published annually by the USDA in the Statistical Bulletin series.

The Technological Payoff

Table 5. Yield Increases per Acre for Corn, Cotton, and Wheat,
Selected Periods, U.S., 1930–63

Crop	1930–39	1940–49	1950–59	1950–63
Corn	22.5%	32.3%	41.6%	78.0%
Cotton	36.2	19.4	67.0	92.0
Wheat	−1.8	5.8	60.4	60.2

in the high-risk area of the Great Plains. But even taking this weather-induced variability into account, we can expect yields of all three of these basic crops to rise in the future.

Yield developments in many other crops are roughly similar to those for corn, cotton, and wheat, some more spectacular, others less so. But the trends are the same: gradual or uneven development up to 1940, and then sharp increases thereafter. It is interesting that several private seed firms are devoting a large part of their research budgets to developing a hybrid wheat; when that hits (it is only a matter of time), wheat yields will take another important step upward.

The aggregate development in the yield per acre for all crops is summarized in the top line of Table 6. The yield, or production, increase per

Table 6. Increases, by Different Measures of Production Efficiency,
Selected Periods, U.S., 1930–63

Measure	1930–39	1940–49	1950–59	1950–63
Crop production per acre	8.8%	15.0%	24.4%	40.6%
Output per man hour	23.3	58.2	80.0	125.0
Output per unit of input	11.8	18.3	20.2	28.4

acre for all crops is 8.8 per cent in the 1930's, 15 per cent in the 1940's, and 24.4 per cent in the 1950's. But crop yields generally are increasing more rapidly in the 1960's than in the '50's, as shown by the large increase for 1950–63 in Table 6. It would appear that increases in crop production per acre in the 1960's will run over 30 per cent. The payoff is getting richer.

The very great increases in worker productivity that have taken place in farming in recent decades are shown in the second line of Table 6. The average farm worker produced nearly 60 per cent more product in 1950 than he did in 1940, and 80 per cent more in 1960 than in 1950. This rate of increase in productivity borders on the miraculous and grows out of two developments we have already observed: the marked increases in total farm output and the concurrent rapid decline in the number of farm workers. Where will it end? In the wild, exciting future described in Chapter 2.

The measure of production efficiency — output per unit of input — in the third line of Table 6 is the most inclusive measure. It measures the change — in this case increase — in output per unit of resources employed. It measures the output forthcoming from a unit of resources when all resources employed in the production of the commodity are accounted for. In this sense the measure is inclusive. It is not like output per man hour, which increases partly because the working force shrinks, and unlike production per acre, which increases partly because a critical resource, fertilizer, is added to the land. The measure output per unit of input takes account of all resource additions and deductions, and thus provides a measure of efficiency in terms of a standard resource unit valued in dollars.

Output per unit of input really measures the magic of technological advance.[2] It tells how much output increases over time from a standard unit of resource inputs, measured in dollars, because the resources in that standard unit have been combined in *new ways*, into new, improved technological configurations. The value of the resources in the standard unit is held constant, but the form and the state of the resources in the standard unit are not. To the extent that the new configuration of resources represents an advance, output per unit of input on the farm will increase, and the index will rise.

From Table 6 we see that production efficiency as measured by output per unit of input increased about 12 per cent during the 1930's, about 18 per cent in the 1940's and about 20 per cent in the 1950's. In other words, a given bundle of resources, measured in constant dollars, employed in farming produced 20 per cent more product in 1960 than it did in 1950. Because of technological advance a bundle of resources of a constant size measured in dollars was 20 per cent more efficient in 1960 than in 1950.

The upward trend in over-all production efficiency, as measured by output per unit of input, should continue during the 1960's. How much it goes up will depend upon how many important new, improved tech-

---

[2] Some economists may want to argue that it may not be measuring technological advance, but rather a general movement by farmers to lower points on their long-run planning curves. Theoretically this is possible, but who really believes that more farmers are in more nearly full adjustment and hence at a lower point on their planning curve in 1960 than in 1950?

nologies reach the farmer in this decade. Simply increasing crop yields through the addition of fertilizer will not cause this measure to rise. But increased yields resulting from the use of additional fertilizer, improved plant varieties, improved cultural practices, and less labor inputs, so that the total value of inputs is held constant, would march this measure of efficiency up several more steps. This will surely happen in the future, but the timing is always difficult to predict.

One final measure of the technological payoff must be considered. It is the number of persons supplied per farm worker (Figure 3). This measure is less precise than the previous one, but in many ways it is more interesting. The number of consumers supplied by one farm worker in 1820 was 4.1, a number that gradually increased to 6.9 by 1900 and 10.7 by 1940. In a hundred years (1820 to 1920), the number of persons supplied by one farm worker just about doubled, and in a hundred and twenty years (to 1940) the number increased one and a half times.

But like all other measures of efficiency we have looked at, this one shoots skyward after 1940. By 1950 one farm worker was supplying the needs of 15.4 consumers for farm products, and by 1963 one farm worker was supplying 30.7 consumers. In other words, the average farm worker was able to feed and clothe 6.6 more people in 1940 than he had in 1820, but he was able to feed and clothe 20 more people in 1963 than he had in 1940.

Probably most of the increase in the number of persons supplied by one farm worker between 1820 and 1900 did not result from tech-

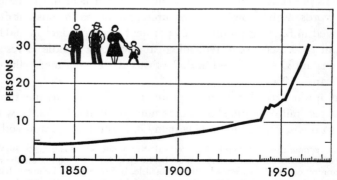

Figure 3. Number of persons supplied per farm worker
(1963 data preliminary)

nological advance; it resulted rather from the addition of fertile land to the average worker. The increase from 1900 to 1940 probably resulted mostly from increased investment in capital of which a part represented technological advance — the tractor, improved planting and harvesting machinery, and improved plant varieties. But after 1940 it is technological advance that shoots up the line in Figure 3 showing the number of persons supplied.

THE MEANING FOR FARMERS

In pure theory, and in the free market, it is perfectly clear who receives the payoff of farm technological advance. The innovators receive the gains of technological advance during the process of industry-wide adoption of the technology, but after the technology has been adopted generally and complete resource adjustment to the new technology has been made, then the full payoff of the technological advance goes to consumers.

The theory is as follows: Price is determined in the market by the workings of supply and demand, and the price so determined is given to the producer. Each producer is so small that he can have no perceptible influence on price. The innovating farmer adopting an improved technology reduces his unit costs of production, but since he has no perceptible influence on price, his net return to each unit produced increases. The innovator holds the gain resulting from the technological advance until it is widely adopted.

When a large number of farmers have adopted the new technology, the aggregate supply of the product increases and its price in the market begins to fall. When the whole industry has adopted the technology, supplies of the commodity may increase so much that the price falls to levels that cause many of the less efficient adopters to lose money. Some go out of business, the supply of the product is reduced, and prices move up to that level where the costs of production of all remaining producers are covered, but where no profits from the adoption of the new and improved technology remain. At this final stage the full payoff from the technological advance is passed on to consumers.

In the pure case, under a free market, then, the consumer is the ultimate gainer. A policy of supporting and advancing agricultural sciences and technology is really, therefore, a consumer-oriented policy. It may be formulated and pursued in the guise of an aid to farmers, as it has, and most consumers may be oblivious to its benefits to them, as they have, but broadly speaking the emphasis on education, research, and development in agriculture since 1862 has been the central core of a low-food-price policy, not a farm-income-assistance policy. Insofar as pure theory holds, farmers have simply been the operating instruments through which the gains of technological advance have been passed along to consumers.

Unfortunately, at least for purposes of exposition, pure theory does not hold without qualification. Since the early 1930's, farm prices have been supported by the government, and thus, for much of the 1930's, the 1950's, and the 1960's there is no question but that farm prices would have been much lower than they were in any particular year, if there had been no price support; [3] excess supplies would have pushed down the level of farm prices 10 to 30 per cent, depending upon the year. Further, it seems obvious to me that farm prices would have gone higher than they did in the war years of the 1940's if it had not been for the increased price support provided in the 1930's and the price certainty provided by price support in the 1940's. The higher, more stable prices provided farmers through governmental actions in the late 1930's and early 1940's certainly helped to trigger the technological revolution of those years.

Let us turn more specifically to the period after the Korean action — 1952–64 — years in which farm technological advance has been rapid, surpluses have been common, and the level of farm prices has ridden on the price-support program. In this situation the farmer remains a price taker; the price may be set in Washington, but as an individual he has no perceptible influence on it; it is given to him. For the innovator nothing is changed. By adopting the improved technology, he has reduced his unit costs of production, the price of the product is unchanged, and his return per unit of product rises. As the technology spreads through the industry, total supply is affected; it increases, caus-

[3] There is always the question of where the level of farm prices would have been in 1963 if there had been no price support program from 1933 on. With lower and less stable prices in the 1930's and the 1950's, it is probable that the rate of adoption of new technology would have been slower than it was, and the pressure of supplies on population less. If that had happened, the level of farm prices in a free market in the 1950's and 1960's would probably have been higher than the level of prices in a free market where that free market followed many years of price support. But no one is ever going to untangle this iffy question to the full satisfaction of all the people involved.

ing a downward pressure on prices, but prices do not fall because of the government support operations. In this case, after industry-wide adoption of the technology, supply increases, price stays at the support level, excess supplies move into government hands, and the economic gains from the technological advance are held by *all* the farmers involved — the average farmer and the laggard as well as the early bird.

But this is not the end of the story. The greater return to all farmers from the technological advance will be taken into account in their thinking and acting — it will be capitalized into the value of the fixed assets of their farms, namely, real estate. Land values will rise to reflect the income gain from the technological advance; thus the gain from a technological advance will be converted into higher land values as farmers and nonfarmers compete for land on which to employ that technological advance. And through the process of competition for land, land prices will rise to a level where unit costs of production are once again equal to price, and there is no profit remaining which is attributable to the technological advance.

Are the facts of the situation consistent with this qualified theory of farm technological advance? First, the level of prices received by farmers has held almost constant since 1954. The pressure of supplies on demand has kept the level of farm prices down to the support level, and price supports have stabilized farm prices and held them constant since 1954. Second, from our earlier analysis we know that farm technological advance has been rapid in this period. Third, land values have risen at about 6 to 7 per cent per year since 1953: farm real estate, land, and buildings, which averaged $82 per acre in 1953, had increased to $140 by 1963.

The facts of the situation are consistent with the theory — or perhaps more than consistent, for it seems unlikely that the substantial increase in land values between 1953 and 1963 is to be explained by technological advance alone. Certainly the very large increases in land values in the Southeast and the Southwest, where farm land is moving into urban developments, is not to be explained by farm technological advance. The demand for land for urban and suburban development is the principal explanation there.

But the steady increases in farm land values in the Dakotas, Minnesota, Iowa, Missouri, and Illinois from 1953 to 1963, when farm prices were not increasing, must have another explanation. We know that the

The Technological Payoff

reason for more than half of land purchases has been for the enlargement of farms. Such purchases are consistent with technological development; one worker is now able to handle more and more acres efficiently. The returns from adding a piece of land to the total farm operation, when the machinery and equipment of that operation are underutilized, are high. The incentive to acquire more land to round out efficient farm units in the 1950's and 1960's was thus an important reason for rising land values.

It is hypothesized here that the full economic gains of farm technological advance become capitalized into land values where product prices are supported through government programs. If this is true, the benefits of farm technological advance ultimately go to landowners. If the farmer is a landowner he benefits; if he is a renter he does not — the doctor, the lawyer, the land speculator, and insurance company do. To turn the gains of technological advance into cash the landowner must, of course, sell the land. But whether he sells or continues to hold, the economic gain is there, and it will move into increased land values so long as product prices do not fall accordingly. In logic and in practice there is no other place for those gains to go.

In summary: the innovators reap the gains of technological advance during the early phases of adoption, but after the improved technology has become industry-wide, the gains to innovators and all other farmers are eroded away either through falling product prices or rising land prices or a combination of the two, and in the long run the specific income gains to farmers are wiped out and farmers are back where they started — in a no-profit position. In this sense, technological advance puts farmers on a treadmill.

THE MEANING FOR CONSUMERS

Widespread technological advance on farms in the United States has meant abundant food supplies for consumers; that is the overriding consequence of the farm technological payoff for Americans. As we saw in Chapter 2, technological advance, combined with the stabilizing influence of price support, has pushed the total output of farm products ahead of domestic population requirements in every year since the early 1930's. This has created a farm problem, but it has eliminated from the United States the age-old fear of hunger. The typical American consumer has eaten well and cheaply, because food supplies have been abundant. And since total resources employed in farming have not increased as population has, the continued abundance must result from farm technological advance.

It may be argued that supplies of farm products have been too abundant in recent years, that government stocks of several important crops have been excessive. This is a justifiable argument. The carryover stocks of wheat in 1961 were 1.4 billion bushels, a sufficient supply to fill domestic needs for two and a half years without any additional production. By any standards wheat stocks were excessive. But in the uncertain world in which we live a large reserve stock of a storeable commodity like wheat is desirable; technicians in the USDA have several times concluded that a reserve stock of between six hundred and seven hundred million bushels of wheat would be in the national interest.

Now the important point for this discussion is not that the goal — adequate reserve stocks — has been consistently overachieved in wheat, cotton, and feed grains, and that this chronic oversupply should be corrected. The important point is that production is adequate to meet annual domestic consumption requirements, a growing volume of commercial trade, a huge volume of foreign food aid, and to maintain without difficulty a desired level of reserve stocks.

In terms of nutrients, food supplies are more than adequate. For more than a decade the supplies available for domestic consumption have been large enough to meet the nutritional requirements of every consumer for every category of nutrient each year. This does not mean that the diet of every man, woman, and child in the United States has been adequate; because of ignorance, bad habits, or sometimes poverty, the diets of many Americans are nutritionally deficient. But the reason is not inadequate supplies.

The housewife may feel after a spree at the supermarket that food prices are high and the city dweller may argue that food prices would be lower if we got rid of those terrible government farm programs — which would be true in the short run, although not to the extent often believed, but which in the long run is open to debate: we do not know how much technological advance would be slowed down with lower farm prices and less stable farm prices in a free market. But the fact is that the food bill of the average consumer in the United States was less, relative to his income, in 1963 than at any earlier time or any other place in the world.

The Technological Payoff

In that year, the average consumer spent 19 per cent of his disposable income on food, a decline from 26 per cent in 1947–49. More importantly, if consumers had bought the same kinds and quantities of food and the same kinds and quantities of food services in 1963 that they bought in the 1930's, their food bill would have been 14 per cent of their income. But consumers have upgraded their diets by substituting meats and vegetables for potatoes and cereals, and they are buying many more services associated with and built into food products than they were in the 1930's. Still, the percentage of their income spent on food is going down.

Compared with other countries, the percentage of income allocated to the purchase of food is lowest in the United States. The average consumer spends about 30 per cent of his income on food in the United Kingdom, between 30 and 40 per cent in Western Europe, 40 per cent in Japan, over 50 per cent in the USSR, and 60 to 70 per cent in some of the less developed countries. Moreover, the percentage in the United States is declining steadily each year.

The real cost of food to the American consumer has declined importantly in recent decades. The material in Figure 4 is given in real terms — loaves, pounds, and hours — because all product prices and wage rates were rising between 1929 and 1963, and it is only by reducing the relations to real terms that one can tell what really happened during

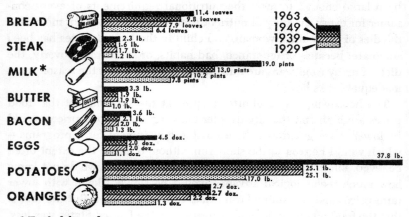

* Fresh delivered.

Figure 4. Quantities of food one hour of factory labor bought, 1963, 1949, 1939, 1929 (length of bars on pound basis)

this dynamic period. Figure 4 shows that an hour of factory labor would buy 6.4 loaves of bread in 1929; but one hour in 1963 would buy 11.4. An hour of factory labor would buy 1.2 pounds of steak in 1929, and 2.3 pounds in 1963. An hour would buy 3.9 quarts of milk in 1929, and 9.5 in 1963. In every important category, an hour of factory labor bought twice as much or more in 1963 as it bought in 1929.

Figure 4 is based on an hour of factory labor, but similar results are found when other categories of labor are used.[4] The real cost of food to the American consumer has declined by a half or more since 1929.

This happened first because wage rates in nonfarm industries generally tripled or quadrupled between 1929 and 1963, and second because prices of farm products did not quite double during the same period. In other words, nonfarm hourly earnings have increased at about twice the rate of farm product prices, so an hour of factory labor bought twice as much food in 1963 as in 1929.

The explanation for the less rapid rise in farm product prices over this long period rests squarely on farm technological advance. New and improved production methods, and the resulting bountiful output, kept farm prices from running wild during the war years of the 1940's, and have held the whole structure of farm prices at price support levels since 1954.

The payoff to consumer from farm technological advance has been the great increases in farm output since 1940, which moderated the wartime price boom of the 1940's and which held farm prices at price-support levels in the 1950's and 1960's. This development, along with rising nonfarm earnings and wage rates, has sharply cut the real cost of food to American consumers, who have been the chief beneficiaries of the century-long policy of research, development, and extension work in agriculture. Such will also be their good fortune in the decades to come.

THE MEANING FOR THE NATIONAL ECONOMY

Rapid, widespread technological advance in American farming has had important implications for resource use and economic growth in the national economy. During the period 1940–63, total farm output in-

---

[4] More information and details about this subject and marketing margins may be found in my testimony in the *Hearings before a Subcommittee of the Committee on Appropriation, House of Representatives, 87th Congress, Second Session Part I*, pp. 280–295, Department of Agricultural Appropriations, 1963.

creased 60 per cent. This was achieved, as we have already observed, with almost no increase in the total resources employed in farming, but rather through technological advance.

But within the constant bundle of total resource inputs there were some significant changes over the period 1940–63. The volume of off-farm-produced inputs employed in farming increased greatly, and the volume of farm labor inputs decreased greatly. The farm sector provided a large, expanding market for such items as tractors and other farm machinery, fuel, fertilizers, chemicals, and packaging materials, and the nonfarm sector had to generate jobs for a large number of displaced workers from farms. The resource adjustment problem resulting from technological change on farms has been and continues to be a big problem — a source of both hardship and benefits for the participants and of potential trouble and reward for society as a whole.

The number of workers employed on farms declined from 11 million in 1940 to 6.5 million in 1963, or by 4.5 million, meaning that the non-farm economy had to provide jobs for 4.5 million displaced farm workers between 1940 and 1963. Accompanying this decline was a net decline in the farm population from 30.5 million to 13.4 million, or by 17.1 million, meaning that the nonfarm sector also had to provide housing, schools, welfare assistance, and other services for 17.1 million migrants from the farm sector.

But the above numbers understate the problem; they describe the net decline in the farm working force and population. Since birth rates are high among farm people, and the farm population has grown rapidly, the absolute numbers of workers and population transferred out of the farming sector greatly exceeds the estimates above. The total number of people transferring out of farming during the period 1940–63 (net of any inflow) ran close to 25 million, or just slightly over a million a year.

In the short run, then, the migration of this large number of workers and their families away from farming and their resettlement and re-employment in the nonfarm sector has created severe strains. Except in wartime, it has added to unemployment and welfare rolls in urban areas. It has contributed to the expansion of city slums, and to all the social adjustment problems associated with slum living. It has wrought havoc in small country towns and forced a reorganization of such rural services as schools, churches, and local government. It has meant business failure and beginning all over again in strange and often degrading circumstances for many families. For these and many other reasons this process of transferring people from farm to city is painful, which explains why even more farm people have not moved to urban areas and nonfarm jobs, as from the purely economic point of view seems so rational and desirable.

But a longer-run implication should not be overlooked: the contribution that the release of more than 4.5 million workers from farming, and their transfer to the nonfarm sector, can make to the growth of the total economy. These workers were released from their farm jobs as new technological processes and capital were substituted for them. Since they were not needed in other farm jobs to produce additional food and fiber products (that addition was forthcoming without their efforts), they in effect were made *surplus* by advancing technology. To the extent that these surplus farm workers were and continue to be re-employed in productive nonfarm jobs — as nurses and stenographers and electricians and mechanics — the total product of the national economy grows and everyone benefits.

This is the positive side of the technological revolution that is sweeping across rural America, throwing more and more men and women off their farms and out of farm jobs. By this process men and women are freed from farming (or made surplus) and become available to produce other goods and services that society wants. Cruel as it may seem to the displaced farm people, it is a part of the growth process of the national economy. It is the particular contribution to national economic growth that farm technological advance has made for two decades and gives promise of continuing to make for the next two.

5

The Domestic Market

THE principal outlet for the produce of American farms is the domestic market, which, in recent years, has taken about 85 per cent of the total product. The characteristics of the domestic market — volume, growth, and elasticity — except in a few commodities, dominate and largely determine the characteristics of the demand confronting the American farmer. These characteristics in turn are themselves determined by the behavior of consumers with respect to the consumption of food and fiber products. To understand the basic determinants of the market for farm products, we must thus understand the behavior of domestic consumers.

FOOD CONSUMPTION

The Changing Composition of Diets. The diet of the average American consumer has changed markedly since 1910, the first year for which data are available on per-capita food consumption. The average American in 1910 was a heavy consumer of cereal products and potatoes, and a reasonably heavy consumer of meats. He consumed 214 pounds of wheat flour, 198 pounds of potatoes, and 146 pounds of red meat in that year. From 1910 to the middle 1930's the per-capita consumption of cereal products and potatoes declined sharply, and the consumption of all meats declined moderately: per-capita consumption fell to 158 pounds of wheat flour, 142 pounds of potatoes, and about 125 pounds of red meat in 1935. During this same period, the per-capita consumption of dairy products, fruits and vegetables, and sugar increased. Basically, the American consumer in the period 1910–35 was moving away from a diet associated with heavy, out-of-doors work to one associated with more sedentary, urban ways of living.

The diet of the average American consumer has continued to change since the middle 1930's, in some unexpected ways. The consumption of red meat, which fell modestly during the earlier period, turned upward in the middle 1930's and has been increasing ever since. In 1963, per-capita red meat consumption was 169 pounds. But of this total, the increase has been primarily in beef; the consumption of lamb and pork has declined slightly since the 1930's. The consumption of milk fat has declined slightly, the consumption of nonfat solids has increased, and the consumption of butter has fallen sharply.

The per-capita consumption of cereal products has continued to decline steadily to the present; potato consumption, on the other hand, declined to the middle 1950's and then leveled off at around 100 pounds per capita. The per-capita consumption of poultry meat increased dramatically during the 1950's, from 20 pounds in 1950 to 31 pounds in 1963, whereas the consumption of eggs has fallen steadily since the end of World War II. Sugar consumption has held almost constant since the middle 1930's, as has the consumption of fats and oils. The per-capita consumption of fresh fruit and vegetables has declined noticeably since the 1930's, but that decline has been just about offset by increases in the consumption of canned and frozen fruits and vegetables.[1]

These changes in the composition of the average consumer's diet were brought about by several forces: rising real incomes, increased urbanization, and nutrition and health information. For example, the continued decline in the consumption of cereal products no doubt resulted from a combination of rising incomes and urbanization; with more money and less outdoor work the desire and the need for bread lessened. This same rise in incomes caused a greater consumption of beef and poultry; the average consumer was able to increase his consumption of a commodity that he liked and wanted.

Nutrition and health information has played a larger role in recent years; it is certainly responsible in part at least for the decline in the consumption of butter and eggs. We can expect nutrition and health information to play an even greater part in the future by influencing eating habits: probably it will de-emphasize the consumption of fat in

[1] For the poundage data involved in these trends, see *Consumption of Food in the United States, 1909–52, Supplement for 1961*, and later supplements, Agricultural Handbook No. 62, Economic Research Service, USDA, September 1962.

general and fat in the expensive red meat cuts in particular, and emphasize special sources of vegetable fat and protein.

It is impossible to say what the diet of the average American consumer will be like in the future, but this much seems clear: it will be consistent with sedentary, urban living; it will not be dictated by grinding poverty; and it will be much influenced by research findings and information about health and nutrition. People may eat more meat per capita, or they may move away from animal products and come to prefer synthetic food products with any desired taste produced from pure nutrients according to scientific formula.

In this world of the future where income restraints are not critical, the potato will be eaten, if at all, because it tastes good and not because it is required to keep body and soul together; similarly with bread. These specific changes will in turn change importantly the demand for specific farm commodities. The workings of the income effect alone will strengthen the demand for meats in general, and beef in particular. But the workings of health and nutrition effect might act to shift demand away from highly marbled meat cuts toward synthesized food products produced from cheaper sources of nutrients — soybeans, for example.

Some strenuous battles may be in the offing, comparable with the butter-versus-margarine fight, for the consumers' allegiance — a battle likely to be fought between producers of animal products and manufacturers of synthetic products. Which products will win cannot now be foretold, because much of the food technology around which these battles will revolve is still to be discovered or developed.

The Stability of Total Per-Capita Consumption. The total food consumption of an individual is dictated by the size of his stomach, or, more precisely, by his requirements for calories and food nutrients. The average consumer does not want to, and probably is physically unable to, increase his total food intake by half, even if his income should increase by half or the price of food fall by half. Nor can he cut his total food intake by half and live, should his income fall by half or the price of food rise by half.

The average American consumer eats about the same total volume of food from about the same categories day after day. He looks for some day-to-day variation — variation within his experience — and his food habits change with time, as we have already noted, but his food consumption in total and by major categories is remarkably constant.

The Domestic Market

Total per-capita food consumption in the United States, measured in pounds, has changed very little since 1910. From 1910 to 1932, it ran just over 1,500 pounds per year. It dipped slightly below that in the depression years of 1933 and 1934, and rose slightly above 1,600 pounds a year in 1944, 1945, and 1946, but otherwise remained just above 1,500 pounds down to 1950. Throughout the 1950's and 1960's total per-capita food consumption ranged between 1,400 and 1,500 pounds per year. The total per-capita consumption of food was almost constant from 1910 to 1950; since 1950 it has declined modestly.

But we know that the composition of the average consumer's diet has changed over the years. Perhaps if we measure total food consumption not in pounds but by a price-weighted index, where each pound of food consumed is weighted by its price, total food consumption will show a greater variation. If meat is weighted in the index at 75 cents a pound and potatoes at 7 cents per pound, a consumption trend which involved an increase in meat consumption and a decrease in potato consumption would cause a price-weighted index of total food consumption to rise. To a degree this is what has happened, but not so much as one might guess. The Index of Per Capita Food Consumption, a price-weighted index, shows that total food consumption measured in this manner was almost constant from 1910 to 1938, increased by 10 to 15 per cent between 1938 and 1946, and again held almost constant from 1946 to 1963 — perhaps increasing slightly in the 1960's.

The explanation for this is as follows: during 1910–38, the large decreases in potato and cereal product consumption and the modest decrease in meat consumption were just about offset by increases in the consumption of fruit and vegetables, dairy products, and sugar, keeping the index constant in value terms. During 1938–46, the consumption of all animal products — red meat, poultry, eggs, and dairy products — as well as of most fruits and vegetables, increased, and these increases in high-valued products more than offset the continued decreases in the consumption of potatoes and cereals. Per-capita food consumption as measured by the Index of Per Capita Food Consumption thus increased during the period 1938–46. During 1946–63, per-capita consumption decreases in dairy products, eggs, potatoes, and cereals just about offset the increases in red meat and poultry, and again the Index held almost constant.

Rapidly rising incomes in 1938–46 are associated with a significant

The Domestic Market

increase in *total* food consumption during that period, as the per-capita consumption of all kinds of animal products increased. But a continued upward movement in personal incomes had almost no effect on total per-capita food consumption from 1946 to the present (Figure 5).

Many people have speculated about the significant increase in per-capita food consumption between 1938 and 1946, and the constancy of consumption between 1946 and 1963, accompanied by rising personal incomes in both periods. The consensus of investigators is that the sharp increases in personal incomes between 1938 and 1946, *in conjunction*

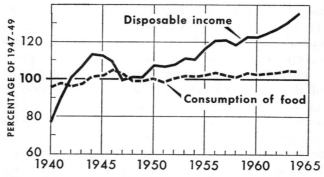

Figure 5. Per-capita food consumption and disposable income (income in constant dollars; 1964 data preliminary)

with the shortage of durable consumer goods during the war years, caused consumers to devote more of their incomes to buying food than they would have if durable goods had been available between 1941 and 1946. With the return of durable goods to the market in 1946, further increases in food consumption through the substitution of high-cost animal products for cheaper potatoes and cereals were slowed down or halted.

Probably the most interesting development since the end of World War II, and certainly the largest in dollars and cents, has been increased purchases by consumers of services associated with and built into food products. The modern supermarket abounds in such products: prepared baby food, boxed spaghetti dinners, sliced and specially wrapped cheeses and lunch meats, cake and biscuit mixes, cans of shelled black walnuts, whipped "cream" preparations, and frozen dinners in trays. Of course, maximum service is acquired by dining out. No matter how much professional consumer groups rail that such services are being pushed onto unsuspecting consumers, housewives and their husbands buy these services in increasing volume because they make preparing meals and cleaning up easier.

The greater purchase of such services does not increase the consumption of food; it increases food expenditures, but it does not involve more consumption of what the farmer produces and sells. When the consumer purchases a new or additional service associated with or built into a food product, he is buying labor, materials, and processing supplied by some firm in the food marketing sector. This is good business for the food marketer and it satisfies the consumer's need or a want, but it does not move more of the products produced by the farmer. It does not expand the market for farm food products.

The big development in the food business in the years since World War II thus has no real meaning for the farmer, except perhaps as it imposes more rigorous specifications on the products that he produces.

THE MARKET DEMAND FOR FOOD PRODUCTS

With respect to the market — the demand — for farm food products we can say first that the domestic market is going to grow about as fast as population grows.[2] This conclusion rests on the fact that rising personal incomes since 1946 have had almost no effect on total per-capita food consumption; that is, the Index of Per Capita Food Consumption was no higher in 1964 than it was in 1946, and there is no reason to believe that it will change in the years to come. If the average consumer is not likely to either increase or decrease his total food consumption, the total domestic market for farm food products will vary in size directly with population growth.

This does not mean that the demand for beef will not continue to expand, and that for pork contract, on a per-capita basis, or that the demand for a new brand of cheese will not expand, and the demand for an old one contract. The demand for some food products will change with advertising, packaging, or nutrition and health information and with changes in personal income. But where the demand for one product

[2] Some economists will argue that personal income has an effect on total food consumption. I would not disagree; income probably still has some effect, but the income elasticity for food in the United States is coming close to zero.

expands, the demand for another will contract — if the past is any guide to the future.

The second conclusion to be drawn from the analysis of food consumption behavior is that the demand for all food by the individual consumer is highly inelastic: the average consumer increases his total food consumption very slightly when the retail price of food declines, and vice versa. This conclusion rests on the observation that per-capita food consumption measured in pounds or by a price-weighted index shows very little change, even when the level of food prices has swung widely.

Many statistical studies of the aggregate demand for food have been made since World War II, all supporting the conclusion that the demand for food is highly inelastic.[3] The estimates of demand or price elasticity in most of these studies vary between —.2 and —.3. An elasticity of —.2 means that per-capita food consumption will increase 2 per cent when the retail price of food declines 10 per cent or decrease 2 per cent with a 10 per cent increase in the price. Similarly, an elasticity of —.3 means an increase or decrease of 3 per cent in per-capita food consumption with a 10 per cent decline or rise in the retail price. The refined statistical estimates support our general observation. The average consumer wants the same total quantity of food day after day; he does not increase his meals to four a day when the price of food falls or cut his meals to two a day when the price rises. His bodily demands for total food tend to be constant over time, thus his money demand also tends to be constant over time.

Within the individual's total demand for food, the elasticity of particular products and categories of food varies considerably, however. In fact, the elasticity of a product varies directly with the extent to which it has close substitutes. There is no close substitute for food, hence the elasticity of demand for food is very low. But pork chops have many substitutes — all the other cuts of red meat, poultry, eggs, fish, and even cheese; its demand elasticity is high, probably approaching —2 or —3. With a 10 per cent increase in the price of pork chops, the consumer reduces his consumption of pork chops by 20 or 30 per cent because he can easily substitute products such as roast beef or chicken that he also likes, whose prices have not risen and which are now cheap relative

[3] The results of many of these studies are summarized in T. W. Schultz, *The Economic Organization of Agriculture*, McGraw-Hill Book Co., 1955, pp. 186–191.

to pork chops. To repeat, the elasticity of demand for a product varies directly with the extent to which it has close substitutes.

The elasticity of demand for all pork (—.75) is lower than the elasticity of demand for pork chops, and the elasticity of demand for red meat (—.60) is lower than that for pork. In each case the elasticity of demand is lower for the more inclusive category because the more inclusive category has fewer substitute commodities remaining to it. The demand elasticities for several other food items are as shown in the accompanying tabulation.[4] The elasticity declines as we move from higher-priced

Chicken	—1.16
Butter	— .85
Eggs	— .30
All vegetables	— .30
Sugar	— .30
Fluid milk	— .28
Potatoes	— .20
Cereal products	— .15

animal products to lower-priced staples. This is not surprising. Consumers shift readily and rapidly among meat items as their relative prices change, because the price change in a highly valued meat item has a noticeable income effect on consumers. But the income effect on the consumer of a price change in potatoes is very small. Further, potatoes have few substitutes — really only rice and bread. Potatoes are a staple, which by definition means they are used regularly. The price elasticity of demand for such commodities as potatoes and bread is very low.

The domestic market demand confronting farmers for food products is the sum of individual consumers' demands, hence it is controlled and determined by the behavior of consumers with respect to food consumption. Between 1946 and 1964 the total demand for food by the individual consumer did not increase at all or increased only slightly (depending upon the exact years selected) concurrent with a substantial increase in personal incomes. Thus, we conclude that total domestic market demand has expanded and will continue to expand with population growth, but very little faster. We are dealing with a slowly growing market. Consumers' tastes and preferences, nutrition and health information, and modes of living will cause the demand for some prod-

[4] Source: G. E. Brandow, *Interrelations among Demands for Farm Products and Implications for Control of Market Supplies*, Pennsylvania State University Experimental Station Bulletin No. 680, August 1961, p. 17.

ucts to grow at the expense of others, but which products will benefit at the expense of which others is hidden in the future.

The market demand for food in the aggregate, the summation of individual consumers' demands, is highly inelastic. A small increase in the total supply of food requires a substantial decline in food prices to move that food into consumption, and, conversely, a small decline in total food supplies can have a substantial price-increasing effect. This is the nature of the market demand for food.

Within the aggregate domestic market demand for food, the price elasticity of individual food products or items tends to be greater than for the aggregate. But the elasticity of demand for most food categories tends to be less than —1.0, that is, inelastic. And the elasticity of demand for staple products such as flour, sugar, potatoes, and milk tends to be very low.

Except for particular brands, particular cuts of meat, or such specialty items as avocados, little additional food can be moved into the average consumer's diet simply by lowering the price. Exquisite packaging, nutritional and other health information (true or false), and associated services are *the* avenue to the consumer's pocket, as modern retailing has discovered. But this avenue of demand expansion for one food product, or item, invariably comes at the expense of other items. Thus, this form of nonprice competition may be profitable to some food processors and retailers, *but it does not move more food in total.*

Two additional points need to be discussed in connection with the domestic market demand for food. First, domestic demand has been expanded in recent years by government programs of feeding poor people. The old, the infirm, and the unemployed have been assisted by programs of direct food distribution; the United States Department of Agriculture has made available surplus food supplies to state and local welfare agencies, which have in turn distributed flour, fats, dried eggs, canned meats, and many other items to needy families. More recently a food stamp program which allows poor families to buy food in retail food markets with food stamps has taken the place of the direct distribution program in many areas.

These have not been small programs. In December 1963 some 515 million poor families received food under the direct distribution program; this food had a retail value of $6 per person per month. At the same time the food stamp program reached 370,000 needy persons. In addition, a million schoolchildren received a free school lunch. These programs have expanded the market demand for food over and above population growth, and they explain the modest increase of 1 or 2 points on the Index of Per Capita Food Consumption during 1961–64.

These programs cut two ways. First, they have helped to expand the domestic market for food in recent years, but if and when the needy people thus aided begin to increase their incomes and drop out of these programs, total food consumption will expand very little, if at all. These former program participants will simply substitute food bought with their own money for food formerly given them by the government. Antipoverty programs designed to raise these people's incomes will not expand the domestic market demand for food; that expansion has already been used up, or largely used up, by existing feeding programs. This fact gives further support to the conclusion that domestic market demand will in the future expand with, but not much faster than, expanding population.

Second, the elasticity estimates presented earlier, and their implications, were at the retail level. The severity of the relation between price and quantity at the retail level intensifies at the farm level. A demand elasticity of —.2 at the retail level converts into an elasticity of close to —.1 at the farm level. In other words, to increase per-capita food consumption by 2 per cent requires a 10 per cent decline in *retail* food prices, but a 20 per cent decline in *farm* food product prices. And the converse is true: a reduction in per-capita food consumption of 2 per cent would increase retail food prices by 10 per cent and increase farm food product prices by some 20 per cent.

The increased inelasticity of demand at the farm level, and the greater price variability associated with a given change in quantity, results from the fact that the absolute change in price associated with a given change in quantity yields a larger percentage change in the farm price than in the retail price. To illustrate, a $.10 decline on a $1.00 retail price is a 10 per cent decline, but a $.10 decline on a $.50 farm price is a 20 per cent decline.

Farmers are at the crack end of the price whip. The extreme inelasticity of the market demand for food makes this so. And the extreme inelasticity of the market demand for food grows out of the constancy in per-capita food consumption. The pressure to maintain food consumption in the face of a food shortage drives farm prices skyward, and a small food surplus unwanted by consumers can cause farm prices to drop into the subbasement. The structure of the domestic market demand for food is such that a little surplus leads to a farm crisis, a little shortage leads to a food crisis. This is true the world around, and is the reason why all governments establish food programs in periods of shortage and farm programs in periods of surplus.

THE MARKET DEMAND FOR FIBER AND TOBACCO PRODUCTS

The behavior of the market demand for cotton is as different from that for food as night is from day. For one thing, the foreign market takes between 35 and 40 per cent of American cotton, and the domestic market therefore does not dominate the demand for cotton as it does for food. The trade policies of importing nations, the specific requirements of foreign mills, and the behavior of foreign consumers are important determinants of the market demand for cotton — its volume, its growth, and its elasticity.

The trade policies that the United Kingdom works out with India, or that Japan works out with the United States may have a critical influence on the volume and expansion rate of the market demand for cotton produced in the United States. Foreign mills' inventory policies can also increase or decrease the demand for American cotton by as much as a million bales in one year. In fact, since the domestic demand for cotton exhibits reasonable stability from year to year, it is changes in the buying policies of foreign buyers that bring about the big fluctuations in the market demand for cotton from year to year. Cotton exports amounted to 5.7 million bales in 1957, dropped to 2.8 million bales in 1958, and jumped back to 7.2 million bales in 1959. Those are big changes in demand, relative to a production of between 11 and 14 million bales per year.

For another thing, cotton has many substitutes: the natural fibers — wool, silk, linen, jute, sisal, and other hard fibers — and the manmade fibers — rayon, nylon, orlon, dacron, and so "-on." Not all of the above products compete with cotton in the production of human wearing apparel; but all compete with cotton as a wrapper and in the manufacture of many products from tires to window draperies. Let the price of cotton become unduly high relative to the price of these other fibers and they will be substituted for cotton, particularly in manufacturing. This means that the demand for cotton is relatively elastic.

The Domestic Market

It is also true that the manmade fibers have been substituting for cotton even when the price of cotton has not increased relatively, thus contracting the demand for cotton; the reason is that manmade fibers are superior in some characteristics, such as strength, for certain purposes. Cotton has had tough competition — price competition and product competition — in recent years from substitute products.

The per-capita consumption of cotton in the United States declined from about 32 pounds a year immediately after World War II to 22 pounds in 1962, while the total per-capita consumption of manmade fibers rose from about 6 pounds per year to nearly 13 pounds during the same period. This is the negative side of the market picture for cotton.

As a final distinguishing characteristic from food, personal income does affect the consumption of cotton goods, particularly wearing apparel. A poor man may be forced to get along with one shirt, a man of moderate means may find it necessary to have fifteen, and a rich man may find that he can use fifty. Furthermore, cotton is often treated by consumers as a superior good; that is, as their incomes rise they substitute pure cotton fabrics for combination fabrics involving some manmade fibers. The domestic market for cotton, like that for food, will continue to expand with expanding population. But as is not true for food, rising real incomes can be expected to cause a significant expansion in the demand for cotton goods. This is the positive side of the market picture for cotton.

In summary, domestic consumption does not dominate the total market demand for cotton. What happens to production in the developing countries, and the trade policies of Europe and the United States, may influence the total demand for cotton more than developments in the domestic market do. But even in the domestic market the future is not clear. Increasing population and rising incomes will certainly act to expand the demand for cotton, but competition from other natural fibers and the manmades may nullify part or all of that potential expansion. The future of cotton rests with technological development: technology in growing cotton, in manufacturing cotton products, and in producing and using manmade fibers. The future market for cotton is thus an unknown quantity.

The market for wool will not be analyzed here because about half the wool used in the United States is imported, and because in terms of the value of what is produced wool is a minor commodity in the United

States. Further, without a sizable government payment on each pound of wool produced, the production of wool in the United States would dwindle to almost nothing.

It is difficult to talk about the market for tobacco as a whole because there are many kinds. But two big-volume cigarette tobaccos (flue-cured, 60 per cent; burley, 30 per cent) make up about 90 per cent of American production and we shall concentrate on them. The domestic market takes about 55 per cent of the flue-cured produced in the United States, and about 85 per cent of the burley. The domestic market therefore dominates the market for burley, but not the market for flue-cured.

Although the per-capita use of tobacco in the United States has not increased in recent years, the total market has widened with population growth. Whether the domestic market will expand or contract in the future depends upon one overriding issue — health. The surgeon general's report published in January 1964 made it clear that cigarette smoking is injurious to health. How injurious, and whether the harmful ingredients can be removed or combated are questions still being studied.

In the meantime, the surgeon general's report and other similar pieces of information have reduced cigarette consumption in the short run. But many analysts believe that such information will not reduce cigarette smoking in the long run (and the evidence in late 1964 was that it will not; most of the quitters were already back on cigarettes). This argument and evidence suggest that smokers will probably simply take their chances with the injurious effects of cigarette smoking. This could be true with respect to habitual smokers. But the health issue, if the harmful evidence continues to build up, could inhibit the taking up of cigarette smoking by young people.

The battle, in the long run, will be fought over the potential smokers — the young people. Cigarette smoking is not a habit acquired at the mother's breast, nor is it associated with rising or falling incomes. It is an acquired taste, and once acquired, the habit is exceedingly difficult to break. What young people do or don't do with respect to smoking cigarettes is all-important to the long-run growth of the tobacco market. Propaganda to win the allegiance of young people will be strong and subtle from both sides — from the health side to keep young men and women from taking up the smoking habit, and from the tobacco side to induce young men and women to take up the habit. Who will win nobody knows, but the future of a big industry rides on the outcome. And again science and technology will probably play a big part in the outcome either by making cigarettes safe or by demonstrating that they are dangerously injurious to health.

THE MEANING FOR FARMERS

The domestic market for *food products* produced by American farmers constitutes 90 to 95 per cent of the total market (as compared with 85 per cent for *all farm* products). Thus, the domestic market for farm food products completely dominates the total market for food products and determines its behavior. And the behavior of the domestic market is in turn determined by the food consumption decisions and habits of individual consumers.

The total of consumers' actions with respect to food consumption yields a total market demand for food products that might be likened to a glacier: the glacier moves slowly but irresistibly; nothing that anyone can do in the short run can speed it up or slow it down. And the face of the glacier is a precipitous cliff.

The market demand for food confronting all farmers is like that glacier. Demand grows in an irresistible fashion with population growth, expanding with population growth but no faster. And nothing anyone can do in the short run can speed up or slow down the growth of population — it is increasing at about 1.7 per cent a year in the United States (a rapid rate for a developed country; population growth in most European countries is less than 1 per cent a year). This is the rate at which the total market for farm food products will expand until the rate of population growth changes. If that happens, the change of population growth is much more likely to be a decline than an increase; in fact there were signs in 1964 that it had already begun to decline.

Now to return to the analogy. The face of market demand is precipitous; supply the market with a little more than it will take and the extra amount tumbles over the edge of the glacier and sells for a price at the bottom of the precipice. Moreover, not only does the extra amount sell at a price at the bottom of the precipice, but *all* the product sells at the price at the foot of the glacier.

It is true that artichoke farmers or Idaho potato farmers or beef producers may successfully advertise their products or consumers may take a liking to them all by themselves, and the demand for those particular products along with the consumption of them will rise. But how do these increases take place? Typically they take place at the expense of close food substitutes: the expansion in artichoke consumption takes place at the expense of other vegetables, the expansion in the consumption of Idaho potatoes at the expense of Red River Valley or Maine potatoes, and the expansion of beef at the expense of pork, lamb, and even possibly bread. By sales promotion or by an unexplained preference, the demand for one product may move out ahead of the glacier — the market demand for all food products — but when that happens the demand for another product contracts, and the movement of the whole glacier remains unchanged: only its face becomes uneven and pitted.

Some farm commodity groups — where the commodity is distinctive and can be differentiated — can expand the market for their commodity and thereby strengthen the price of their commodity by purposive sales promotion or by being lucky with respect to consumer preferences. But all farmers cannot take this road to the promised land. They cannot because the per-capita consumption of *total* food is constant over time. Promotion will not put more total food in the stomach of the average consumer. This fact farmers, their leaders, and interested city people must come to appreciate.

All farmers must take what the market gives them in the way of a farm price level, given the glacier-like movement of aggregate market demand, or they must adjust their production to that demand. Farmers can make resource adjustments to this glacier-like demand and in that way influence farm prices. But the glacier will not be hurried.

Around this glacier, the aggregate demand for farm food products, there are lesser but still important domestic demands for farm commodities, for cotton and tobacco, to name the two most important. The future development of the markets for these two is highly uncertain. With sustained economic prosperity, the demand for cotton could expand rapidly in the years to come, or it could contract with continued improvements in the manmade fibers and an adverse export picture. The market demand for tobacco could similarly go in either direction. These are things that man can do something about, however, and he will. Commercial wars will be waged around these commodities, with purposive policies and counter-policies manipulating the markets. There is a place for market development and market management in these commodities.

A FINAL COMMENT

Intelligent decision-making by farmers and by city men about farm problems requires that they understand consumers' behavior. Without that understanding policy decisions are sometimes made to take action where the possibilities of success are near zero, and action is not taken where demand manipulation is feasible. There is nothing more pitiful than a group of farmers wasting their money on the promotion of a product that lacks distinctive features, hence does not lend itself to promotion, or a national leader asking every consumer to crowd an additional glass of milk a day into his stomach, and crowd out who knows what, to solve a dairy surplus. But nothing is more exciting than the promotion story of Sunkist oranges, or a group of producers recognizing that the market demands that they make adjustments in their use of resources.

6

The Foreign Market

THE foreign market has long been viewed as an overflow market for American farmers. This is not to say that it has been an unimportant market; it is an important market for agriculture as a whole and for wheat, cotton, and tobacco in particular. But its role in American thought and action has been different from that of the domestic market, which has always had the first claim on the products of American farms. During the 1950's and 1960's the domestic market took 85 or 90 per cent of the product coming from those farms. As a consequence the foreign market has typically been treated as a residual market — an overflow market to take what the domestic market could not use. Its policy role has been to clear the domestic market of its surpluses and permit the domestic farm economy to operate unhindered by price-depressing commodity surpluses.

In this role the foreign market has a record that is sometimes good, sometimes bad. When it swallows up the exportable surplus without difficulty, the American farm economy runs smoothly and beautifully: witness the happy years during and right after the two world wars. But when the foreign market has failed to absorb the exportable surplus with dispatch, as was true between the wars and during the 1950's and 1960's, the American farm economy runs into trouble and everyone becomes unhappy with it and with the foreign market. In other words, what happens to the exportable surplus is critically important to the farm economy. If the surplus moves out, the farm economy prospers; if it dams up, or moves sluggishly, the farm economy drags and encounters price, income, and surplus problems.

The Foreign Market

The size of the exportable surplus is, of course, a key element. When the rate of population growth in the United States is running ahead of the rate of farm output expansion, the size of the exportable surplus decreases, making it easier to move the surplus into foreign channels. But when population grows more slowly than farm output expands, the exportable surplus increases in size and it becomes more difficult to move the surplus into the foreign market. The size of the exportable surplus can increase or decrease, depending upon this relation, but historically there has always been a surplus to move.

Now the question at issue is whether the foreign market can serve effectively as a residual outlet for the farm surplus of the United States. That it can serve as a residual or overflow market is not the question; it has done so by default or by intention for a century. But can it serve *effectively*? Can it take with speed and dispatch the exportable farm surplus, whatever it may be, and permit the United States farm economy to generate good, stable prices and incomes? Or does the farm export market have an independent structure and unique characteristics that must be recognized? And if the foreign market has an independent structure and characteristics of its own, which seems likely in the light of history, what are those characteristics and what are their implications for American farmers?

TRADE TRENDS

The export market for farm commodities has varied greatly in importance over the long run. In 1910, it accounted for 16 per cent of total cash receipts from farm marketings in the United States; in 1919–21, it took 25 per cent or more each year. After 1921, the export market for farm commodities withered away; in 1940 and 1941 it accounted for only 6 per cent of farm marketings. During the war years of the 1940's it widened again, accounting for 13 per cent in 1949. With relative peace after the Korean action, farm exports slumped again to 9 per cent of farm marketings in 1953. But the slump did not last long: exports increased steadily in the second half of the 1950's and the early 1960's to become 16 per cent of total farm marketings in 1964.[1]

In dollars, farm commodity exports amounted to $2.8 billion in 1953 and about $6 billion in 1964. With a farm price level almost constant over this period, this meant a big increase in the physical volume of

[1] See Appendix Table 4 for more details about these trends.

The Foreign Market

farm commodity exports. Exports served as an important additional outlet for American farm commodities at a time when domestic farm production was increasing rapidly and an expanded market was much needed. Without this expanded foreign market in the late 1950's and early 1960's, surpluses in the United States would have become intolerable.

Five farm commodities — wheat, feed grains, cotton, soybeans, and tobacco — accounted for about two thirds of total farm exports in the early 1960's. The dollar value of exports for these five commodities for fiscal 1963–64 were as shown in the accompanying tabulation. Three of

Wheat and wheat flour	$1,519,000,000
Feed grains	850,000,000
Cotton	670,000,000
Soybeans	516,000,000
Tobacco, unmanufactured	421,000,000

these commodities — wheat, cotton, and tobacco — have long been at the top of the export list, but that position is something new for feed grains and soybeans. Soybeans are a new crop, not produced in volume or exported before the middle 1930's. Moreover, the dollar value of soybean exports for 1963–64 given in the tabulation is for uncrushed beans; if the value of soybean oil and meal exports for that fiscal year were added, the total soybean products export figure would reach to $728 million.

Though feed grains for livestock and human use have long been exported, their export value reached $500 million for the first time in 1958. The industrial countries of Western Europe and Japan, where meat production and consumption are increasing rapidly, are turning increasingly to the largest and most efficient producer of feed grains, soybeans, and protein meal, the United States, for supplies. To the extent that economic development continues around the world and more and more people increase their consumption of meat, the demand for the raw materials of meat production will increase, which means that exports of feed grains, soybeans, and protein meal from the United States will increase. Thus, in the years to come, it could well be the case that the leading farm commodity exports will be feed grains and soybeans (as whole beans and as protein meal and oil); in fact the exports of these commodities could in time dwarf all other farm commodity exports.

The question might be asked — Will meat exports expand to fill the needs of the rapidly developing countries of Western Europe and Japan? This could take place — particularly with respect to beef, since these countries do not have the pasture land required to produce the cattle carcasses, and they can ill afford to use their valuable land in such an extensive manner. But important increases in exports of poultry and hog meat to those countries seem unlikely. Both economics and politics dictate that the meat production take place within the importing country. Feed concentrates can be shipped as cheaply as, or in some cases more cheaply than, the live animals or meat; labor costs are lower in the countries under consideration; and the income generated from meat production is, of course, welcome — that is the economics of the issue. And all countries try to protect and expand their agricultural industries, both production and processing, where they can — that is the politics of the issue.

With continued economic development around the world the following picture makes sense: per-capita and total meat consumption will increase; to supply that meat, broiler factories, hog factories, and beef-fattening operations will develop in those countries, and to supply the raw materials — feed grains and protein meals — the United States as the leading and most efficient producer of feed grains and soybeans will export larger and larger quantities of those commodities.

American wheat, cotton, and tobacco farmers will be confronted with very strong competition in the years ahead. Canada and Australia, both of which live off their agricultural exports, hope to expand their wheat exports in the future; the Soviet Union hopes to become a consistent wheat exporter; and the Common Market countries expect to increase their wheat production and reduce their imports of wheat. Someone is going to get hurt in that traffic, particularly since per-capita cereal product consumption will at the same time be declining in the developed, importing countries.

The hopes of much of the underdeveloped world rest on increasing their production and export of cotton and tobacco. Many of the developing countries also hope to increase their production and exports of sugar, citrus fruits, vegetable oils, and such tropical products as bananas, coffee, and cocoa. Through expanding the production and export of some or all of these commodities, most underdeveloped countries hope to earn the foreign exchange necessary to develop their economies industrially.

In other words, these countries hope to produce a farm surplus, ex-

The Foreign Market

port it, earn foreign exchange, and in that way develop. This is the tried, true, and recommended route to economic growth for underdeveloped economies; the United States once trod this route. But whether it is still the way when many countries are using it and when there is no shortage of food in world *commercial* markets is a question. A second question is what the United States will do when increased supplies of cotton, tobacco, sugar, and vegetable oils from the underdeveloped countries begin to encroach upon its traditional markets. Will the United States accept this competition without resorting to government action such as state trading, increased export subsidies, and increased import controls, or will it employ these measures to hold and expand its markets? If it does the latter, what kind of production and trade policies remain open to the underdeveloped nations? These are questions that give responsible political leaders around the world sleepless nights.

Two Foreign Markets. Between 1953–54 and 1963–64 the total value of farm commodity exports rose by slightly over $3 billion. Of this total, commercial exports increased by some $2 billion and government-programed exports by about $1 billion. That is, both private commercial trade and foreign food aid (Food for Peace) played important roles in expanding farm commodity exports during this time, but the increase in commercial trade was about double that of foreign food aid (Figure 6).

Because both commercial trade and foreign food aid increased in the 1950's and 1960's, farm exports to two very different kinds of country

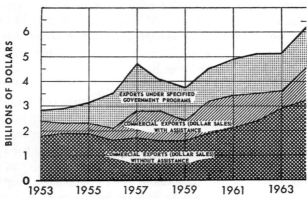

Figure 6. Exports of farm commodities from the United States, fiscal 1953 to fiscal 1964

increased during this period. Private commercial exports to the prosperous, rapidly developing countries increased importantly. Canada, Japan, West Germany, and the Netherlands, all among the top ten markets for United States farm products, increased their commercial imports of farm products from the United States by 80 per cent or more between 1954–55 and 1963–64. At the same time a new category of country entered the top ten. These countries became important outlets for American farm products through their participation in our foreign food aid program. The two countries entering the top ten in 1963–64 primarily through their imports under Public Law 480 were India and the United Arab Republic.

In the early 1960's the foreign markets for American farm products were thus primarily of two kinds: commercial trade with the industrialized and rapidly developing countries, and shipments under P.L. 480 — that is, foreign food aid (see footnote, p. 101). Farm commodity exports under private, commercial trade in 1963–64 amounted to $4.5 billion, foreign food aid to $1.6 billion. The former dominates the export picture, and in recent years has increased more rapidly than foreign food aid, but the latter has become a solid segment of the total export market.

Commercial exports of farm products in 1963–64 earned $4.5 billion of foreign exchange — dollars earned abroad free to be used to pay for exports to the United States from the importing countries or any other country. The food aid exports do not earn free foreign exchange, but they do earn nonconvertible, or blocked, currency of the importing country which can be used to pay for expenses of the United States in the recipient country (the maintenance of the United States embassy, for example). In the financial accounting of United States trade, it should be recognized further that subsidy payments of $800 million or more were paid by the United States government to United States firms in 1963–64 to make domestic, price-supported commodities competitive with foreign-produced commodities. These payments represent, however, a domestic charge against the United States treasury, and do not affect the international balance of payments.

Agricultural imports in fiscal 1964 amounted to $4.1 billion, some $2 billion less than exports. The gap between farm commodity exports and imports was a little larger in 1964 than in earlier years, but in the typical year farm commodity exports exceed imports. More important, just about half, or $1.9 billion worth, were complementary farm products in 1964; that is, about half the imports were things like coffee, tea, and bananas that do not in any way compete with the products of American producers, but rather complement domestically produced farm products.

This situation is typical of trade trends during the decade 1955–64: imports of complementary farm products have varied between $2.4 and $1.7 billion since 1955. From time to time imports of beef, lamb, butterfat, cheese, tomatoes, and other supplementary products have caused concern and a demand by farmers for more protection. But in the main, competition from imports of farm products has not created serious problems for American farmers. Their real problem has been and is likely to continue to be protectionism abroad — the loss of existing and potential markets by the erection of barriers to trade abroad.

THE COMMERCIAL POTENTIAL

As already noted, commercial exports increased by about $2 billion between 1953 and 1964, reaching an all-time high of $4.5 billion in 1963–64. Part of this increase in farm exports resulted from forces beyond the control of American farmers, businessmen, and government administrators. It resulted from the rapid economic growth of Western Europe and Japan and the corresponding increase in the demand of their populations for a richer, costlier diet. This strong demand enabled the United States to increase importantly its exports of wheat, feed grains, soybeans, and protein meal to those two areas, and at least not lose markets in cotton and tobacco. Further, bad weather in the Soviet Union for several consecutive years in the early 1960's, and in Western Europe in 1963, helped to push commercial exports of farm products from the United States to an all-time high in 1963–64.

But part of the increase in farm exports resulted from hard, dedicated work by many people at four levels: in private export firms, in trade development groups, in the United States departments of Agriculture and State, and in Congress. Basically, there is no world market for farm commodities in the nineteenth-century sense, no market where export firms simply sell for delivery. The United Kingdom and the Netherlands were essentially free markets for the grains up to 1962, but since then they have slipped from that natural state: the Netherlands has moved under the protective system of the Common Market and the United Kingdom has established a price system that, with the aid of import levies, fixes the minimum prices at which grains may be imported.

Thus *every* important trading nation of the world now has a barrage of control devices through which farm commodities must pass: old-fashioned tariffs, all manner of quantitative import restrictions, variable levies to bring the import price up to some minimum import price, plant and animal sanitary and quarantine practices, state purchasing agencies and state trading monopolies, and, finally, customs union or common market regulations.

Every country does not use every one of these devices; if a country makes use of a government purchasing agency, that really becomes the import control device; but if it relies on private traders, it will use a combination of import restrictions — import quotas, minimum import prices in combination with variable levies, and the subtler plant and animal quarantine practices. Each foreign sale really becomes an adventure in which the exporter must beat the competition from other countries, and, more important, find the secret door through which his commodity may pass into the importing country.

In the successful efforts between 1953 and 1964, it was the responsibility of private firms in the United States to seek out buyers abroad, to acquire knowledge of the import control measures relevant to their commodities, to find ways through or around those measures, and to reach agreements about details of each sale. All this American firms have learned to do with skill and patience.

But actually to expand exports the private traders have required support and assistance in many ways. Such private trade development groups operating abroad, as the Soybean Council, the Feed Grain Council, Great Plains Wheat, have displayed American products, sought out new users, induced foreign governments to interpret regulations favorably, and influenced the form of new regulations. These groups have kept American farm products before potential users, expedited the movement of products, developed new markets, and helped hold open old ones.

At times, however, commodities simply cannot move, as when state purchasing agencies will not consider United States products, or when quantitative trade restrictions are in force, or when tariff rates are prohibitively high. When this happens, the leverage of government must be brought to bear, and on this problem officials of the departments of

The Foreign Market

Agriculture and State have worked long and diligently in recent years, negotiating to make quantitative controls less restrictive, to reduce tariff barriers and minimum import prices, and to induce state purchasing agencies to buy American products. These efforts have been effective in lowering barriers and in interesting foreign purchasing agencies.

Finally, American farm products will not move into foreign markets when their price is higher than that of competing exporters. The price-support program in the United States has held the domestic price of numerous farm commodities well above the level of world prices, particularly in those important commodities cotton and wheat. To move these two commodities in foreign markets Congress has directed the USDA to subsidize their export at world prices, and authorized the use of government funds to cover the subsidies. That is, Congress has directed the USDA to pay American export firms a subsidy equal to the difference between the domestic price and the going world price of wheat and cotton, and thereby enable them to compete effectively abroad. Although the export subsidy device has been used primarily for cotton and wheat, it can be used on other price-supported commodities when necessary to make them competitive in world markets.

This subsidy weapon has been much criticized by competitors of the United States in world trade, and there is no question but that it is open to abuse. If the United States wanted to use its treasury in that way it could *try* to expand its markets at the expense of third countries by increasing the size of the export subsidies on its products. But insofar as other countries lowered their prices to hold markets, the result would be lower prices to all, and higher costs to the United States. The United States must get the prices of its price-supported commodities down to world levels if it is to sell anything abroad; but to push prices lower by an increased export subsidy to capture the markets of competing suppliers is self-defeating, and a practice the United States has not followed.

Through hard work by Americans at several levels to expand the sales of farm products abroad, and vigorous economic growth in Japan and Western Europe, farm commodity exports have, in fact, increased in a sustained way over the period 1953–64; and there is reason to believe that these two forces will continue to operate in the same way in the near future. The workings of these two forces by themselves should support a continued expansion of commercial farm commodity exports from the United States into the early 1970's, with perhaps the greatest increases in the feed grains and protein meals.

But other forces must be taken into consideration in appraising the growth potential of the commercial export market. The first and most disconcerting to Americans is the protectionist tendencies in the Common Market. The establishment of a Common Agricultural Policy in the Common Market — with a high internal grain price structure, a minimum import price slightly above the internal price, and a variable fee to make up the difference between the world price and the minimum import price — gives American farm leaders cold chills. Such a policy, vigorously pursued, could importantly expand grain production in the Common Market countries — France in particular — causing traditional grain suppliers to lose part or all of that market. Such a high grain price policy and protectionist system would also reduce the potential expansion in meat production and consumption in the Common Market area, with adverse effects on European consumers on the one hand and on feed grain exporters to that area on the other.

How this institutional development will turn out cannot be foretold. In the winter of 1964–65 the forces of agricultural protectionism seemed to be winning the battle. The Council of Ministers of the European Economic Community, at France's urging, adopted a schedule of relatively high internal grain prices in December 1964. The soft wheat target price to become effective July 1, 1967, in the Community is $2.89 per bushel. This price and the corresponding internal target prices for rye and barley provide a powerful incentive to French farmers to increase grain production. It thus seems probable that total grain production will be increased and total imports reduced in the Common Market in the late 1960's and 1970's. In this situation commercial grain exports from the United States will be reduced.

One more negative force must be reviewed, the hoped-for and very likely increase in the exportable surplus of raw agricultural products from the underdeveloped nations. These countries are trying to increase their production and consequently their exportable surplus of such commodities as sugar, cotton, tobacco, vegetable oils, protein meal, rice, and tropical products. This surplus they want to export to Western Europe, the United States, Japan, and other hard-currency markets to earn the foreign exchange that will enable them to buy the hard goods that their development plans call for. Their agricultural surplus, if it materializes, will run head on into the exportable surpluses of the United States and the traditional export trade of Australia, Canada, and Argentina. The results of this collision, unless they are counteracted in some way, will be increased competition for the import markets of the industrialized countries and a lower level of world commodity prices.

This is truly a difficult economic and moral problem. The economically advanced nations advise trade, not aid; the underdeveloped nations prefer trade, not aid, or perhaps trade *and* aid. But many of the commodities in which they are best equipped to increase production, hence exports, are commodities that are commonly in world surplus — sugar and the vegetable oils; or they are commodities that run squarely into the export aspirations of the United States — cotton and tobacco.

As a leader of the free world with a vital interest in the successful development of many of these economically underdeveloped countries, the United States cannot ignore their export aspirations and requirements. But American cotton farmers are not going to lose markets to cotton farmers in Pakistan and India with a smile. So the economic noose tightens, but it is not yet clear whose head is going into it. It is only clear that much trouble lies ahead in commercial trade policy for such commodities as cotton and tobacco.

It is sometimes argued by agricultural economists, and often argued by urban economists, that the United States should get rid of farm price supports, get farm prices down, and really expand the export market through vigorous price competition. Such an argument completely ignores the structure of world trade in farm commodities since World War II. There is no free market arena in which to engage in "friendly" price competition.

In the first place, most major importing nations now protect their producers through a minimum import price coupled with a variable levy. If, for example, the minimum import price for wheat in a Common Market country is $3 per bushel, the importer of wheat in that country must pay $3 whether the exporter sells for $3, $2, or $1; at the first price the variable fee is zero, at the second $1, and at the third $2. The importing country simply levies a fee equal to the difference between the sales price and the minimum import price; the price to the importer remains the same regardless of the price competition outside the importing country.

Exporters gain nothing from price competition in this situation; the gainer is the public treasury of the importing country, which collects the skimmings, or variable fee. Price competition leads to income losses for the exporters and achieves no expansion in the market, because the price to the ultimate buyer does not come down. Price competition by exporters in this situation is pure nonsense.

Where domestic producers are not protected by a minimum import price, price competition is not likely to be highly productive in the long run, because almost every important exporter of farm products except the United States sells its products abroad through a National Marketing Board, or Commission, which has an export sales monopoly on the product or products of that country. Prices of commodities such as wheat are set in the world market in much the same way as the price of steel is set within the United States — not by collusion, but by mutual understanding. By tradition, or convention, one big fellow sets the price and all the others follow, because all understand that price competition leads to a situation where all get hurt, and the total expansion of the market is very small.

But should one country move its selling price down in wheat to gain a market advantage, all the others would follow in self-protection. Price competition leads to lower prices, but rarely to a capturing of the other fellow's market, because he lowers his price to protect his export sales: price competition is therefore frowned upon in the oligopolistic commodity markets of the modern world. Competition takes the form rather of better credit terms, advantages in transportation, maintenance of product quality, or forward price commitments.

In summary: the size and growth of commercial exports of farm products from the United States is going to depend upon four major developments: (1) the rate of economic growth in Japan, Western Europe, and possibly the Soviet bloc; (2) the skill and diligence of all Americans engaged in foreign trade, both private firms and government; (3) the extent to which highly protectionist policies come to dominate the European Common Market; and (4) the extent to which the underdeveloped countries develop exportable surpluses of sugar, cotton, oilseeds, and tobacco and thereby become important suppliers of those commodities in world markets.

The first two developments are definite forces toward expanding commercial farm exports from the United States into the foreseeable future. The Common Market policy could go either way; farmers and farm organizations in France and Germany are working for a strong protectionist policy with a high internal grain price, a minimum import price slightly above the internal price level, and a variable levy system to effectuate those price policies. If they win (and in 1964–65 it would appear that they are winning) Western Europe could become self-sufficient, or nearly so, in grain production, and an important market would be lost to the United States and other exporters. But if those groups with an interest in relatively low grain prices, a big increase in meat production, and abundant food supplies at reasonable prices — labor and urban consumers — ultimately carry the day, then an important and expanding export market for feed grains and wheat will be maintained for the United States and other suppliers outside the Common Market.

Unless the underdeveloped countries fail completely in their development plans, something the United States for political reasons cannot let happen, the fourth development listed above will certainly work against future American farm export interests. How strong a deterrent it becomes depends, of course, upon the size of the exportable surpluses those countries produce, and the extent to which international programs and agreements are developed to cope with and ease this problem. But the export ambitions of the underdeveloped nations, potential and realized, in commodities such as cotton, tobacco, vegetable oils, and rice are almost certain to complicate and deter American export activities, causing a nasty, nagging problem that will be with the United States for many years to come.

On balance, it would seem that commercial exports of farm products from the United States will continue to increase in the foreseeable future. The economic forces associated with economic growth have been supporting, and give promise of continuing to support, expanded trade in farm products around the world. But whether American exports expand rapidly or slowly depends in large measure upon developments in the trade policy of Western Europe and the Soviet bloc countries.

THE FOOD AID POTENTIAL

Since 1961 foreign food aid exports (Food for Peace) have been running a little over $1.5 billion a year. At one time these exports moved under several different governmental authorizations, but now almost all are under Public Law 480.[2] The full costs of these exports are met from the United States treasury, and the specific expenditures are carried in the budget of the Department of Agriculture. In national bookkeeping the cost of foreign food aid is thus charged to the USDA, but to confuse the issue P.L. 480 expenditures appear in the printed federal budget under the heading "international affairs and finance."

Wheat and wheat flour has been the largest single item in this category of exports, accounting for just about half the value of food aid exports since the program began in 1954. Other important commodities are feed grains, rice, vegetable oils, dairy products, tobacco, and cotton.[3]

Though political pressure to reduce federal expenditures for foreign economic aid has risen in recent years, a level of P.L. 480 exports at $1.5 to $1.7 billion seems to be firmly established in American policy. This is the case for a number of reasons. First, if the level of these exports were lowered, either the volume of government-held stocks would increase or production controls would have to take a bigger bite. Neither of these alternatives is something that American political and farm leaders wish to contemplate. Second, many church and charitable organizations strongly support and actively participate in the foreign food aid programs of the United States. Third, foreign food aid has made an important contribution to the development efforts of many underdeveloped countries, and this is increasingly understood and appreciated in both the United States and the recipient countries. There are many lines of support for the foreign food aid programs under consideration here: special economic interests, good will, and enlightened national self-interest.

But where present levels of foreign food aid are accepted, and some modest increases are possible, it must also be recognized that giving away food to needy countries (or selling it to them for their soft, nonconvertible currencies, which is technically the procedure employed) is not easy. For a number of reasons it is neither feasible nor possible to expand these food aid exports importantly in the short run. First, these countries have their own farm producers and food marketers who take

[2] For a good and complete description of P.L. 480 and the activities conducted under it, see the latest "Semiannual Report on Activities Carried on under Public Law 480," submitted regularly by the White House to Congress.

[3] These last two, of course, are not food products, but they are farm products and with some poetic license can be included under the heading of foreign food aid.

a dim view of such imports, which at best (from their point of view) keep farm prices and food prices from rising and at worst lower farm and food prices. Second, competing export nations fear that our food aid exports will be substituted for their commercial exports and thus reduce their exports absolutely and hinder their potential growth. The United States has been aware of this problem from the inception of the program and taken considerable care to insure that the food aid we give is additional to the country's regular commercial imports. But in fact our food aid exports do, to some degree, substitute for commercial exports in many cases, and the question of the legitimate growth in commercial exports from third country suppliers is impossible to resolve satisfactorily. American food aid exports remain a constant sore spot in our relations with other exporting nations.

Third, and probably most important, the countries that need food aid the most lack the storage, handling, and transportation facilities to handle and effectively distribute any substantially larger volume of food than they are currently getting. They usually also lack the governmental and private organizations, and particularly the skilled personnel, to distribute more food products effectively. The bottleneck which prevents a big increase in food aid exports to most underdeveloped countries is inadequate storage, handling, and transportation. Until this bottleneck is enlarged, increased food aid to these countries would result in scandalous waste.

If this bottleneck is enlarged or broken by the countries themselves or with the technical and financial assistance of industrially advanced countries, then the story of potential food aid exports will come to a different conclusion. The current need for more food for millions of people in the underdeveloped world has been demonstrated in numerous studies; the most recent and probably the best study to date summarizes the situation as follows:

Two-thirds of the world's people live in countries with nutritionally inadequate national average diets. The diet-deficit areas include all of Asia except Japan and Israel, all but the southern tip of Africa, the northern part of South America, and almost all of Central America and the Caribbean.

The diet of people in these areas averaged 900 calories per day below the level of the one-third of the world living in countries with adequate national average diets in 1959–61, and 300 calories below the average nutritional standard for the diet-deficit areas. The daily consumption of protein was less than two-thirds of the level in the diet-adequate countries; the fat consumption rate was less than one-third.[4]

The diet-deficit areas of the world may be seen in Figure 7; the diet-deficit areas of the world overlap almost perfectly the underdeveloped areas. The world food deficit is likely to widen in the future rather than narrow unless action is taken to correct or alleviate it. This generalization is based on the following reasoning. Population will continue to increase by between 2 and 3 per cent a year in the underdeveloped countries. These countries will experience economic growth, some rapid, some slow; with this growth, per-capita incomes will rise by as much as 3 per cent a year in the rapidly growing countries; with a high income elasticity for food in these countries, the rising per-capita income will expand the demand for food in a rapid fashion.

The expected rates of population increase and income increase will cause the demand for food to rise by as much as 4.3 per cent a year in the rapidly growing countries, and by 3.5 per cent a year in the slower-growing countries. But food production is not likely to exceed 3.3 per cent a year in the rapidly growing countries and 3.0 per cent a year in the slower countries. The hopes, plans, and realities of the situation in the underdeveloped countries add up to a rate of demand expansion for food that outpaces the rate of production increase by up to 1 per cent a year. In making the above comparison, moreover, a rate of food production increase is assumed that, though physically possible, is well above the actual rate in those countries during 1953–60.

The quantitative results of the above analysis of possible economic growth, food production, and food consumption projected to the year 1980 for the aggregate of ninety-three nations are shown in the ac-

```
Consumption .........................$153.6 billion
Production ..........................$128.0
    Deficit ..........................$ 25.6
Increase in commercial imports ..........$ 10.9
    Remaining deficit ...................$ 14.7
```

companying tabulation. We thus conclude from the above analysis and projection that increased food production in the ninety-three countries must be the principal solution to meeting their potential food deficit,

[4] *The World Food Budget, 1970,* Foreign Agricultural Economic Report No. 19, Economic Research Service, USDA, October 1964, p. iii. This report is an excellent source of information about the present and expected world food situation.

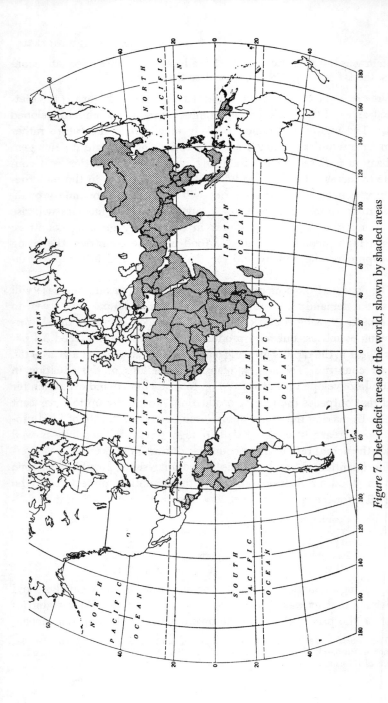

Figure 7. Diet-deficit areas of the world, shown by shaded areas

but that very large increases in commercial imports and food aid must also be a part of the solution.[5]

More positively, food aid exports to the underdeveloped countries could easily reach a level of $14.7 billion by 1980, because the production projections are optimistic on the basis of past experience, and the national economic growth rates are below the planned rates in most instances. Since the United States is the only country in the world engaged in foreign food aid in an important way, and since, further, its annual level of food aid exports is currently running at $1.6 billion, the potential expansion in this food aid market for the United States could be $13 billion as of 1980.

It seems improbable at this writing that the United States would expand its "give-away" market for farm products by $13 billion by 1980, first because of budget considerations at home and second because the recipient countries will still probably be lagging in the storage, handling, and transportation facilities needed to handle this volume of semi-perishable products. It is possible, moreover, that Western Europe will be in a serious surplus condition with respect to some farm products by 1980 and will want to share in this market.

But this much is certain. If food and fiber supplies amounting to at least $13 billion have not materialized from somewhere to fill this deficit by 1980 there are going to be some dashed economic plans and broken political systems as per-capita economic growth falls far short of expectations in many underdeveloped countries. Those food and fiber supplies are unlikely to come either from greater rates of production or from greater commercial imports than those projected above. And if these supplies are not forthcoming, the conservative rates of economic growth cited above cannot be realized; they will be eroded away by inflation and blocked by the necessity of using scarce foreign exchange to buy urgently needed food supplies.

The long-run situation of the underdeveloped countries is truly desperate. If they achieve a reasonable rate of over-all economic development, the demand for food, based on a high income elasticity of demand for food, gives promise of running away from food production. If, on the other hand, they do not achieve a reasonable rate of over-all economic

[5] The above conclusion, projections, and analysis are from Willard W. Cochrane, Arthur B. Mackie, and Grover C. Chappell, "Potential Uses of Farm Products as Aid to Developing Countries," *Journal of Farm Economics*, Proceedings Issue, December 1963.

growth, they are faced with grinding poverty, actual hunger, and the likelihood of political disaster.

Once removed, the situation is also desperate for the free world. Certainly the United States and other nations of the free world cannot seriously consider a course of action that leads to economic failure and political disaster for large numbers of the underdeveloped nations. This being true, the United States and Western Europe must be prepared to think very big indeed about economic assistance in general and food aid exports in particular.

THE EXPORT MARKET REAPPRAISED

There once was a time — in the years before World War I — when it made sense to view and treat the foreign market as an overflow market. A free world market, for the grains, at least, was centered at Liverpool. It was a world market in that men around the world traded on the price quotations of the Liverpool market, and it was a free market in that any legitimate trader could buy or sell on that market at any time, provided he abided by its rules. There were similar, although perhaps somewhat less formal, markets for other staple agricultural commodities: cotton, sugar, tobacco, and wool.

The individual grain trader viewed the Liverpool market in the same way that the individual farmer views the domestic market today. If he were a law-abiding citizen there was nothing — no import quotas, no minimum import prices, not even a tariff — to stop him from shipping to that market and selling his grain there. And his shipment to this market would typically be so small relative to the volume of grain traded there that it would have no perceptible influence on the price in the market.

In fact, however, most grain in the world market did not physically move through the Liverpool market; Liverpool was the accounting center of a worldwide organization of grain markets, which took account of world demand and supplies and all purchases and sales, and determined the prices of grain, spot and future, on which trading around the world took place. Thus, if at any time a grain trader in the United States could not find what he considered a satisfactory outlet in the home market, he could within minutes sell his grain for export, to go physically he knew not where, on the Liverpool market. It was a wondrous and wonderful arrangement to which economists have given the technical name "a perfect market."

The Foreign Market

But the world market served as an overflow market in a larger sense. The perfect market conditions in the grains made possible an overflow market, but the perfect market itself did not constitute the overflow market. The overflow concept derived from two unrelated, but nicely complementary, relations. First, the domestic market was a large and rapidly growing market which could and should be satisfactorily supplied from domestic production; after it was supplied there was a need to put the unplanned surplus somewhere. Second, the world market turned out to be an ideal place to put the surplus, because it was so large relative to the size of the surplus that disposing of the surplus in it did not depress grain prices so much as disposing of the surplus in the domestic market would have.[6]

In other words, the price of the surplus grain, and all other units of grain in the market involved, would not decline by as much when the surplus was pushed onto the great worldwide market as it would if it had been put on the smaller domestic market. Thus, because the real market was the home market, because fertile land and improved technology have always tended to yield a surplus, and, further, because price losses could be minimized in the export market, the export market has traditionally been viewed as an overflow market for the surplus products of American farmers.

But the free world market in the grains and other important farm commodities withered away, or was strangled (depending upon your point of view) between the two world wars, and since World War II has ceased to exist. No longer can an exporter simply sell grain or cotton on the world market for physical delivery he knows not where. In the present world situation he must find a specific buyer — government purchasing agency or private firm — and deal with that buyer under the specific trading regulations that pertain to the import country. And when an importing nation's domestic price is below the minimum import price, or the import quota is full, or the government purchasing agency has obtained its supplies from another seller nation, there is no way to move products from the export nation X to the import nation Y. Farm products simply cannot move in this situation.

The mission of the exporter of farm products in the present world

[6] Or as economists might put it: the realized demand curve confronting the suppliers of the surplus at the world level is much more elastic than that at the domestic level.

situation is to find a way to worm his products through the protectionist devices of each country. Sometimes the private exporter can succeed in moving a farm product through the barrage of restrictions all by himself; and, of course, the job becomes relatively easy when the importing country is in need of the product. But sometimes the barriers are such that the product simply cannot move, as in the situation outlined above. Then the private trader requires the help of his government to negotiate more favorable import regulations and interpretations of regulations to open the door to trade; this has been the course of action followed by the United States in recent years.

The world commercial market in the 1960's cannot serve as an effective overflow market for the exportable surplus of American farms; it is not an unlimited void to be filled at the pleasure of American farmers. The commercial export market may expand slowly before the onslaught of the American team of staff workers, traders, and negotiators. Or it may contract. But its present structure does not permit it to serve as an outlet for whatever surplus may have come into being for whatever commodity. Each importing country takes from foreign suppliers each year what it needs to satisfy its requirements, *and no more*. Those takings may be modified over time by the diligent efforts of the traders from a particular export country. But each importing country takes what it needs, and no more.

The foreign food aid market is another story. Basically it has served as an overflow market since 1954. But it is far from a perfect overflow market. The United States government must pay the full bill. Competing commercial export nations complain bitterly about American food aid, and the quantities that each recipient country can or will take are limited by the political pressures exerted by their own farmers and the availability of storage, handling, and transportation facilities in those countries.

On the other hand, the food needs of the underdeveloped countries are great, and are going to increase; the potential consumers are there. Thus, the extent to which the foreign food aid market can serve as an effective overflow market for the exportable surplus of the United States really depends upon how far the American public and its congressional representatives are ready to go in footing the bill.

If the American public is willing to give the underdeveloped countries both financing and technical assistance to build adequate storage, handling, and transportation facilities, and if it is willing to cover the cost of the commodities moved into this market (that is, purchase the commodities and distribute them abroad), then the foreign food aid market can serve as an effective overflow outlet for the surplus farm products of the United States.

The foreign food aid market can effectively use now and in the foreseeable future the level and composition of exportable surplus generated on American farms in the early 1960's. The issue is the cost of the program — the cost of developing the handling facilities in the underdeveloped countries, of moving the products to those countries, and of acquiring the surplus commodities in the United States. The bill is not small.

What are the alternatives? The first is not let the exportable surplus be produced. By careful planning and rigorous production controls it would be possible to gear the annual production of the farm plant to the requirements of the domestic and commercial export markets. But so far this has not had any great appeal to farmers. The second alternative is a system of loose production controls to dampen down farm production, move some part of the exportable surplus into foreign food aid, and let the balance flow into the hands of the Commodity Credit Corporation (the agent of the federal government for taking over the surplus stocks of farmers). This is the alternative that has been followed for many years, and it is the current practice.

The many and varied implications of this latter policy will be discussed and analyzed in the chapters that follow. The point to be made here is that the Commodity Credit Corporation has since the 1930's served as the ultimate overflow market for the surplus of American farms. The overseas market really ceased to serve as an overflow market in the 1930's, when its structure changed so radically that it could no longer take the surplus regardless of price. This alteration forced the surplus back on the domestic market. But the adverse price implications of disposing of the surplus in the domestic market were so great that a new residual or overflow market was created, the Commodity Credit Corporation.

7

𝔭

The Basic Problem

TO THIS point, we have analyzed different strands of the commercial farm problem. The technological revolution occurring on American farms has been described and its driving force in expanding farm output analyzed. The growth and behavior of the domestic market has been described and its implications for demand expansion analyzed. And the foreign market with its uncertainties and potentials has been described and analyzed. Now we need to pull these different strands of the problem together in one integrated analysis; that is the purpose of this chapter.

THE PROBLEM: EXCESS CAPACITY

Since 1930 farm output has run ahead of population growth (see Table 4). During the war years of the 1940's and the period of rehabilitation that followed, this imbalance created no problem; first our allies and later the defeated countries swallowed up the American surplus of food and fiber products and cried for more. But during the 1930's, the 1950's, and again in the 1960's food and fiber supplies have pressed against domestic demand, causing farm prices to fall disastrously in the 1930's, and government stocks to build up under price support in the 1950's and 1960's even as the government tried to reduce or hold down production. Except in wartime there have been too many resources producing too much product — excess productive capacity — on American farms since 1930; this is the basic problem of the commercial farm sector.

During the 1950's farm output increased about 2.1 per cent a year despite programs to limit production. During the same period popula-

110

tion in the United States increased about 1.7 per cent a year. That is, total farm output increased about one half of one per cent faster than population growth during the 1950's.

Per-capita food consumption remained almost constant during this period; thus increased per-capita food consumption did not absorb any significant part of the excess production. Commercial exports did increase, and did absorb a part of the excess. Foreign food aid (Food for Peace) came into being in 1954 and helped absorb an important part of the excess. But increased exports did not succeed in absorbing all of the excess in farm production over population requirements.

Government-owned stocks of farm commodities grew from about $1.3 billion in 1952 to $7.7 billion in 1959, as government acquired stocks in price-supporting operations. Since 1959, the government stock position has improved modestly, but this has occurred through expanded production control programs which keep an increased number of productive acres out of production.

We know that the excess productive capacity of the national farm plant has not continued in being since 1930 because the farmers maintained the status quo. Millions of them have left farming since 1930, and the number of acres devoted to crops has declined importantly since 1949. But new and improved capital and practices have been so effectively substituted for labor and land that total output has continued to increase — and to increase enough to hold the farm economy in a chronic state of surplus.

It is not that labor and land have not moved out of farming in the past three and a half decades; it is rather that they have not poured out of farming in the volume necessary to offset the inflow of new and improved capital and practices. The national farm economy simply has not been able to make the rapid resource adjustment required by the rapid inflow of new and improved capital and practices. It therefore remains in a constant state of excess productive capacity.

What has been the extent or size of this continuous excess productive capacity of the national farm plant? Several studies that measure the excess productive capacity or the surplus production of the national farm plant for the 1950's are available.[1] One places the estimate as low

[1] See James T. Bonnen, "American Agriculture in 1965," *Policy for Commercial Agriculture, Its Relation to Economic Growth and Stability,* 85th Congress, 1st Session, November 22, 1957, p. 146; R. G. Bressler, Jr., "Farm Technology and the Race with Population," *Journal of Farm Economics,* November 1957, p. 851;

as 5 per cent of total production. Other estimates run as high as 8 and 9 per cent of production. A part of this discrepancy in the size of estimates is due to the different assumptions of the different studies, but a part is due to different periods studied. Excess productive capacity increased during most of the 1950's, reaching a peak in 1958–59. It may therefore be concluded that between 5 and 9 per cent of total farm production each year during the 1950's was surplus — that it could not find a commercial home at the supported farm price level.

Surplus production, or excess productive capacity, must be measured at some price level above the free, equilibrium price level, for at the free, equilibrium price level there is no surplus. At the equilibrium price supply equals demand. But some idea of the magnitude of surplus farm production at the level of support prices in the 1950's may be obtained by considering what level farm prices would have had to drop to in order to wipe out a surplus of, say, 7 per cent (the median of the above estimates). With an elasticity of aggregate demand for all farm products of −.3 at retail, farm product prices would have had to fall by over 20 per cent at retail and by 40 per cent or more at the farm level. Measured in price terms the excess productive capacity of the national farm plant in the 1950's was breathtaking.

A recent and thorough study of excess capacity in American agriculture by Tyner and Tweeten throws additional light on the problem, particularly for the early 1960's.[2] Taking account of commodity acquisitions by the CCC (the government), commodities that would have been produced on land withdrawn from production under various control programs, and all government subsidized exports, these investigators conclude that surplus production in 1961–62 amounted to as much as 10 per cent of total production. Then, taking into account certain value received by the United States from subsidized farm exports, they conclude that a realistic estimate of surplus farm production for 1961–62 would be 7 per cent of total production. This means that the best estimate of the excess productive capacity of the national farm plant for the early 1960's is just about the same as that for the middle 1950's, namely, 7 per cent.

Nathan Koffsky, "The Long-Term Price Outlook and Its Impact on American Agriculture," *Journal of Farm Economics*, December 1954, p. 797.

[2] See Fred H. Tyner and Luther G. Tweeten, "Excess Capacity in U.S. Agriculture," *Agricultural Economics Research*, Economic Research Service, USDA, January 1964.

But with the same realistic assumptions about exports, the Tyner-Tweeten estimate of excess capacity goes as high as 11 per cent in 1958–59. And if crop yields increase as rapidly in the second half of the 1960's as they did in 1961–63, the level of excess productive capacity in farming could once again move up to 11 or 12 per cent of total production. This means that one of three things or a combination of them can happen in the second half of the 1960's: (1) stocks in government hands may begin to build up again; (2) the cost of government control programs may rise still further; (3) the volume and cost of P.L. 480 shipments may increase still further. Assuming that the farm price level holds constant, increased but unneeded productive capacity for commercial purposes must come out in one of these three ways, all of which mean increased costs. Increased productive capacity unneeded for commercial purposes thus leads by one avenue or another to increased government program costs. And the rate of crop yield increases of 1961–63 projected through the 1960's certainly leads to *increased* excess productive capacity in the farm sector.

A GENERAL THEORY OF CHRONIC EXCESS CAPACITY

The farm economy has been out of adjustment, except possibly during World War II, since the early 1930's. The question is, Why? Why is there chronic excess productive capacity in farming? Why are there too many resources producing too much product at a reasonable level of prices year in and year out?

This chronic condition grows out of four related circumstances: (1) the high value that American society places on scientific research and technological development; (2) the market organization or structure within which farmers operate; (3) the extreme inelasticity of the aggregate demand for food; and (4) the inability of resources previously committed to farm production to shift easily and readily out of farming. These are the components of a general theory which explains the chronic excess capacity in American farming.[3]

The American people have not singled out agriculture in general and farming in particular to carry the burden of scientific and technological advances; Americans prize science and technology highly, expect it, and demand it in all segments of the economy. And as we ob-

[3] This analysis is adapted from my earlier work, *Farm Prices: Myth and Reality*, pp. 105–107.

served in Chapters 2 and 3, they are getting rapid scientific and technological development in agriculture, and its widespread adoption in farming.

There is no question about the general acceptance by the public, by farmers, and by the scientists and technicians of the essential goodness and correctness of broad, sustained efforts to develop science and technology in agriculture. Anyone in government or out who questions the wisdom of spending as much money as we currently are on research and development in agriculture (as I have) is hooted down as being against progress. The fact that very rapid technological development and advancement also requires very rapid resource and institutional adjustments in the farm sector is not understood by many, and those who do understand simply believe that technological advances and the associated gains in production efficiency are desirable, and that the resulting resource and social adjustments must be made, whatever the cost.

So in the name of progress vast sums are poured into scientific and technological development in agriculture. These research and development efforts are now efficient and effective and the new and improved technologies are produced and disseminated with the capacity to increase total farm output in a sustained manner. The belief is there, the money is there, and the trained research workers and technicians are there — so the new and improved technologies pour forth. And they will continue to pour forth in the future, with the result that farming will be totally different in 2000 from what it is today, just as today's farming is vastly different from what it was in 1900 or even 1940.

The market structure under which the typical farmer operates is highly conducive to the farm adoption of new and improved technologies. The typical farmer operates in a market so large that he can have no perceptible influence on it, and must take as given to him the prices generated there; he is a price taker.

Confronted with this situation, he reasons, "I can't influence price, but I can influence my own costs. I can get my costs down." So the typical farmer is always searching for some way to get his costs down. By definition, an improved technology is cost-reducing (that is, it increases output per unit of input). The typical farmer is thus on the lookout for new, cost-reducing technologies; built into the market organization of farming is a powerful incentive for adopting new and improved technologies — the incentive of reducing costs on the individual farm. And it works: farmers generally adopt new and improved technologies to reduce costs; this widespread adoption increases farm output in the aggregate, and thus farm technological advance pushes total output before it in an expanding action.

If the demand for food were highly elastic all would be well in farming. If the aggregate demand for food were elastic, the bountiful and expanding supplies of food that farmers want to produce would sell in the market at only slightly reduced prices, gross incomes to farmers in the aggregate and individually would increase, and the surplus resources would be employed to produce the additional product that would be taken by consumers at only slightly reduced prices. If the aggregate demand for food were elastic, farming would be an expanding industry as more men and more land were combined with improved technological practices to produce an increased total product that sold for such modest price decreases that gross receipts to farmers increased as a result. This is the happy situation confronting an industry with an elastic demand for its product.

But the aggregate demand for food is not elastic; it is inelastic and extremely so. For this reason, a little too much total output drives down the farm price level in a dramatic fashion. In other words, with a severely inelastic demand confronting the producers of food, it is very easy to develop a condition of excess capacity, or surplus production; a small surplus can have an extreme effect on farm prices and gross farm income.

The severely inelastic aggregate demand for food would not be devastating, however, if the aggregate supply of farm food products were elastic. If the aggregate supply were elastic, then with a surplus situation and a downward movement in farm prices, productive resources would quickly move out of farming, production would be reduced, and a bottom would be placed under the price decline. Through an adjustment in resource use the surplus would be eliminated and the drastic price decline avoided.

The aggregate supply of farm food products is not elastic; it is inelastic and extremely so. It is inelastic because productive resources cannot easily and readily leave farming and move to other industries in response to changes in the farm price level. Farm labor is tied to family patterns of living and increases and decreases in response to family growth cycles rather than to price level changes, except when the whole family decides to move. Farm land cannot pick up and move to urban areas when farm prices fall; it shifts into nonfarm uses only when those uses come to it. Capital sunk into farm buildings, irrigation and drainage works, tractors, and combines does not move easily or have ready uses in nonfarm industries. Most resources employed in farming move only slowly, as they are worn out and not replaced, or as they become of age and break away from the family. Consequently, the short-run aggregate supply of farm food products is highly inelastic and provides no brake to falling prices in a surplus situation.

What we have in farming is, then, the following: (1) a generous publicly-supported research and development effort which effectively turns out an array of new and improved technological practices year after year; (2) the widespread adoption of these technologies by farmers, resulting in a sustained increase in the aggregate production of farm food products; (3) expanding supplies which press against a slowly expanding and inelastic aggregate demand for food and create a strong downward pressure on farm prices; (4) a downward movement in farm food product prices which is not able to bring about readily a reduction in supplies offered on the market and thus put a brake on falling prices, because resources employed in farming move sluggishly in response to changes in price level; and (5) since the inflow of new and improved technologies has exceeded the outflow of conventional resources employed in farming, there has, except in wartime, been a price-depressing surplus year after year. This is the general theory of a chronically maladjusted farm sector.

In the 1930's the surplus of farm products actually came onto the market and drove farm prices down to disastrous levels. In the 1950's and 1960's, the surplus has been kept off the market by two devices: the withdrawal of land from production through government programs and the acquisition of supplies by government at support price levels. Farm prices have therefore not fallen disastrously in the 1950's and 1960's as the result of excess productive capacity; that excess productive capacity has been absorbed by government programs.

THE SYMPTOMS OF THE PROBLEM

Reading about the commercial farm problem in a newspaper, one is not likely to find excess productive capacity referred to as the core of the problem. The reader may run across a statement that there are too many workers in farming or too many resources employed in farming, but this is not likely to be billed as the basic problem. The farm problem is more likely to be described in the newspaper as involving "low farm incomes," or "a mountain of surplus stocks in government hands," or "the high cost of farm programs." The average reader has been conditioned to these phrases.

Now what is the relation of these phrases to what we have described as the basic aspects of the problem, namely, excess productive capacity? The catchphrases describe symptoms of the problem; excess capacity is its cause. Under one set of institutions, excess productive capacity in farming causes low farm prices and incomes, under another set of institutions excess productive capacity in farming causes large stocks in government hands and/or high-cost government programs. Too many resources in farming producing too much product is the basic cause; low farm incomes or expensive government programs are the symptoms.

Assuming that there were no farm programs in operation to support farm prices and protect farm incomes — that is, no programs to control production and no programs (domestic or foreign) to dispose of products acquired in price-supporting operations — and the excess productive capacity in farming, amounting to about 7 per cent of total production in the early 1960's, was fully utilized to produce and then sell products, what would be the price and income consequences to American farmers? They would be disastrous. Given the very low elasticities of aggregate demand and supply, and the almost total absence of a braking action to a price decline on either the demand or the supply side, an additional supply amounting to 7 per cent of current production dumped onto the market could lower farm product prices at retail by 20 per cent or more and at the farm level by 40 per cent or more. Since in this situation production costs would change very little — the prices of nonfarm inputs would not be affected, and increases in production costs due to increased production would be about offset by the lower prices of farm produced inputs — the squeeze on net farm incomes would be terrific: aggregate net farm income could fall by as much as 60 to 70 per cent.

This, of course, is the short-run result. With the farm prices and incomes outlined above, *resource adjustments would take place.* Capital items would not be replaced as they wore out, new production practices

117

involving out-of-pocket costs would not be instituted, and labor would race out of farming if jobs were available in the nonfarm sector. Whether the level of farm prices would rise again to the level of the early 1960's, say in six to eight years, is anybody's guess. I am inclined to guess that it would not. An average level of farm prices halfway between the early 1960 price level and the short-run bottom described above would seem more probable for the long run. But this average level would involve a high degree of variability from year to year. And this price variability and the consequent price uncertainty that accompanied a free market for farm products would probably be more damaging to rational economic action than the initial price drop.

But we do have farm programs that support prices and protect incomes. The excess productive capacity of 7 per cent is not used to produce products to be placed on the commercial market. Surplus farm production, actual and potential, is held off the commercial market by a series of devices: the purchase and acquisition of surplus stocks under price-support operations, the withdrawal of land from production under control programs, and the disposal of surplus stocks outside commercial channels of trade at home and abroad. By means of these devices farm prices are not permitted to fall to the disastrous levels that would obtain in a free market.

The symptoms of the basic disease — too many productive resources in farming — are thus in practice converted from very low prices and incomes to surplus stocks in government warehouses and expensive farm programs. The physical problem of handling large stocks of food and fiber products seems to worry many people, but that handling problem is readily reducible to money costs. The overt symptom of the commercial farm problem under price and income supports is therefore best summarized as government costs of farm programs of price and income support and commodity disposal.

Government expenditures for these programs reached a high of $5.4 billion in the Eisenhower administration in fiscal 1959; during most years in the late 1950's government outlays under these programs were running between $3 and $4 billion. Under the Kennedy-Johnson administration expenditure by the federal government on these programs was $4.8 billion in fiscal 1962 and $5.9 billion in fiscal 1964.

The government costs of these programs were higher in the early 1960's than in the late 1950's for three reasons. First, the excessive stocks of grain in government hands were reduced through expanded control programs — through expanded withdrawals of land from production; this action in effect transformed increased storage costs in future years into increased costs of production control in 1961–64. Second, the Kennedy-Johnson administration raised net farm incomes by means of modestly higher price support and production payments to farmers. Third, and most important, the cost of holding down production through withdrawing land from production rose with increased yields per acre. With rising yields the farmer must be paid more to induce him to hold his land idle, and more acres must be kept out of production to hold total production constant.

This third point is going to be of critical importance in the future. As crop yields continue to increase, it will cost more and more under voluntary programs to induce farmers to let their acres lie idle; and as crop production outraces commercial requirements, more and more acres will have to be withheld from production to support prices at any given level. We can expect with a high degree of probability that the cost of price and income support will increase during the late 1960's and the 1970's, if farm prices are maintained at their present levels.

Rising program costs resulting from increasing productivity are likely to lead to a farm policy crisis over the next decade (see pp. 29–31). Thus, the symptom, government costs of farm programs, like a high fever, could, as the result of rapid increases in farm productivity, get out of hand in the decade ahead, and force major changes in American farm policy.

A NOTE ON FARM INCOME AND LAND VALUES

In thinking and talking about the current level of farm income, the most important single point to keep in mind is that current farm incomes are riding on a massive program of surplus acquisition, removal from the market, and disposition in noncommercial channels; without that program net farm incomes would be 40 to 70 per cent below the 1961–64 level (depending upon what kind of free market is assumed). Whether farm incomes in 1961–64 are fair and equitable may be debated, but one point is not open to debate: farm incomes would fall to disaster levels if programs of price and income support were done away with. This farmers and city men should not ignore or forget.

But now the question must be faced: Are farm incomes at their present level and distribution fair and equitable, or are they low and poorly distributed? The average farm worker earns less than half what an average factory worker earns in a year. The net income from farming (in money and in kind) for the average farm operator and his family in 1963 was $3,643; not much by any standard, and certainly not big in terms of the large investments involved in farming.

But the income picture changes somewhat when we take into account size of operation. Net farm incomes for 1963, by the farm sales categories used in Chapter 1, are shown in the accompanying tabulation.[4] The net

Annual Sales	Net Incomes
$20,000 and over	$10,180
$10,000–$19,999	6,207
$5,000–$9,999	3,731
$2,500–$4,999	2,337
Less than $2,500	1,406

incomes of families operating farms grossing over $10,000 per year, commercial farms by our definition, are not excitingly large, but neither are they disgracefully small. The average net farm income for the group in transition, farms with sales between $5,000 and $9,999, is getting pretty low, and the net incomes for the last two sales categories put the operators and their families squarely in the poverty class, unless they have substantial income from nonfarm sources.

Given this distribution of net farm incomes, to what extent are the incomes for the different sales categories fair and reasonable, and by what criteria? The late Robert H. Masucci, in an important study, estimated the extent to which farmers in different economic groupings are receiving or not receiving parity incomes.[5] His study assumes that a return of 5 per cent on productive assets, a minimum wage of $1.25 an hour to hired labor, and a return of $2.32 an hour for operator and family labor, constitutes a parity of return to capital and labor employed in farming. The results of the study show that as of 1961, the average farm with annual sales of $5,000 and over earned a gross income that fell 9 per cent short of the parity income goal. In other words, the average farm grossing over $5,000 per year would in 1961 have had to receive a 9 per cent increase in gross income to provide a parity of returns on cap-

[4] These estimates, computed from Appendix Table 2, measure total net farm income (in money and in kind) of farm operator families and were arrived at by subtracting the figures in the fifth column from those in the seventh of that table.

[5] See "Income Parity Standards for Agriculture," *Agricultural Economics Research*, Economic Research Service, USDA, October 1962.

ital and labor. Gross receipts to commercial farmers in 1961 fell short of a reasonable measure of a fair level of income — but not badly short.

Farms with sales of less than $5,000 a year are, however, in desperate shape. Farms with sales between $2,500 and $4,999 would require an increase in gross income of 74 per cent to provide a parity of return for the resources employed on those farms. And an increase of 193 per cent in gross income would be required to provide parity returns to farms with sales less than $2,500 a year.

Updating this parity income analysis to 1963 and developing estimates for more economic groupings, we get the following results. The average farm with sales $20,000 and over fell short of the parity income goal by only 2 per cent; with a 2 per cent increase in gross income the average farm in this size group would realize a parity of income. The average farm with annual sales between $10,000 and $19,999 would require a 10 per cent increase in gross income to realize the parity income goal, the average farm with sales between $5,000 and $9,999 a 34 per cent increase, and the average farm with sales of less than $5,000 a year fell short of the parity income goal by the dramatic figure of 129 per cent.

Farmers operating farms with sales $20,000 and over in the early 1960's were coming very close to earning fair and equitable incomes — by at least one set of criteria. Farmers with sales between $10,000 and $19,999 were on the average falling about 10 per cent short of the goal of fair and equitable incomes. We can say, therefore, that some 27 per cent of all farmers, those producing 78 per cent of the total farm product, are at or fairly close to a reasonable measure of parity of income.

The transition group, the six hundred thousand farmers grossing between $5,000 and $9,999 per year, is another story. They have a long, long way to go to reach parity of income. And most farms and farmers grossing less than $5,000 have an impossible task; hence we shall consider their case separately in Part III of this book.

Although the above evidence suggests that the income picture of truly commercial farmers is not bad, this does not mean that a lot of commercial farmers, who are acquiring highly valued assets, are not in financial trouble. Many of them are. Many are buying high-priced land faster than is consistent with their reasonable but not exorbitant incomes. But that is a different problem. Many a city man, and certainly many a college professor, would be in financial difficulty, if on his present income he were trying to acquire productive assets as rapidly as many commercial farmers are.

This leads to that difficult question of land values. The price of farm land has risen persistently and substantially since 1940. As our analysis in Chapter 4 showed, this must happen where farm technological advance is widespread and farm prices do not fall to reflect the gains in productivity. And the rising cost of farm land, with the heavy investment required to buy enough acres for an economic-sized farm unit, means that the typical farmer will have great trouble paying for that land in ten years, or twenty years, or even in his lifetime.

Table 7. Value of Farm Real Estate in Billions of Dollars, U.S., 1940–64

Year	Valued in Current Prices	Valued in Constant 1940 Prices	Increase in Value Due to Land Price Increases
1940	$33.6	$33.6	..
1950	75.3	35.8	$39.5
1960	129.9	38.1	91.8
1964	150.8	38.7	112.1

Source: *The Balance Sheet of Agriculture*, 1964 and previous years, Agricultural Information Bulletin No. 290, Economic Research Service, USDA.

But there is another side to this land value question. Because of rising land prices, the value of farm real estate, over and above the physical improvements, has increased tremendously since 1940 (see Table 7). Capital gains in farm real estate due to rising land prices amounted to $112 billion between 1940 and 1964. Since farmers own about 78 per cent of all farm real estate, this means that farm operators received capital gains from farm real estate of about $87 billion between 1940 and 1964, or about $3.5 billion each year. That is not a small gain.

It is true that a person cannot buy groceries with capital gains, or make monthly payments on a new tractor. But it is also true that when capital gains are realized through the sale of the asset such gains are better than earned income, because they are taxed at a much lower rate. Further, as assets appreciate in value, the credit base of a businessman is increased — very important in the modern business world. Farmers have been the beneficiaries of a very large gain over the past twenty-five years, call it what you will.

Assuming arbitrarily that the annual capital gain to farmers of $3.5 billion was worth $2.5 billion to them as some kind of income, it follows that total net income to all farmers was really some 20 per cent greater each year than the published net income figures in the 1950's and 1960's. And the income of the average commercial farmer, the farmer with annual sales of $10,000 and over, more than met the parity income standard.

The land-values issue cuts two ways. Rising land values are making it increasingly difficult for the young man to get started in farming, if he expects to become an owner of land in the same sense that his father and grandfather did. But to farmers who own land, rising land values have brought important gains that cannot and should not be ignored. Those gains are increasing the net worth of owner-operators faster than equal amounts earned as income would.

In sum and in short, taking account of both net income from farming and capital gains on farm real estate, the average commercial farm operator has not done badly in terms of economic return. Where he is prone to get into financial difficulty, if he does, is in his attempt to acquire high-valued real estate more rapidly than his reasonable but not exorbitant income permits. But once again, farmer and city man alike must recognize that the whole structure of farm incomes in the 1960's is riding on government programs of price and income support.

8

The Economic Solutions

THE basic problem of commercial farming, excess productive capacity, is an economic problem involving the proper allocation of research and development resources, the adjustment of conventional farm resources, and the growth and elasticity of the aggregate demand for and supply of farm products. A consideration of the relevant economic solutions to the commercial problem is thus in order at this point; this then will be the subject matter of this chapter: the unvarnished economic solutions.

THE RELEVANT SOLUTIONS

The Free Market. The surplus problem in American farming could be solved by simply letting prices fall to that level where the market is cleared of the surplus. This solution is effected by consumers demanding and taking more product at a lower price on one hand, and producers offering less on the market at a lower price on the other. There is some price for every commodity or group of commodities — in this case a lower price — where the expanded demand and the contracted supply reach equality, and the surplus in the market is eliminated. This is the free market solution.

The difficulty with the free market solution in farming is that in correcting the surplus problem, it creates another, the farm income problem. As we have already observed, American consumers expand their consumption of total food very little with lower food prices; and family farmers contract the total product on each farm very little with falling farm prices. The aggregate demand for food is inelastic and the aggregate supply of farm food products is very inelastic. In this state of affairs farm prices must fall a long way to bring about a balance between demand and supply when the surplus condition in farming approaches 7 per cent. It is this requirement that farm prices fall a long way to bring about a balance or equality that creates a farm income problem.

Before we can say how far farm product prices must fall, and how much farm income will decline as a result, under a free market solution, we must know what kind of a free market we are talking about. Any free market must have government involved, if for no other reason than to establish and enforce the rules under which buying and selling take place. But most people in thinking about a free market for farming have in mind a great deal more government involvement than the establishment and enforcement of trading rules. Most often they have in mind government-supported research and extension work, foreign food aid and domestic food distribution, and marketing orders and agreements and government inspection and grading of commodities. Turned around, the most commonly held concept of a free market for farming is one where price support and production control programs are eliminated, but all other government activities in the agricultural complex are maintained.

In this concept of a *modified* free market, the measure of excess productive capacity falls from a range of 7 to 10 per cent to a range of 4 to 7 per cent. The measure declines because food and fiber products acquired by government and distributed under domestic food distribution programs and foreign food aid are not considered a part of excess capacity under this concept; these programs are built into the permanent demand structure for food and fiber products.

It is estimated that farm prices would decline by 20 to 25 per cent and that total net farm income would fall by about 50 per cent, under a modified free market in a three-to-five-year period.[1] Of course, all farm prices would not fall equally. Beef cattle prices would fall by about 15 per cent, hog prices by 26 per cent, broiler prices by 21 per cent, milk at wholesale by 11 per cent, wheat by 50 per cent, corn by 31 per cent, and cotton by 38 per cent; farm income reductions would vary directly with the magnitude of the commodity price declines. But over all, the

---

[1] See the Committee Print, *Farm Program Benefits and Costs in Recent Years*, prepared by Walter W. Wilcox of the Legislative Reference Service, Library of Congress, and printed by the Senate Committee on Agriculture and Forestry, October 6, 1964, for a summary and discussion of the price-income consequences of having no price-support programs.

modified free market effects a solution to the surplus problem that reduces the net income to all farmers by something over 50 per cent.

But if we have in mind a concept of a *pure* free market where all government programs are abolished, and the full excess capacity in farming is eliminated by lower prices, then the price and income declines are more spectacular than those above. As we saw in Chapter 7, if the full excess productive capacity of American farming of the early 1960's were to be eliminated by lower prices, the decline in the level of farm prices could be as much as 40 per cent, and the decline in aggregate net farm income as much as 60 to 70 per cent.

The estimates presented above for both concepts of a free market are for the short run of three to five years. In the longer run of six to eight years, with a continuous expansion of demand through population growth, and an adjustment in resource use through the out-migration of farm labor and the failure to replace worn-out capital items, it is probable that prices and incomes in farming would turn upward again. But conditions become so tenuous in the long run that it is impossible to make realistic estimates of price developments. The best that can be said is that it is probable that farm prices would rise again following the short-run havoc.

The economics are clear. Removing price-support and production-control programs would correct the excess capacity problem. But the correction of the surplus problem by the free market route creates a farm income problem that at least the body politic judges to be worse than the original surplus problem. It will be remembered that the price-support and production-control programs came into being in the 1930's and have been maintained since then for the very purpose of avoiding the income consequences of surplus production in farming.

Production Control. Theoretically, it is possible by manmade controls to adjust supplies to demand at a previously determined fair price, and in that way eliminate the production surplus in farming. The first step on this route is to estimate total demand (commercial demand plus quantities needed for food aid programs) at the determined fair price; this establishes the quantity that can be used, hence the total quantity that needs to be produced. With the total quantity established the second step is the allotment of that total quantity among farmers. This is probably best done on the basis of each farmer's historical record of production.

The Economic Solutions

The third step involves getting farmers to agree to subject themselves to an equitable set of production restrictions that will yield an outturn of product that fills the national quota *and no more*. This step probably would mean presenting the program to farmers, in terms of the level of price support and the nature and extent of the individual restrictions, for their approval or rejection by referendum. If approved the regulations for the commodity involved would become binding on all farmers through the use of the police powers of the state.

The straitjacketing effect of production controls can be minimized if the production allotment to each farm is made in the form of a marketing quota expressed in bushels, pounds, or bales, and the marketing quota is made negotiable. By these twin devices the individual farmer is free to combine his resource inputs to fill his quota in any way that is desirable and economic in his operation, and he can expand or contract his operation by buying and selling quota in the same way that he would any other resources. By these quota devices the total output of the national farm plant is controlled, and the surplus production eliminated, but the individual farmer has a high degree of freedom in the planning and actual use of his productive resources. Finally, since production in farming varies unpredictably with the weather and other uncontrolled elements, adequate storage should be built into the total management program to meet such contingencies as a bad crop or an unexpected wartime demand.[2]

But this is not the way that production control or supply management programs have developed in practice. Farmers have sought and obtained a looser structure of controls on total output, but controls in many ways more binding at the farm operating level. The following has emerged in practice. First, to support farm incomes, prices have been supported by government action. In this action, the government has accumulated stocks of farm commodities. Second, to stop the build-up of stocks in government hands, and possibly reduce these stocks, controls over the use of productive land on farms have been instituted. In the typical commodity control program the producers are asked or required (depending on the nature of the program) to hold 15, or 20, or 25 per cent of their *base acreage* of that crop out of production.

[2] This is the kind of program I recommended to farmers in the late 1950's, and to the Kennedy administration in the early 1960's. See also my *Farm Prices: Myth and Reality*, Chapter 8.

The Economic Solutions

Acreage control is a pretty leaky vessel in which to float a production control program for at least two reasons. For one thing, the producer substitutes improved plant varieties, increased fertilizer, and improved cultural practices on his uncontrolled acres and increases production there — increases it enough within a few years to more than offset the outturn lost from the acreage taken out of production. For another thing, the acreage withheld from production in the crop being controlled, wheat, for example, is planted to a second best alternative, perhaps sorghum grain. Total production is thus reduced very little; productive resources are simply diverted from a crop heavily in surplus to crops which were in less trouble. In time the alternative crops move into a surplus condition, too, as happened to sorghum grains when wheat land in the 1950's was shifted to sorghum production as the result of the acreage control program on wheat.

This shifting of productive resources from crop A to crop B as the result of an acreage control program on crop A was brought to an end under the Soil Bank Program in the late 1950's and under the commodity programs of the Kennedy administration. Under those programs the acres taken out of production had to be held in a nonproductive use — had to be held idle. But for many years commodity control programs simply meant shifting productive resources from one crop to the next and had almost no effect on total farm production, hence upon total excess capacity.

With the tightening of the control features of commodity programs, farmers have become increasingly disenchanted with the programs. To get control programs through Congress in recent years and to get farmers to participate in them it has been necessary to pay farmers to take land out of production. Under the Soil Bank plan of the Eisenhower administration farmers were paid to keep part or all of their farms out of production. In the commodity control programs of the Kennedy administration this was again true.

Attempts were made during the Kennedy administration to get wheat and feed grain farmers to accept mandatory acreage control programs, but this they would not do. What has evolved in the middle 1960's are voluntary control programs where each producer, on the basis of payment rates for holding cropland out of production, decides whether or not to take part — whether or not to hold idle a part of his base acreage for the particular crop. This he will do, if, when he figures the alterna-

The Economic Solutions

tives, he determines that the economic return is greater from holding land out of production than from farming it. Under this type of voluntary commodity program, plus a few million lingering Soil Bank acres, some fifty-six million acres were held out of production in 1963–64 at a cost to the public treasury of about $1.4 billion.

There is nothing wrong with buying land out of production as a means of controlling surplus production — if cost is no object. Enough acres can always be removed from production to eliminate the surplus — at a price. But if cost is a consideration, which obviously it is, then the control of production through buying land out of production is an inefficient and costly route.

It is inefficient first because crop yields in general are increasing year after year, which means that more land must be bought out of production to hold total output constant, and second because the drive to increase yields on the producing acres of the controlled crop is particularly great. It is costly first because farmers are being paid to do what they would do for nothing under a free market or under the theoretical control system described at the beginning of this section, and second because the cost of buying land out of production increases as crop yields increase and as the level of price support increases.

In summary, the surplus production of the national farm plant at the 1961–64 level of prices can be contained and controlled by either the theoretical system described at the beginning of this section or the actual system that has evolved. The theoretical system is analytically clean, it provides a high degree of flexibility at the production level, and it costs the government little or nothing. But it has one great defect; it is unacceptable to farmers.

The voluntary acreage control programs that have evolved will also control the surplus, but at a cost. There are numerous minor difficulties with present-day acreage control programs, including administrative problems at the local level and impediments to desirable adjustments in resource use. But the important limitation of present-day programs is cost to the government; they are costly as they stand and with rapid technological advance they are becoming more costly. The free market solves the surplus problem at the expense of farmers; present-day control measures solve the problem at the expense of the federal budget.

An Optimum Allocation of Research and Development Resources. The total product of American farms is produced by the conventional resources — land, labor, and capital — employed on those farms, *plus the research, development, and extension resources* that produce new technologies and extend them to farmers. An important change in composition of this total mix of resource inputs has been occurring in the 1950's and 1960's: research and development resources in increasing volume have been added, capital goods embodying the product of the research and development resources have been added, and the employment of land and labor has been reduced. This changing mix of total resources has, as we have observed, increased total farm output more rapidly than the expansion in the commercial market, and hence kept the farm economy in a continuous state of excess productive capacity.

As we saw in Chapter 3, the engine driving this development has been research and development. Research and development resources added to the agricultural complex have produced the new technologies — the new and improved production practices and the capital goods — which have been substituted for both land and labor, thereby forcing those resources out of farming and increasing the total farm output. The national farm plant should thus be viewed as a continuously changing organizational structure, with dynamic research and development resources flowing in to produce new and improved technologies that are adopted on farms, and land and labor flowing out as new and improved technologies are substituted for them.

With this view of the national farm plant in mind, it should be possible to conceptualize an optimum application of these research and development resources — an application that would turn out just the desired quantity of farm product at the established support price level. Granted that this optimum would be exceedingly difficult to achieve in practice, because the technological product of any set of those resources actually adopted is unpredictable as regards its time of appearance and its output-increasing potential. But the problem is not impossible to solve. When hundreds of millions of dollars are invested in research and development, as is the case in the agricultural complex, the outturn of new technologies ready for adoption can be viewed in a probability sense where the total outturn of new technologies (but not a particular technology) is directly dependent on the total research and development budget. And since the total budget is controllable through the federal government's contribution, the total outturn of new technologies is controllable in a probability sense.

The Economic Solutions

At the least, a conscious consideration of the problem in this sense would help. At present there is almost no concept of an optimum application of research and development resources in agriculture. The current and accepted view is that the research and development resources which have been applied to farm production problems have worked wonders; therefore a greater application would be good. But good for what? Certainly increased application of research and development resources to the production problems of farming would turn out more improved technologies that would lower unit costs of production in the short run, increase total output, and force a more rapid adjustment of productive resources in farming.

But do we need a faster rate of output expansion and a faster rate of resource adjustment on farms during the next ten years than we had in the last ten? The answer would seem to be no. What is needed is a *slightly* slower rate of farm output expansion and resource adjustment in the next ten years. A contribution could be made to the achieving of a slightly slower rate of farm output expansion and to solving the excess capacity problem if the total mix of productive farm resources, including the part that research and development play in that mix, were analyzed in this economic sense of an optimum allocation. It might well be determined that a slower rate of increase in the application of research and development resources to farm production would be in the national interest.

FARMERS' ATTITUDES

One segment of farmers would like to try some variation of a free market. It is hard to say how large the segment is, but it certainly includes far less than a majority. Some farmers are in this segment because they do not understand the price-income consequences of a free market. The entire structure of farm prices has been riding for so long on price supports in the basic crops that some farmers, particularly the younger ones, have forgotten what a little surplus production can do to prices in a free market.

Further, because the price of every farm commodity is not supported, hog and cattle prices for example, producers of those commodities ignore or do not understand the fact that their commodity is supported *indirectly* through the process of resource substitution among commodities. Such wild and irrational arguments as that the price of wheat would actually rise if price supports were eliminated circulate in farming communities. But when this group of farmers comes to understand the price and income consequences of a free market, or they get a small taste of the consequences in the form of a price decline, they quickly lose interest in that policy.

But there are other farmers who are "true believers" in a free market — who believe either that the welfare of the nation and farming is dependent upon a return to the free market and are willing to suffer the consequences whatever they may be, or that they can weather the short-run price storm and come out in an improved economic position in the long run. For this small but vocal minority a return to the invigorating climate of a free market is an absolute must.

The overwhelming majority of farmers want nothing to do with a free market. The older ones remember what happened in the early 1930's under a free market, and the younger ones have read the analyses by various departments of agricultural economics in the land-grant colleges of the price-income consequences of a return to the free market. This larger group of farmers firmly holds that a return to the free market would be disastrous. A multitude of different views are held by these farmers as to what should be the content of a protective price and income policy for farming, but on the undesirability of a free market they are unanimous.

Concerning the production control route, it is probably safe to say that no farmer likes controls as they impinge upon him as an operator. But a minority group, possibly about the size of the free-market group but at the opposite end of the ideological spectrum, believes that it is altogether necessary to control production to achieve good and stable prices. These farmers usually reason by analogy that the supply management policies pursued by big business with success as far as income returns are concerned can and should be adapted to farming. These farmers would accept the annoyance of controls to get good, stable prices and incomes, which, they reason correctly, can only be achieved where the actual or potential surplus output of farming is in fact held off the commercial market.

But the overwhelming majority of farmers are opposed to mandatory production controls — controls binding on each producer which may or may not involve some kind of payment to them. Most will accept voluntary production controls where each producer, on the basis of the payment offered for withdrawing land from production, decides whether to come into the program or stay out. But farmers indicated both through their elected representatives and in referendum during the early 1960's that they were not willing to accept mandatory controls binding on each producer of a commodity with only modest government payments. That is, they were unwilling to accept tight controls, with at least the initial cost of reducing the surplus production capacity to be borne by themselves.

Stated somewhat differently, the discipline of manmade controls, as a means of solving the excess capacity problem, farmers find about as obnoxious as the discipline of lower prices under a free market. They have been helped for a long time in coping with the surplus problem in farming, and they are going to continue to request that help as long as there is a chance of getting it.

Probably most farmers have never given serious thought to the optimum allocation of research and development resources as a policy solution to the excess capacity problem. To the extent that they have considered it as a solution to the excess capacity problem, they have probably rejected it. The modern commercial farmer is a technologist; he sees new technologies as a means of dealing with his individual economic and financial problem, and he works with, plans, thinks about, and repairs technological processes daily. Because he tends to ignore the aggregate effects of farm technological advance and to concentrate on the application of new technologies to his own farm, he is inclined to think that the more research and technological development there is, the better.

Further, the typical commercial farmer would probably feel that it was "against progress" if not downright immoral to question the rate of application of research and development resources to farming. It may thus be concluded that there would be little, if any, support among farmers for a conscious policy of analyzing and appraising the rate of application of research and development resources in agriculture, with the possibility of that analysis leading to a reduced rate of application.

In summary, none of the strict economic solutions with the capacity to deal effectively with the surplus production problem in farming appeals to the majority of farmers. Each rubs the pocketbook or value system the wrong way. As a solution, each has therefore fared rather poorly in practice.

The Economic Solutions

Most urban or general economists believe that it would be desirable to move to a free market in farming, either immediately or gradually over, for example, a five-year period. They have adopted this point of view for a number of reasons, some good, some bad. First, the present program of price support and production control is costly, and the funds spent on the program would be more wisely spent on such things as education, anti-poverty programs, and medical care. Second, the high level of price support and the consequent farm income protection slow down resource adjustments in farming, i.e., slow down the transfer of human resources out of farming. Stated conversely: the decline in farm prices under a free market would speed up the flow of resources out of farming, wash away the excess capacity problem in farming, and transfer the excess resources into nonfarm employment where they are needed. Third, the high level of price support — high relative to world prices — hinders the export of farm commodities, restricting price competition among sellers and making necessary unneeded government expenditures in the form of export subsidies. And fourth, the actual production of surplus foods followed by the distribution of those foods in special aid programs domestically and abroad is an undesirable and inefficient form of economic aid; in this view it would be a better policy to take the money now used to acquire and distribute surplus foods and issue it directly in the form of cash payments to the recipients, whether individuals or nations. For these reasons, which could be developed at length, most nonfarm economists favor a policy of moving gradually toward a free market for farming.

For many years most agricultural economists agreed with the general economists that it would be desirable to move toward a free market for farming. But in more recent years, in the 1950's and 1960's, many agricultural economists have changed their view about the desirability of this free market policy. First, they have become keenly aware of the extreme price and income consequences of a free market for the farm sector, and the havoc it would create throughout the agricultural complex. Second, they doubt the wisdom and the equity of farmers' trying to operate a free market while all segments of the nonfarm economy surrounding them are governed by bigness, monopoly power, and restricted competition.

Some farm economists would subscribe to a modest lowering of price-support levels to reduce program costs modestly, but few would advocate a return to the free market. Farm economists are a lot like farmers; they know that a free market spells disaster, and each one knows how to improve some mechanical aspect of existing programs, but they get vague and fuzzy when it comes to laying out an internally consistent policy that will get government costs down and hold farm income up.

Most general economists are opposed to the production control route as a means of coping with the surplus problem. They would agree that program mechanics can be developed which effectively hold surplus production resources out of production, and which permit considerable flexibility in the use of resources at the farm level. But they argue that such programs do not *correct* the excess capacity problem, but merely hold the excess productive resources in place and idle. They argue further that a desirable program would transfer those surplus resources out of farming and into useful nonfarm employment.

At this point, the nonfarm economists are also likely to buttress their logical arguments with arguments of political expediency — namely, that farmers will not accept or support effective control programs anyway. Thus, it becomes foolish or wrong or both to offer farmers effective control programs. In summary, then, most nonfarm economists oppose a production control policy in farming, and most are radically opposed to the rather slippery acreage controls that have evolved over time.

Agricultural economists are all over the lot with regard to production controls. Most recognize that if there are to be price supports, then there must also be some kind of controls to hold the excess productive resources out of production or limit their use in some way. But when it comes down to the formulation of controls that will work in practice and have the capacity to deal with the surplus problem, most farm economists would prefer to be doing other things.

The farm economist who admits the need of price support typically does not oppose production control as a matter of principle as does the nonfarm economist. He recognizes production control as a necessary evil. Having gone that far he either busies himself with some other kind of problem or develops a pure theory of resource transfers that would require some whole region far from his home state to go out of production. In either case the practical problem of developing production controls that have some degree of acceptability and the capacity to cope with the surplus in farming is left to the politicians and the program administrators.

In the cavalier treatment that general economists typically give the farm sector, it is probably true that few, if any, have considered the policy solution of achieving an optimum allocation of research and development resources as a means of dealing with the excess capacity problem. This is probably the case, because few general economists are aware of the breadth and depth of the technological revolution that is taking place in farming. Consequently, it is likely that few, if any, general economists have expressed themselves with regard to this general approach.

Among the farm economists, a few serious students of the farm problem are beginning to explore gingerly the implications of this policy. And gingerly is the word, for no economist in a public institution can afford to take a position of being against progress.

But the concept of an optimum use of resources which has been used in economic analysis for a century or more with respect to conventional resources — land, labor, and capital — should be applicable to research and development resources as well. It is not a question of being for or against progress, but a question of using scarce resources where they will produce the greatest return to society. Since research and development resources are among the most scarce in modern America, it follows that they should be allocated among *all* productive uses so as to provide the greatest benefit to society. And because the present rate of application of research and development resources to farming, in combination with the conventional resources, yields a chronic surplus, there is evidence that the present rate of application is too rapid. This is the kind of policy problem that a few farm economists are beginning to look at with considerable care. But as yet no rigorous analysis has been made to support either a slower or a faster rate of application.

THE SOLUTIONS REVISITED

At this point the question may be fairly asked: Have all the relevant solutions to the excess productive capacity problem been considered? Many people hold, politicians particularly, what might be called "The Flat Rock Theory of the Farm Problem"; if you turn over enough flat rocks, you will find the perfect solution to the commercial farm problem under one. This optimistic theory is based on the premise that the perfect solution exists, and if students of the farm problem would look long enough and do enough research, they would find it.

Unfortunately, the problem of too many resources producing too much in farming is not analogous to the problem of finding the lost key to a locked door. Rather, this problem is analogous to the problem of lifting water in opposition to the forces of gravity. So long as men want to lift water, for whatever purpose, they are going to have to expend energy to overcome the ever present forces of gravity. True, pumps may be designed in many different shapes and sizes to do the lifting job, but there is no avoiding the use of power in those pumps to overcome the forces of gravity.

The commercial farm problem is comparable to the water lifting problem. An infinite number of program mechanics can be devised to reduce or offset the excess productive capacity of farming. But in each instance the mechanics must have the power, the capacity, to overcome the economic and social incentives that are pulling new and more productive resources into farming and holding established resources in farming. The solution to the problem of *too many resources producing too much* in farming cannot take the form of a gimmick found under a flat rock; it must have *the power* to hold resource inputs out of productive operations by stopping resources from entering farming, or by pulling established resources out of farming, or by simply holding those resources idle.

To the extent that there is a real excess capacity problem which needs correction, there are only two general approaches, or possibly three, which have the capacity to deal with the problem. The first is a return to the free market, immediately or gradually. Here the falling product prices induce some expansion in consumption, induce some resources to leave farming, and act to limit the entry of new and improved resources. The second is the establishing of effective man-made controls over the use of productive resources, where the controls have the sanction of law and are enforceable through the police powers of the state. Here the power of the state is substituted for the power of the price incentive in directing and regulating resource use. The third approach, which may or may not be a realistic possibility, is the achievement of an optimum inflow of research and de-

The Economic Solutions

velopment resources into agriculture through the management of the expenditure of public funds. Whether this approach can be made operational remains to be seen. But in theory at least it should be possible to achieve a flow of research and development resources into farming through budget management that is optimum in the sense of bringing about a rate of increase in output that is in balance with the rate of increase in demand at some desired level of prices.

Now someone may say that another realistic possibility exists: the expansion of demand, particularly in the foreign market. In the largest sense of the problem, this is a possibility. When demand expands at any point in time through increased private trade or government food aid programs, the measure of excess productive capacity is reduced. We followed this approach ourselves earlier in this chapter; in the modified free market it was assumed that foreign and domestic food aid programs would be continued — that they were a part of legitimate demand. By this assumption we cut the magnitude of the excess capacity problem to be solved through falling prices roughly in half. To the extent that demand expands relative to supply at any particular time, the problem of commercial farming — excess productive capacity — is reduced and the balance between aggregate demand and total supplies is improved.

But to the extent that a commercial problem exists — too many resources producing too much in farming — then some means must be employed which has the power to remove the excess resources from production. And this means will not involve a sleight-of-hand trick or a change in program mechanics; it must involve the pursuit of a policy with the capacity to effect needed resource adjustments.

9

𝕗

The Political Stalemate

WHAT is the political solution to the commercial farm problem? How does it differ from the economic solutions? What forces have played a role in the political solution? And how is the political solution likely to change with the passage of time? These are interesting questions, and knowledge leading to answers to them will be basic to intelligent and effective political action in the future. We therefore turn to political action and the nature of the political solution in this chapter.

THE GROUP PRESSURES

Farm legislation is usually first formulated in the Department of Agriculture, moves through the Council of Economic Advisers, the Bureau of the Budget, and the White House staff; it is transmitted to the Congress by the President; in Congress it runs the gauntlet of the Agricultural committees, both Houses, and the Conference Committee from both Houses. With luck something is ultimately enacted into law that had its origin in the Department of Agriculture, but it will have been changed, modified, and reshaped many times in the tortuous legislative process.

The content of the proposed piece of legislation and of its many revisions throughout the legislative process is heavily influenced by different groups that have an interest in the legislation. The views, concerns, and pressures of interest groups are important in shaping legislation at all levels, but they are particularly important at the congressional level. The organization of Congress, with its great reliance on hearings in committees, the obligation of congressmen to represent their constituents, and the need of congressmen for financial and community support in elections give this power to interest groups. The content of a piece of legislation in its formative stages may be determined by a national need or the need of some particular economic or social interest group, but the final law is the result of the efforts of contending interest groups and compromises effected among those groups. At least this is true for farm legislation.

Farm legislation typically begins its weary way in the Department of Agriculture in response to the need of some commodity group or farm organization. But before it is enacted into law many pressures from many different sources will have "contributed" to its final content. One classification of the key pressures bearing on farm legislation is as follows: (1) farm groups; (2) nonfarm suppliers, processors, and marketers; (3) church and charity groups; (4) program personnel and allied organizations; (5) consumer groups and the general public. With more time and space each of the above categories could be broken down, but I shall attempt to portray the part played by the principal interest groups in formulating farm policy and farm legislation by means of these five categories.

Farm Groups. The overriding interest or objective of farm groups is good and stable prices for the products they produce and sell. This general goal tends to convert into a farm-policy aspiration of "reasonable to high-level price supports and weak to no production controls." But since this aspiration is impossible of achievement, the different farm groups must develop and support more realistic policies and programs of farm price and income support. It is at this point that the farm groups and organizations fall apart.

In the 1920's, the 1930's, and during part of the 1940's a recognizable farm bloc worked together reasonably well in the interest of *commercial* farmers in general. But this bloc no longer exists. Among the major farm organizations, the largest, the American Farm Bureau Federation, now stands for lowering farm price supports and as little production control as possible. The National Farmers Union, on the other hand, stands for a higher level of price support and tighter production controls. The Grange is somewhere in between the Farm Bureau and the Farmers Union, but in recent years it has moved closer to the Farmers Union's position.

Among the farm commodity groups, the policy views are more varied and farther apart. Wheat growers, at least until recently, were willing to accept effective controls in return for a high level of price support. The tobacco and rice producers readily accept production controls in return for price support. But the cattlemen want no part of price support or domestic production controls, though they do want import controls. Cotton producers are split several ways: some want high price support and strict production controls, others want something close to a free market, and still others want something in between. Milk producers embrace a form of supply management in fluid milk markets, but hold fiercely to the best of all possible worlds for manufacturing milk, namely, price support and no controls. The broiler and turkey people were willing to accept a private cartel arrangement under the Marketing Order concept, but they would not accept "government interference" in that arrangement. Some potato growers want controls, others do not. The feed grain producers are reasonably happy with voluntary acreage controls with payments, but they are violently opposed to mandatory controls. And so it goes.

There are also strong regional differences in farm policy attitudes. The small higher-cost cotton producers in the Southeast, almost to a man, support the position of high-level price supports and strict controls, whereas the cotton producers in the irrigated valleys of the West want something close to a free market. A major difference of opinion regarding production control over feed grains separates the deficit South and the surplus Middle West. And the long-time alliance between winter wheat producers and spring wheat producers is in danger of coming apart, because most of the wheat surplus is winter wheat.

Clearly there is no longer a single, or general, point of view on commercial farm policy among farmers and their organizations. In fact, the antagonism among farm groups runs high in the 1960's; what we have now in the farm sector is not a bloc — it is more like a jungle.

Farm interest groups play the following roles in the legislative process. In the 1950's the Farm Bureau Federation and certain of its commodity allies worked with the Republican administration to formulate legislation; the Farmers Union, the Grange, and their commodity allies fought that legislation in the Congress. In the early 1960's the latter combination worked with the Democratic administration to formulate legislation and the Farm Bureau and its commodity allies fought

141

it in the Congress. This situation does not lead to the easy passage of farm legislation, and the legislation that is passed does not meet with the general acceptance and support of farmers.

What we have among farm groups in the 1960's are many and deep differences of opinion about price and income policy for commercial farming, ranging from the goal of high-level price supports and strict production controls to some variation of the free market. The many different and contending farm groups are not perfectly balanced, but they are balanced in a rough way; it is therefore difficult to achieve any major change in farm policy. The interest groups within farming, together with the other pressure groups to be discussed, have reached that state of balance where a redirection in farm policy has not been possible. A stalemate has been reached.

Nonfarm Suppliers, Processors, and Marketers. As a part of the agricultural complex, suppliers, processors, and marketers have a close and vital interest in the farm sector. Firms in this group supply the producer goods and operating supplies required in farming, process the raw products, and handle and distribute the finished products. There is no question about the policy goal of firms in this group; they want volume, the maximum farm production possible. High-level farm production enables them to expand the market for farm producer goods and supplies and the volume of product processed and handled. This interest group persistently opposes all forms of supply management, or production control, programs.

Nonfarm suppliers on the one hand and processors and marketers on the other sometimes differ with regard to the desirable level of price support. The nonfarm suppliers do not object to reasonably high price supports, since this enhances the purchasing power of their customers, the farmers. But processors and marketers favor low farm prices because they are purchasers of farm products. But this issue is minor compared with the question of volume. All these agribusiness groups want farmers producing at full throttle; the question of a little or a big surplus, and who bears the cost of carrying it, does not disturb them.

Since it is not politic to be working against the income interest of farmers, the representatives of agribusiness are not always obvious on the political scene. But the various components are well organized and well financed, and they know exactly what they want. Hence, they are effective in a quiet sort of way.

142

Church and Charity Groups. Members of church and charity groups perform in several different capacities. Some serve as the conscience of commercial farmers concerning wages and living conditions of hired labor, particularly migrant labor. Some are highly knowledgeable about the problems of the small commercial farmer and about poverty in rural America, and work to protect the interests of these otherwise largely unrepresented people. Still others are concerned with furthering the work of food aid programs at home and abroad — with obtaining the legislative authority to acquire surplus food products free of charge for distribution in the aid programs.

In the first two capacities representatives of church and charitable organizations have not endeared themselves to commercial farm groups, since the achievement of their objectives means increased labor costs and possibly increased tax loads. But the persistent efforts of these people have prevailed, and the lot of hired workers and many small farmers has improved in recent years. In their third capacity, representatives of church and charity organizations usually line up against strict control programs. This is true for a number of reasons. For one thing, these men of good will feel that it is morally wrong to restrict food production so long as people anywhere in the world are hungry. For another, they know that surplus foods for their aid programs are easier to obtain when there are physical surpluses in being than when excess resources are held out of production by control programs.

At one time representatives of church and charitable organizations may have been ineffectual, but not any more. They too know what they want: they want improved living conditions for the downtrodden at home and abroad. This means that they push and support programs of improved wages and living conditions for hired workers, improved credit and education in low-production rural areas, and more abundant food for use among the poor at home and abroad. In these efforts, armed with the cause of justice and with tireless energy, they have met with considerable success.

Program Personnel and Allied Organizations. Every important program builds its own lobby, and farm programs are no exception. Farm programs may in fact be the leading species of a larger genus, since the programs involve so much government support and so many producers. In any event, farm programs tend to build up a permanent and dedicated staff, or secretariat, within each program and an associated extragovernmental organization outside the program. The extra-governmental organization often establishes a Washington office and maintains a trained staff to hold before the eyes of political decision-makers the goals and achievements of the program. Administrators within the program and leaders in the extragovernmental organization thus work together to protect and enhance the budget of the program, expand the program's capacity to fulfill the mission assigned to it, and protect their program from the encroachment of other programs.[1]

The purpose of representatives of this interest group is, then, to per-petuate the existing program — to protect and expand its budget, to expand its capacity to fulfill its mission or possibly enlarge the concept of its mission, and to improve its operation. There is nothing insidious or illegal about this form of interest group representation; it is com-mon practice with respect to programs for the armed forces, the de-partments of Interior and Health, Education, and Welfare. It does, however, have an important influence that should be recognized here: it supports the continuance of existing policies and makes changing policies and initiating new programs most difficult. Once a program is successfully launched and an associated extragovernmental organi-zation established, it becomes exceedingly difficult to change that pro-gram in any important way except expanding it. This lesson each Sec-retary of Agriculture must learn whether the program is concerned with conservation, extension, credit, or farm price support. Each pro-gram develops self-perpetuating forces inside it and beside it.

Consumer Groups and the General Public. The goal of consumer groups in farm policy and farm legislation is clear and bold: to keep food prices from rising and reduce them if possible. This is the constant position of consumer groups. But American consumer organizations tend to be weak and poorly organized and their position is rarely pressed with skill and vigor.

If organized labor decided to espouse the cause of the consumer, this would change. But organized labor prefers to push for higher incomes for workers rather than try to hold a lid on consumer prices. In fact, organized labor sometimes tries to work with farm groups to raise the incomes of both farmers and laborers, but this alliance has

[1] For an interesting analysis of the workings of this interest group phenomenon see Theodore Lowi, "How the Farmers Get What They Want," *The Reporter*, May 21, 1964, pp. 34–37.

The Political Stalemate

never paid rich dividends to labor. In any event, without labor's support, efforts by consumer groups to reduce food prices generally have not been crowned with success.

Nonetheless, most consumers worry about food prices, and the one man elected by all the people, the President, is well aware of this. Retail food prices were certainly in President Johnson's mind when he appointed Esther Peterson chairman of the President's Committee on Consumer Interests in January 1964. Though professional consumer groups have not been successful in bucking producer-minded groups in the halls of Congress, the interest of fifty-five million households across the nation in reasonable food prices does impress the White House. This is a fact that farm organizations have learned to their sorrow in their drives for higher levels of price support.

Besides food prices, the general public has one other important interest in farm programs: their cost. The typical urban congressman asks only one question about a new piece of farm legislation: Will it increase government costs or reduce them? If it increases government costs he is opposed to it; if it reduces them he is for it. He reacts thus because he knows that his constituents are strongly opposed to spending more money on farm programs — that they really want government expenditures on farm programs reduced so that their taxes can be reduced or they can benefit from increased social services. The full force of urban opinion, which is nearly the same in the 1960's as general public opinion, is thus pressing for a reduced government expenditure on farm programs.

No paid Washington representative advances this cause with Congress and the President, but every urban congressman and the President are fully aware of the desire of the average urban voter to get the costs of farm programs down. This imperative hangs over every discussion of farm programs in the nation's capitol, the planning activities in the Department of Agriculture, the policy decisions in the White House, and congressional roll calls like a great pall.

THE COMPROMISE SOLUTION

The interaction of the above groups, each pressing its own interest or interests vigorously, has produced a compromise program for dealing with the surplus problem of commercial farming. This compro-

145

mise program has been alluded to in previous chapters, but here it will be given the full treatment. It took the following form in the early 1960's:

1. The prices of the principal crops, of some minor crops, and of milk are supported at the farm level by the purchase of surplus products and the making of nonrecourse loans to producers.

2. The take-over of surplus products by the government is held within reasonable bounds by acreage controls in the principal crops.

3. Surplus products coming into government hands are distributed outside commercial channels at home and abroad as food aid.

4. The ultimate reservoir of surplus farm products is the Commodity Credit Corporation.

The level of price support under this program represents a compromise in all cases. For example, the average level of price support on the corn crop produced in 1964 and utilized in 1965 was $1.25 per bushel, of which $1.10 was received as a guaranteed price and $.15 as a payment. This average level of price support equaled 80 per cent of parity — full parity being the legal definition of a fair farm price. Many, if not most, corn producers believe they should get full parity for their product, which in 1964 was $1.56 per bushel for corn. But groups concerned with lower government costs would have preferred to see a support level of perhaps $1.00 per bushel on the 1963–64 corn crop, with more acres in production. And so it goes.

Domestic wheat in 1964–65 was supported at $2.00 per bushel, of which $1.30 was received in a guaranteed price and $.70 as a payment. Export wheat was supported at $1.55 per bushel of which $1.30 per bushel was received as a guaranteed price and $.25 as a payment. Depending upon how you look at wheat prices, the level of price support varies as a percentage of parity: the $2.00 figure is close to 80 per cent of parity, whereas the $1.30 figure is fairly close to 50 per cent.

All cotton of average quality was supported in the market in 1964–65 by loans to farmers at 29.3 cents per pound or 72 per cent of parity. Small growers with fifteen acres or less of cotton and other growers who produced within the domestic share of their total allotment also received a price support payment of 3.5 cents a pound, bringing their guaranteed price to 32.8 cents per pound or about 80 per cent of parity. Thus, in 1964–65 small cotton growers received a higher level of price support than did large growers.

In every case the level of price support falls below the legal definition of full parity, for most commodities between 70 and 80 per cent of parity; and the support price guarantee for each of the three great commodities — corn, wheat, and cotton — takes the form of part price guarantee and part payment.

Most farm groups, but not all, contend that this level of price support is a rank miscarriage of justice. On the other hand, price-support and disposal operations at these levels give rise to government program costs that have not been below $4 billion annually since fiscal 1961, and which reached a high of $5.9 billion in fiscal 1964. These cost data provide fuel for those groups that want to lower the levels of price support and thereby reduce government costs.

The result is a compromise — a compromise that has produced a structure of commodity price supports that does in fact support farm prices, but at levels satisfactory to few if any of the contending groups. Whether it is judged high or low, this support price structure is holding the actual level of farm prices at about 75 per cent of parity; and when production payments are added in, the level is equal to about 80 per cent of parity.

The acreage control program is a leaky and inefficient means of controlling production. The men that operate and administer the program know that. But most farmers want it that way, and their allies, suppliers of producer goods and the processors and distributors of farm products, are only too happy to support this weak control position. All the important interests involved support acreage controls because they know that through the adoption and increased use of new and improved technologies, production can be expanded on the uncontrolled acres. What farmers fail to see is that when one man fudges in a game he gains if he is not caught, but when fudging is made legal and widespread no one gains and the game could be ruined. But farmers generally don't see this, and the suppliers of producer goods and processors are glad they don't. Farm price- and income-support policy thus struggles along in a crippled condition.

One important gain has, however, been made in program efficiency in recent years. That gain is with respect to the use made of acres diverted under the control program. First under the Soil Bank program and second under the Kennedy-Johnson administration commodity programs, acres taken out of production had to be kept in a nonproductive, soil-conserving use — that is, idle. Under these programs, acres taken out of the production of one crop could no longer simply be diverted to another crop. This tightening of acreage control programs made an important contribution to the reduction of *total* surplus production. The problem now is to hold this gain against those groups who have an interest in increasing total production regardless of the cost.

The surplus production of American farms acquired through price-supporting operations has been used effectively at home and abroad as food aid. There are definite limits to the use of surplus food as aid to the needy domestically — and we are close to those limits. But for practical purposes there are no limits abroad, *if the United States is prepared to assist in the storage, handling, and distribution of those surplus products in the needy, recipient countries.* The policy question confronting the United States is therefore really to decide what it wants to do about food aid to the underdeveloped countries. To this point, we have simply stood ready to ship to needy nations whatever commodities we had on hand in physical surplus. This has worked pretty well, although not perfectly. In some cases, countries have needed commodities of which our surplus stocks were low — for example, rice and milk powder — but could not use all the wheat we wanted to ship them.

In the cases of wheat, sorghum grains, and cotton, where we have not been able to dispose of the visible surplus through foreign aid programs, the ultimate residual outlet is the Commodity Credit Corporation. Building stocks in the CCC is the "use" of last resort. In the first half of the 1950's stocks were building up rapidly in this residual outlet, but with the passage of P.L. 480 in 1954 and the expansion and modest tightening of acreage controls in the late 1950's, stock-building came to an end in 1959; this expansion and tightening continued in the early 1960's and the total value of stocks in CCC hands was reduced somewhat between 1959 and 1964.

The total program for coping with the excess capacity problem in commercial farming may be said to be in an operating equilibrium as of the early 1960's. The combination of acreage controls and food aid programs, at the going level of price support, is dealing with the problem in a way such that stocks in the ultimate outlet are not increasing. It is an uneasy equilibrium, possibly saved in 1964 only by a poor growing season in the Middle West and the consequent reduced crop yields. But uneasy or stable, it is in being, and it is the result of a series of compromises among many and varied contending interest groups.

THE STALEMATE

The compromise program described above has been in existence in about that form since 1954, when the last major component of the program, P.L. 480, or institutionalized foreign food aid, was added to the total program. There have been many changes in the total program, and some not so minor, since 1954, but the basic program components have not changed since that date.

Some of the not so minor changes in the total program since 1954 have included (1) the addition and then the closing out of the Soil Bank; (2) the establishment of a voluntary feed grain program in 1961; (3) the tenuous acceptance of the principle that acres taken out of the production of one crop should not be shifted to producing another crop; and (4) the increased use of production payments to induce participation in voluntary programs.

Further, each time a commodity control program comes up for passage or re-enactment in the Congress, there also arises the many-sided question of exceptions and loopholes for particular areas and regions: whether there should be some form of exemption to the control of feed grain production in the deficit Southeast, whether oats should be controlled anywhere, and whether such minor crops as flax and sunflowers should be grown on diverted acres in the upper Midwest. Each producing area has some "small" exception to the general control program that it "must" have, and these "small" exceptions or goodies are fought over, changed, and rechanged from year to year. Even though the basic framework of the total program has not changed since 1954, many problems, some minor and some not so minor, have occupied the attention of the interest groups, the administrators, and the legislators in the annual struggle over farm price and income policy.

The fact that the basic structure of the compromise program has not changed in ten years does not mean, however, that people, firms, and groups have not been trying to change it. The major farm organizations, each in its own way, have been trying desperately to make significant changes in the program. As we have already observed, the American Farm Bureau Federation has been trying to reduce the level of price support and minimize the use of controls, whereas the Na-

149

tional Farmers Union has been trying to raise the level of price support and accept stricter controls where necessary.

But more important, two presidential administrations have tried without any real success to redirect the course of commercial farm policy. What we have had in commercial farm policy for a decade is a political stalemate. The many and contending interest groups have surrounded the farm price and income policy ball on all sides, and the pressures have been so close to equal that no group or administration has been able to move the ball to any significant degree.

Secretary Benson in the Eisenhower administration saw the solution to the excess capacity problem in freer prices and less production control. Benson never made it completely clear how free a market he was seeking, but certainly all his statements and recommendations moved in the direction of free market prices. He asked Congress for the authority to lower the level of price support, and he opposed production control in all forms. But Congress, reflecting the pressures acting on it, did not give him the freedom he wanted to lower the level of price support and in that way reduce the farm surplus.

After eight strenuous years, Secretary Benson ended his term of office with the over-all structure of price support down somewhat from where it was when he took office, but not down to the level required to eliminate the excess productive capacity in commercial farming. Further, he ended his term with one of the largest, though voluntary, acreage control programs of all times in force, the Soil Bank. This was the result, because Secretary Benson and the Eisenhower administration could not break the political stalemate and put their policy views into operation.

Secretary Freeman, in the Kennedy-Johnson administration, 1961–64, saw the problem differently. He wanted to increase price supports, make increased use of production payments, and eliminate the excess capacity problem through effective production controls — effective supply management. Freeman repeatedly asked Congress for the authority to eliminate the excess capacity problem in commercial farming through the use of effective control measures and to increase farm income through a combination of higher prices and production payments. And repeatedly Congress, again reflecting the pressures on it, refused to grant him the authority to institute mandatory controls with the capacity to solve the surplus production problem.

The Political Stalemate

Secretary Freeman and the Kennedy-Johnson administration, too, were unable to break the political stalemate in commercial farming and put their policy into operation. Thus, in the summer of 1964 the Kennedy-Johnson administration found itself in the following general position: the level of price support (including payments) was somewhat higher than in 1960 and a set of voluntary commodity control programs had been substituted for the one large voluntary Soil Bank program.

Both secretaries were able to win the authority for large-scale voluntary programs, each of which has advantages and disadvantages. But Secretary Benson could not win the authority to reduce prices sufficiently to eliminate the surplus problem. And Secretary Freeman in the period 1961–64 could not win the authority to institute the controls necessary to eliminate the surplus problem without heavy expenditures of public funds. In both cases the stalemate prevailed.

It may be, however, that the political stalemate is taking a new form, and if so, the results for commercial farming would be startlingly different. The new stalemate may result from the inability of farm interest groups to pass any commodity legislation at all. In the past several years, it has become increasingly difficult to pass farm commodity legislation requiring heavy budgetary outlays. And with three major commodity programs — wheat, feed grains, and cotton — coming up for re-enactment in 1965, some fear that it will prove impossible to put three such large and costly programs through Congress in the same year.

The problem is this: The existing legislation is written for each of these three commodities in such a way that the failure to re-enact the existing legislation or pass new legislation would have or could have serious and adverse price and income consequences for the producers of those commodities. This new stalemate, then, would not have a neutral effect, but a serious price-damaging effect.

The existing voluntary control wheat program comes to an end with the 1965 crop; if new legislation is not passed or the old legislation extended a referendum must be held before August 15, 1965. The choice in this referendum is the same as that in the 1963 referendum: (1) mandatory controls and a high level of price support or (2) a low level of price support — 50 per cent of parity or about $1.25 per bushel — for those who stay within their acreage allotment and no price support for those that exceed their acreage allotment. The second choice is very close to a free market situation, and the one which farmers elected in the 1963 referendum. But they expected to be saved, and were saved, in that instance by the passage of legislation giving them the present voluntary program.

If, however, wheat legislation is not passed in the spring of 1965, and farmers again choose the second alternative, and then no further legislation is passed, wheat growers would be operating on something very close to a free market.

In the case of feed grains, if new legislation is not passed, the Secretary of Agriculture is required by existing law to lower price support to that level where stocks will not accumulate in government hands, but at not less than 50 per cent of parity. For corn, 50 per cent of parity is equal to about 80 cents a bushel.

Though each case will probably be resolved in one way or another shortly before or after this book goes to press, the principle that they illustrate is nevertheless an important one. In the case of both wheat and feed grains (and cotton too, but it has complexities all of its own) failure to pass new legislation or extend old legislation means an important drop in the level of price support and a loosening of controls. And so long as farm policy legislation is framed in this form, a legislative stalemate means a basic shift in farm policy — means that the old political stalemate has been broken.

If in the spring of 1965 or in later years the farm interest groups fail to move commodity legislation successfully through the Congress, it will be evidence that the power alignments that produced the compromise program from 1954 to 1964 have shifted in some way. And it probably means that the power alignments have changed in several ways: first, that the political strength of the nonfarm groups has increased, and that of the farm groups has decreased; second, that the deep divisions and antagonisms among the various farm groups have reduced the total effectiveness of farm groups in moving legislation through the congressional mill; third, that the policy position of some farm groups has become similar to that of the nonfarm groups.

The realignment of power among the interest groups concerned with commercial farm policy legislation along the above lines is not beyond the realm of possibility. It has been going on for some time and is likely to continue. As it goes on, a point must be reached where a significant change in farm policy will result. The way existing farm legislation is written, a simple strategy to effect this change would be to create a stalemate in the passage of farm legislation. And it could be that political power among the interest groups has already been sufficiently realigned to cause this stalemate strategy to come to the fore.

THE EROSION OF FARM POLITICAL POWER

It has often been said in recent years that the political power of farmers is waning. This statement rests on the obvious fact that the farm population is declining and the urban population increasing. The representation of farm people in the Congress is declining as a consequence while that of urban people increases. This was documented dramatically by Wayne Darrow after the 1964 election. As he pointed out, there were 251 seats in the House of Representatives from farm districts, districts with a farm population of 20 per cent or more, after the elections of 1924, but the number of seats from farm districts was reduced to 53 after the elections of 1964.[2] Further, the decisions of the Supreme Court with regard to equal representation are speeding up the redistricting process, which will further increase the representation of urban areas at the expense of rural areas.

But we also need to be careful with respect to the conclusions we draw on this subject. To repeat: the representation of farmers in the Congress is declining absolutely and relatively; that is one measure of the decline of farm political power. With the divisions that exist among farm interest groups plus the reduced farm representation, it is becoming more and more difficult to pass any important piece of farm legislation; this is another measure of the decline of farm political power.

Political power has other aspects, however. A well-organized, well-financed interest group with unity of purpose, even though its constituent base is small, can be highly successful in obtaining certain kinds of legislation — witness the success of the sugar lobby over the years. And a well-organized, well-financed cattlemen's group obtained legislation restricting the importation of beef into the United States in 1964, following a period of excess supplies that resulted almost entirely from increases in domestic production. In sum and in short, spe-

---

[2] *Washington Farmletter*, No. 1106, November 27, 1964.

cial interest groups can be very successful in getting certain kinds of legislation if they know what they want and if they are well financed.

In what areas have well-organized special interest groups met with legislative success? Really in two areas: first, in getting legislation providing services for their industry — market news, inspection and grading, and research and development; second, in obtaining monopolistic restrictions for the protection of markets — for example, import quotas, licensing to control entry, and patent laws and regulations. These two areas have certain things in common. Both involve the granting of rights or privileges or services to some group, and they do not entail large government budgets.

An economic interest group does not have too much trouble getting legislation passed granting a right or a privilege or a service to itself, provided that grant does not *obviously* hurt some other group, and provided it does not require a major outlay of public funds. Well-organized, well-financed interest groups, including certain agricultural interest groups, have learned how to obtain legislation that aids and protects their industry where government expenditures are small or nonexistent.

Where the political power of farmers has been eroding away is in the passage of major pieces of farm legislation that transfer millions, even billions, of dollars of income from the nonfarm sector to the farm sector, hence run up the federal budget. The day when farmers, their elected representatives, and their interest groups can pass this kind of legislation is fast coming to an end, if the end is not already here.

This decline in the power of farmers and farm groups to pass legislation transferring real money from the nonfarm sector to the farm sector rests on two developments already observed: first, the decline in farm population and the accompanying decline in farm representation in the Congress, and second, the deep policy divisions among farm groups. The first of these is obviously going to continue, and probably speed up; the future of the second cannot be predicted with certainty, but the policy differences among farm organizations have increased rather than lessened since 1955. It seems highly unlikely that these differences will be resolved and the farm bloc resolidified in the foreseeable future. In this sense the political power of farmers has declined: the power to pass major pieces of legislation year after year to support farm prices and incomes is no longer there.

10

𝔭

The City Man and the Commercial Problem

IN ONE sense farmers and other sectors of the agricultural complex have the greatest interest in the solution of the commercial farm problem. Their incomes are involved. But the city man, the urbanite, also has a vital interest in its solution: his food supply is involved — its adequacy and its cost.

Clearly it is to the advantage of the city man to have an abundant, low-cost food supply rather than a tight, high-cost food supply. This means that he must be concerned with policies that affect the efficiency of production in farming, the use of resources in farming, and the extent of reserve stocks in food and fiber products. Stated more positively, it is better, far better, for the city man for the agricultural complex to operate in a state of chronic surplus than in a chronic food shortage. And as we know full well, a chronic surplus with its attendant price-depressing consequences has been the fate of the farm sector, except in wartime, for several decades.

But the city man and the nonfarm components of the agricultural complex have responsibilities too. Holding the farm sector in a chronic state of surplus, however the holding is done, involves a cost, a cost that must be borne by someone. In recent years, with widespread and rapid technological advance, those costs have been shared in some proportion by urbanites and farmers. Urbanites have paid most of the money costs of the programs of price support and production control. Farmers generally have borne the full cost of human suffering involved in the rapid resource adjustments in farming, and the small-to average-sized farmer has paid a high price in terms of low income and business failure.

The questions that have been before the nation for some time without being satisfactorily resolved, that currently remain before the nation, and that are likely to become more acute in the future, are the following: How much abundance do we want in food and agriculture — how much of a surplus do we want year after year? Having answered that question, in what form do we want to carry that surplus — in unused excess productive capacity, in physical surplus stocks, or in some other form? And having answered that question, how do we want to bear and share the costs of running a farm sector that produces abundantly — that produces a little too much rather than a little too little year after year?

The city man has long avoided taking clear, overt positions on these farm issues of national importance. He has simply grumbled about the high cost of government programs. But he can no longer avoid taking a position; he can no longer simply go along for the ride on farm policy issues. He must work out and support a policy position on the commercial farm problem that is first in his own self-interest and second responsible, in terms of the national interest. It is the purpose of this chapter to discuss such a position and its possible content.

THE POLITICAL SITUATION

Farmers and their organizations are hopelessly divided on the question of the solution to the commercial problem and how to go about reaching a solution. The number of farmers in the total population is now very small, and their political representation in the Congress is vanishing. From these basic facts of the political situation several conclusions, of varying degrees of firmness, follow.

First, it is absolutely clear that no aggregation of farm interest groups has sufficient power to break the stalemate in commercial farm policy and redirect that policy into a significantly new line. Different farm groups working with different presidential administrations between 1954 and 1964 made strenuous efforts to break the stalemates without success.

Second, the power alignments that produced and supported the stalemate from 1954 to 1964 appear to be shifting, with the traditional price-support position losing strength through increased disunity among farm groups, reduced representation in Congress, and the movement of some farm groups closer to the policy position of suppliers, processors, and marketers and other nonfarm groups. Thus it seems likely that the stalemate will be broken in the not too distant future, and that commercial farm policy will take a new direction.

Third, the power to break the stalemate and redirect farm policy will in the future be in the hands of an aggregation of nonfarm groups — suppliers of farmers' producer goods, processors, and distributors; such other urban-based groups as bankers' associations, labor organizations, and the national Chamber of Commerce; groups concerned with public affairs such as the National Planning Association and the Committee for Economic Development; and last but not least, urban public opinion reflected in congressional and presidential actions. This is a loose and essentially undirected agglomeration of political power that will act positively with great difficulty. But this is where the political power to resolve in one way or another the commercial farm problem now resides.

For many years, nonfarm interest groups have grumbled about the ineptitude of farm programs of price support and production control, and have exerted a negative kind of power which, combined with the pressures of suppliers of farmers' producer goods, processors, and distributors, and the divergent but positive aspirations of the farm groups, produced the farm policy stalemate running from 1954 to 1964.

But if this analysis is correct, the situation is now changed or changing. The power to act, to change things, is now in the hands of a loose confederation of nonfarm interest groups. *With that power comes responsibility.* The urban congressman can no longer simply ask whether a piece of farm legislation will cost more. The supply, processing, and marketing sectors of the agricultural complex cannot simply press for more and more volume. These nonfarm groups must now take the lead in forging a policy that does not tear farmers apart, that leads to abundant food supplies in both the short run and the long run, that involves some reasonable sharing of the costs of running a national farm plant that produces abundantly at all times, and that both expands markets abroad and behaves responsibly toward the trade needs and aspirations of foreign nations.

It is not an easy task. And it will not go away by the mouthing of such catchphrases as "supply and demand" and "return to the free market." The forces and actions implied in such phrases may be included in an effective solution to the commercial farm problem, but many other forces and actions will be included too. The resolution of the varied and conflicting forces and actions, and the forging of a new commercial farm policy, now reside where the power resides — in the hands of the city man.

The goals of food and agriculture can be set forth in detail to cover the aspirations of the many and varied groups in society, and for some purposes such a detailed list of goals may be desirable. But that will not be the approach here. Here the major composite goals of society with regard to food and agriculture are presented — those goals that *must* be reached to maintain the society of the United States in a strong, viable, and happy condition.

The number of these major goals and their specific formulation will vary somewhat with the author. But history, a common Western culture, and a commonly shared system of values make society's goals in this area almost self-evident. Some people may argue that certain important goals are omitted from the following list, but controversy over those presented does not seem likely.

Four major goals are set forth here that must be achieved if the Great Society is to be realized. They are:

1. The provision of abundant food supplies for the domestic population at reasonable cost.

2. The creation of a situation where resources employed in farming receive a return equal to that earned by comparable resources employed in nonfarm pursuits.

3. The establishment of a set of family and social institutions in rural areas consistent with the aspirations of the people and equal in quality to those in urban areas.

4. The establishment of a foreign policy with respect to food and agriculture that increases commercial exports, meets foreign food aid commitments, and expands markets for the developing nations.

The first goal is a simple statement of the obvious fact that Americans have enjoyed an abundant food supply in the past and expect to do so in the future. With the land, labor, capital, and technical knowledge available to them, any lesser goal would be unthinkable. The problem is not with the goal or its achievement; the problem results from chronically overachieving the goal. Who is to bear the costs of chronic overabundance?

The second goal is a corollary of the first; in a sense it says that the economic return from resources employed in farming should not be jeopardized by the achievement or overachievement of the first goal. But it says more than *should.* The second goal states that a situation is to be created wherein resources of equal ability and capacity employed in farm and nonfarm pursuits do in fact earn equal incomes. It does not say that *all* men who may want to be employed in farming should, insofar as they are of equal quality to nonfarm workers, earn incomes equal to the nonfarm workers. This is impossible of achievement in a rational economic world. But it does say that we need a system that can effect needed adjustments in resources and as a result provide equitable returns to those resources employed in farming. The second goal implies a sequence of events: (a) the development of a situation or program or system in which the realization of equitable returns is possible, (b) the adjustment in the use of resources required to achieve an equity of incomes, and (c) the realization of a parity of returns for resources employed in farming.

The third goal is concerned with establishment of those institutions in rural America — the business organization of farms, school systems, health services, road systems, church organizations — that can make rural communities pleasant, productive, viable, and interesting places in which to live and work. The third goal says that the time has come to eliminate rural slums and to raise the quality of social services in rural areas to that of urban areas.

The fourth goal states both a need and responsibility. The increased productivity of the national farm plant requires that vigorous efforts be made to expand the overseas markets for its products. But American foreign policy requires that world markets for the farm products of the underdeveloped countries be opened and expanded; if this does not happen, many a developing country will sink back into despair and dictatorship. At the same time, the United States must continue to offer food aid to many developing countries and be prepared to expand it from present levels. All this the United States must do without destroying commercial markets for itself and its traditional competitors. These requirements will certainly test the souls and imagination of political and business leaders in the international field.

The City Man and the Commercial Problem

The charge might be made that one important goal has been omitted: the conservation of soil and water resources. For those who believe that this goal should be added, let it be added. Certainly I am not disposed to advocate the waste or destruction of natural resources. But this goal was not included because the conservation of land is not the important problem it once was. Conservation programs have been spectacularly successful over the past three decades in stopping erosion and inducing farmers to accept soil conserving practices, making the urgency to conserve the land less great than it was. Further, advancing technology substitutes for natural resources. Poor land in 1964 can be made into good land by grading and leveling, by improved tillage practices, and by adding the needed plant nutrients.

Water is a different matter, but it is a national problem involving urban and industrial needs as well as food and agricultural needs. A solution to the water problem requires more than conservation; it must take into account such matters as efficient use and regional distribution. The water problem is wider than the issue of conservation and may someday require the formulation of a national policy comparable with that under discussion for food and agriculture.

Perhaps other goals of food and agriculture should be included, but the four presented here are important goals — goals that any general policy for the commercial farm sector must ensure the achievement of, if it is to be called a success. Abundant food supplies at reasonable cost, parity returns for resources employed in farming, stable and viable family and social institutions in rural America, and an effective and responsible trade policy for farm products — these are goals that commercial farm policy must take into account, and provide the means of achievement.

SEVEN POLICY IDEAS

A set of policy ideas is presented here as the constituent parts of a possible commercial farm policy, for the consideration and discussion of the city man, his interest groups, and organizations, and, of course, for anyone else who might care to use them. These ideas are not formulated into specific recommendations for at least two good reasons. First, no group or body has asked for recommendations, or is in being to receive them. Second, it is a waste of time for anyone not an integral part of the legislative process to offer a specific plan or to make specific recommendations, because the specifics of a plan or a program or a

The City Man and the Commercial Problem

policy are what get forged in the give and take and compromise of the legislative process.

But ideas that suggest a fresh approach to a policy problem, or consistent lines of action, or lines of action that have the capacity to cope with the problem do play a useful role in policy formation. Such ideas help the decision-maker in the legislative process to think creatively, consistently, and realistically. That is the spirit in which the following ideas are presented; they do not constitute a plan; they are ideas that are internally consistent, that, I hope, have the capacity to cope effectively with the commercial farm problem, and that have some possibility of acceptance. These ideas may be viewed as a "study paper" to serve as the basis of policy discussions and future program development.

1. Level of National Economic Activity. A necessary condition for solving the commercial farm problem is a high level of national economic activity. This alone will not solve the commercial problem, but without it, no solution is possible. This is true for two important reasons.

First, a high level of economic activity is basic to the maintenance of a strong domestic demand for food. Though rising personal incomes no longer serve as an important source of demand expansion for food in the United States, depressed economic activity with widespread unemployment would cut back somewhat the total demand for food. And a contraction in aggregate demand of 2 or 3 per cent on top of an excess productive capacity in farming of 7 to 10 per cent would aggravate an already difficult problem.

Second, and more important in the United States, a high level of economic activity is necessary to provide employment for the surplus workers, the displaced workers, of modern commercial farming. Farm workers displaced, as new and improved technologies have substituted for them, have been flowing out of farming, and must continue to do so if the excess productive capacity of farming is to be held within bounds and reduced to a desired level. These displaced workers must have jobs and those jobs are available only when the economy is running at a high level.

Stated conversely, when the economy runs with slack in it, and unemployment is widespread, the flow of excess workers off the farms is dammed up, and the excess capacity problem in commercial farm-

161

ing is intensified. A prerequisite to solving the excess capacity problem is the availability of nonfarm jobs, and that availability is directly related to the level of national economic activity. At high levels of national economic activity, displaced farm workers can find nonfarm jobs; at low levels they cannot.

2. *Resource Mobility.* The resource mobility problem is not difficult with respect to producer goods. Cement, fertilizer, gasoline, feed grains, and packaging materials move easily and readily in any direction. Even tractors and trucks move into farming and among various regions without difficulty. Land, on the other hand, has zero mobility. New, nonfarm uses must move to it; no one has yet thought of a way of moving farm land to town.

The *resource mobility* problem centers on the *human resource.* People move, but unlike sacks of cement, they do not move easily. There are human costs involved in uprooting a family from familiar surroundings and re-establishing it in new surroundings. There are the money costs of moving, often coming on top of business failure in the case of farm families. And there are the uncertainties of a new job, or even finding a new job. All these things reduce and restrict the mobility of labor and particularly farm workers, who must usually make both an occupational and a geographical shift.

Political and farm leaders have not helped the situation. They have usually treated the out-migration of farm people as a mentally ill child was once treated: don't mention it, hide it, and leave it alone. And leave it alone they have. Although there has been a heavy net migration from rural to urban areas for decades, almost nothing has been done to facilitate or ease the process.

One possible exception to the above charge is the land-grant university, which was, of course, originally established for training rural youth to return to the farm. But things have not worked out that way; for sixty years the land-grant university has been one of the principal escape routes from the farm. For the young man or woman who has not gone to college, however, almost nothing has been done, and for the farm family facing business failure nothing has been done.

In fact a stronger indictment against political and farm leaders on this issue should be made. In more than a few cases they have blocked efforts, such as the operation of a Federal Employment Service in rural areas, which would have facilitated the ongoing process of out-migration. The time has come for these leaders to face the reality of farm to city migration and support programs and actions which contribute to worker mobility.

At a very minimum these programs should include extending the Federal Employment Service to rural areas. As a next step, rural education in general should be improved, and nonfarm vocational training provided for that majority of farm youth who do not plan to stay on the farm. For the young man or woman who does not plan to stay on the farm, vocational training in stenography, business, electricity, or mechanics is much more valuable than vocational training in agriculture. After that grants and loans might be made to farm families to finance the cost of moving to a new location, and to finance the cost of vocational training for family members to learn new skills and new jobs. In sum, the migration of workers from farm to city could be improved, eased, and facilitated in many ways, *if the will existed*. And since the welfare and training costs of unskilled and poorly educated farm families that migrate to the city are largely borne by urban dwellers, it would certainly be in the interest of the city man to provide that will.

3. *The Use of Research and Development Resources.* The time has come to stop viewing research and development as magic, heavensent, and always representing progress. Research and development resources are like any other resources; their use is subject to analysis; you can have too many research and development resources in one economic area and too few in another, and since those resources are costly to produce and scarce relative to their needs, the analytical problem confronting the United States is to allocate those resources among competing uses so as to maximize the economic and social well-being of society. Granted that this is not an easy problem to solve, but it is conceptually no different from the one with which economists have been wrestling with respect to conventional resources for nearly two centuries.

It may turn out after an objective analysis that just the right amount of research and development resources is being applied to farm production problems. But if this is the case, it will be owing to pure chance, because systematic analysis and conscious direction have been conspicuously lacking in this resource use problem. It seems more reasonable to assume, on the basis of supply data, that the application of research and development resources to farm production problems has been somewhat greater than the optimum, at the farm product price level of the early 1960's. On the other hand, the purpose of an analysis of this resource use problem should not be to cut expenditures for research and development in food and agriculture; it should rather be to ascertain the optimum expenditure of funds on research and development in food and agriculture. When full consideration is given to needs and uncertainties in the decades ahead, perhaps the present rate of application will be found not excessive.

The discussion above, however, raises new questions: How much excess production capacity should be tolerated in any given period, with what rate of current application of research and development resources, to be certain that there will be food enough in some future period?

In any event the analysis should be made. To be useful for policy purposes it should be made by an independent and competent economic research organization, perhaps by the Council of Economic Advisers. As a staff agency to the President, this council sits at the center of the resource allocation process in the federal government, with access to data and information from all federal agencies, but beholden to none.

Another possible place to make such a study is a private university or research foundation, such as Harvard University, the University of Chicago, Resources for the Future, Inc., or the National Planning Association. There are agencies to do the job, and good ones, too. Again the problem is one of attitude. Will the governmental agencies, the interest groups, and the congressional committees permit and support a rational analysis of a resource allocation process that has been proceeding exclusively by pressure and compromise? And again the city man, who in large measure pays the bill for maintaining excess capacity in commercial farming, has the incentive to see that such a study is undertaken.

4. Price Policy. Price policy is at the heart of the commercial problem. A lowering of the level of price support — and consequently the whole structure of farm prices — would have two desirable effects. First, it would dampen down the rate of aggregate output expansion and in that way reduce the annual farm surplus. Second, it would reduce the governmental costs of the programs of price support and production control. But it would have one undesirable effect: it would reduce farm income.

Net government expenditures for the feed grain program could be reduced about $400 million annually by reducing the support rate, and thereby the market price, by ten cents per bushel on corn and an equivalent amount on the other grains including wheat. But such a reduction in the support level in feed grains, with the consequent increased production of beef, pork, poultry, and dairy products, would cause the cash receipts from livestock products to fall about $1 billion after full adjustment to the lower price had been achieved. This is the meaning of increased food supplies with an inelastic demand. Further, cash receipts from the sale of feeds would be reduced by $300 to $400 million, reducing the total receipts in the feed-livestock economy by $1.3 to $1.4 billion.

The economic problem facing commercial farmers *as a whole* comes into sharp focus in this analysis. In the context of surplus production, where the entire feed-livestock economy is riding on the support price of grains, a ten-cent decline in the support price of corn (and an equivalent decline in the other grains) results in a $400 million saving in program costs, but a $1.4 billion reduction in the gross return of feed-livestock producers. These relations cause me to suggest the following two-step price policy for the commercial farm sector.

First, hold the structure of farm prices at the 1961–64 level by maintaining the general level of price support at the 1961–64 level, if farmers will accept effective supply controls.

Second, if farmers will not accept effective supply controls, lower the level of price support gradually, say 2 per cent per year, for 7 straight years, or by a total of 15 per cent.

In this connection, one question needs to be answered: What is meant by effective supply control? No single specific mechanism is involved, but the acceptance of mechanisms which control efficiently and reduce program costs is necessary. Depending on the commodity and the situation, accepting effective supply controls means accepting some combination of the following measures: marketing quotas measured in bushels, bales, or pounds; individual quotas that are negotiable; controls that are binding on all producers of a commodity if the majority of the producers approve; retirement of marginal land on a long-term basis at low cost; and retirement of whole farms on a long-term basis at low cost. The acceptance of some combination of the above measures would enable the government to hold total farm production in line with total requirements at reasonable cost.

The logic of the first step above is to provide commercial farmers the opportunity to continue to protect their incomes — to provide commercial farmers with the opportunity to avoid the drastic income consequences that flow from a correction of the surplus production problem through lower prices. The protection of commercial farm incomes by a continuance of the present level of price support seems reasonable on several grounds. For one thing the present level is not generating exorbitant farm incomes. At the present level of support the large, efficient producer is, on the average, receiving something close to a parity of income, and something over a parity of income when capital gains are taken into consideration. But the medium-sized to small farmer is a long way from earning a parity of income.

Second, a decline in farm prices would reduce food prices somewhat, but marketing margins have a way of increasing, through the provision of more services to consumers, when farm prices fall. The decline in farm prices that would spell income disaster to thousands of farm families would cause only a modest decline in retail prices, or perhaps no decline at all if the margin were absorbed in the form of more service built into finished food products.

Third, continuing the 1961–64 level of price support *with effective supply controls* would mean that the cost of maintaining excess capacity in commercial farming, hence the assurance of future food abundance, was being shared by producers and consumers. The acceptance of effective supply controls, and the loss of production control payments and the consequent reduction in government expenditures, would be borne by farmers, and the maintenance of food prices at 1961–64 levels, or the failure to realize increased services, would be borne by consumers.

In other words, the first step is suggested as a compromise to avoid the disaster of putting farmers through the long-run economic wringer where food prices to consumers are not increased and government costs of production control programs are reduced. Such a program would seem to represent a net gain to the economy as a whole.

Raising the level of farm price support is not considered here for two important reasons. First, raising the level would increase the costs

The City Man and the Commercial Problem

of price support and production control programs. Second, increased farm incomes resulting from increased levels of price support would quickly be capitalized into increased land values. In sum, holding the level of price support constant at the 1961–64 level would prove least disruptive to the commercial farm economy — would minimize problems of asset valuation — and would bring tangible gains to the nonfarm sector, if farmers would accept effective controls over their production.

But the acceptance of effective controls by commercial farmers is indeed doubtful. Certainly the action of farm organizations before Congress and the action of farmers in referendum during 1961–64 suggest that they would not accept effective controls. Except in a few commodities, such as tobacco and rice, farmers have shown an unwillingness to accept controls except when the payments received from taking land out of production yield a better return than farming the land.

The probability that the majority of farmers will not accept effective controls provides the logic of the second step. To reduce the annual surplus and the cost of the price support and production control programs when controls are inefficient and ineffective, the level of price support must be lowered. There is no other alternative if the excess capacity problem is to be corrected and program costs reduced.

A reduction in the level of price support — say 2 per cent a year — is suggested for two reasons. First, a gradual rate of reduction in the level of price support would give farm operators the time and opportunity to make adjustments in the use of resources under nondistressed conditions. The less efficient operators might want to sell out to the more efficient — sell out before they were forced out. And the more efficient might want to make shifts among enterprises and employ productive resources in different combinations given a general price deflation, but one in which individual commodity prices did not fall equally.[1]

Second, a gradual decline of 2 per cent a year in the general level of farm prices should be pretty close to the annual gain in production efficiency. Such a price decline should not therefore reduce the return per unit of product in the short run (cost per unit and price per unit

[1] One specific formulation of this general approach is to be found in the Committee for Economic Development publication *An Adaptive Program for Agriculture*, 1962. The C.E.D. program suggestion is more drastic than that suggested here, but it indicates the view of one important nonfarm organization on this subject.

would be falling by about the same amount), or create a downward pressure on asset values, particularly land values, in the long run. In other words, commercial farming should be able to escape a general deflation in land values if the product price level falls no more than 2 per cent a year. The gain in production efficiency resulting from farm technological advance that previously was capitalized into increased land values would be wiped out by this decline, leaving no gain to be received as profit or to be capitalized into land values.

A decline of some 15 per cent over a seven-year period is suggested. At the end of that time the full implications of this price policy should be reviewed to discover the efficacy and desirability of this approach. But from the 1964 vantage point an over-all decline of 15 per cent is suggested, and not more, because a price decline of something less than the full amount that would occur under a free market would appear to be consistent with the national welfare and other national policies.

A price support structure about 15 per cent below the 1961–64 level should, five to seven years from now, still be generating some surplus, particularly in the grains, which seems desirable for several reasons. First, this result represents a continuation of a policy of erring modestly on the side of food abundance rather than trying to produce the precise annual market requirement, with the possibility of erring on the short side. Where food is concerned, it is better as a matter of national policy to err on the long side than on the short side. Second, the generation of physical surpluses at a level of support prices somewhat above the free market equilibrium would make it easier in practice to acquire products for distribution in foreign food aid programs (Food for Peace). Foreign food aid can and should be a part of the long-run foreign policy of the United States. Third, the generation of physical surpluses would also make it easier to maintain a reasonable and legitimate reserve stock program. Thus, there are good reasons for not moving to a complete, bare-shelf, free market policy.

Whether a 15 per cent decline in the over-all structure of price support over a seven-year period is the perfect formula cannot be known before the fact. The numbers and the direction of change do, however, illustrate a principle: Move toward a lower level of price support gradually, but don't go all the way to the free market level. The policy of gradualness is suggested to avoid the forcing of resource adjustments under crisis conditions, and a general deflation in land values. The 15 per cent limit is suggested to hold the farm economy in a continuing state of abundance, which is consistent with other food and agricultural programs to be discussed.

5. *Reserve Stocks.* The Commodity Credit Corporation has long been the outlet of last resort in American farm policy, and in this capacity the CCC has accumulated, at various times, very large stocks of wheat, feed grains, cotton, dairy products, and other farm commodities. Stocks accumulated in price support operations have borne no relation to the reserve needs of the nation; the government simply accumulated whatever it had to acquire to hold market prices at the support levels. But on several occasions — the Korean War, the Suez crisis, the Cuban crisis — and in years of poor crops at home or abroad, the nation has discovered how comfortable it is to hold large stocks of foodstuffs. "Surplus" stocks accumulated under price support operations quickly become a valuable asset in periods of international crisis. It is fair to say that part of the CCC holdings, which are called "surplus" stocks by the press, should be labeled "needed reserve" stocks.

The inelasticity of demand for food, which in the case of a little too much can drive farm food prices down to disaster levels, can in the case of a little too little force food prices skyward. The United States, for its own protection and as the leader of the free world, must be prepared to move supplies into situations of short supply resulting from international crises or crop failures, and thereby moderate panic buying and dampen skyrocketing prices. And we can do this only if we have the stocks on hand. The United States should therefore establish and pursue a legitimate reserve-stock policy for food and fiber products geared to the needs that are likely to confront the nation.

How large the reserve stocks of food and fiber should be is to some degree a question of judgment and open to debate. As in any insurance problem, how complete or how full a coverage should be maintained depends upon current capacities and future expectations of the persons involved. But if the magnitude of the possible contingencies is established, then realistic judgments of the size of the reserve stocks can be made. Using this approach, technicians in the Department of Agriculture have on several occasions set forth a desirable level of reserve stocks for the United States for some of the more important commodities. Their judgments are as shown in the accompanying tabulation.

Wheat	600–700 million bushels
Feed grains	40–50 million tons
Cotton	6–7 million bales
Soybeans	75–100 million bushels

These stock levels should not be viewed as a miser views his money hoard. Reserve stocks are meant to be used, and stock levels should be pulled down to zero if necessary to meet or moderate a short food supply situation. The point to be made here is simple, but one that managers of reserve stocks don't always seem to understand. The desired stock level is not meant to be maintained at any cost; if it is, stocks will not be used for the purpose for which they were created. Reserve stocks are in being to be *used* to meet a contingency, and once the contingency is passed, the stock should be rebuilt to the desired level to meet new contingencies.

The establishment and implementation of a national reserve-stock policy means, in turn, that production and price policy must be related to the stock policy. Under the discussion of price policy, it was suggested that some surplus be generated every year to meet the continuing requirements of foreign food aid and the intermittent requirements of the reserve-stock program. That is good as far as it goes. But an effective reserve-stock policy, where stocks must be rebuilt from time to time, means also that price and production policies need to be sufficiently flexible to permit the expansion of production in one year to rebuild stocks and a contraction after the desired level of stocks has been reached.

6. *Foreign Food Aid.* The United States has excess productive capacity in food and fiber products. Many developing countries have an acute need for increased food supplies, but lack the foreign exchange to buy what they need in the commercial market. To an important degree this gap has been bridged by the foreign food aid programs (Food for Peace) of the United States. During the early 1960's shipments under this program have run at an annual rate of $1.5 to $1.7 billion dollars.

Although many people do not realize it, this is a big program. And though each country's program has its faults and limitations, this aid has saved many a developing country from extreme food shortages and political disaster, and contributed importantly to the development of many more, while draining off the surplus production from the

American farm plant and making deeper production cuts unnecessary. It has been an ideal program for both the rich and the poor.

The question confronting Americans is where to go from here with respect to foreign food aid. Opposing pressures to expand and to restrict it are developing simultaneously. It would be a crime against humanity to restrict this program seriously. Cutting off or seriously restricting food aid to certain developing countries could precipitate political crises that would topple their governments; in most of the developing countries, moreover, such action would mean that more people would go hungry. Furthermore, such a restricting action would complicate the excess capacity problem at home. Foreign food aid programs should be maintained, improved, and expanded in a realistic manner.

What about expanding the program? As we said in Chapter 6, food needs around the world are great and increasing every day. But the physical facilities — storage, handling, and transportation — for reaching those people with more food are limited. And with the exception of a few commodities, notably milk powder and rice, shipments under P.L. 480 cannot be expanded greatly until the facilities bottleneck is broken. Those men of good will and special interest who want to shove surplus supplies into poor, underdeveloped countries where adequate facilities are lacking are doing the program a disservice. Nothing can destroy a food aid program as fast as rotting food and a public scandal, which must be the result when shipments are increased to countries lacking the facilities to handle them.

What is needed in this foreign food aid area is the following. First, information and intelligence about food needs around the world. And this phase of the work is completed.[2] Second, information and intelligence with respect to storage, handling, and transportation needs and costs in the food recipient countries, which is almost totally lacking in a rigorous, quantitative sense. Third, the formulation of a policy with regard to what the United States is prepared to do in the way of breaking the facilities bottleneck.

If the United States is prepared to help importantly to build and operate food handling facilities in the developing countries, the foreign food aid program can be expanded to almost any size — doubled,

[2] See *The World Food Budget: 1970*, Foreign Agricultural Economic Report No. 19, Economic Research Service, USDA, October 1964.

tripled, or even quadrupled during the next decade. In so doing foreign food aid would serve as effective economic aid in the developing countries, and act to solve the excess capacity problem in the United States. But the foreign food aid program cannot be expanded importantly from its present level until the physical handling problem is licked.

Surplus food products cannot be wished overseas any more than they can be wished away at home. But they can be used with great effectiveness in many developing countries in the 1960's, 1970's, and 1980's if ways can be found to store, handle, and transport them. The sooner the United States turns its attention to this problem, the sooner this avenue of economic aid will be widened to the benefit of all concerned.

7. *Commercial Trade.* Several forces are working to expand the trade of farm products in international commerce: rapid economic growth and rising personal incomes in the industrial countries; the high income elasticity of demand for meats in those same countries; the slower but nonetheless important economic growth in the less developed countries; and the high income elasticity of demand for food in total in this latter group of countries.

But growing barriers to trade and problems of competition must be overcome if exports of farm products from the United States are to increase in a sustained way. These include the emerging Common Market and its drive for self-sufficiency; farm protectionist policies in almost every industrialized country in the world; increased use of monopolistic sales practices among traditional exporters; and the development of exportable surpluses of farm products in many less developed countries.

In this situation, commercial exports of American farm products could expand or contract in the long run. The struggle for overseas markets in farm products is rough and tough, and it will be won, with expanded exports as the result, if and only if a strong, intelligent, and sustained effort is made at many levels. This means that the federal government must continue its present determined policy of trade expansion and strengthen it not with more vigor, but with more *imagination* and *skill*.

Markets for farm products are not won in Western Europe by publicly denouncing the agricultural policy of the Common Market as evil; markets are won rather by working out trading relations that are in the interest of both the Common Market union and the United States. Admittedly this is not easy, but it is the only way foreign trade is expanded. Foreign countries do not respond favorably to public criticism of their trade policies.

If exports of farm products are to be increased, the federal government must also encourage and work with commodity development groups and private firms in their overseas efforts. The efforts of commodity groups must be encouraged and supported; these groups perform a useful role in placing American products before prospective buyers. The specific needs of private firms with respect to handling and commercial practices and individual country barriers to shipments must also be learned and acted upon. Modern foreign trade is a cooperative endeavor among government, quasi-private groups, and private firms; this cooperation must be real and effective if commercial trade is to flourish.

What happens to the volume of commercial farm exports from the United States over the next decade will depend upon the nature of the policy effort adopted by the United States. If that effort is strong intelligent, and *sustained*, given the economic forces that seem likely to be operating, exports should expand — perhaps modestly, perhaps greatly, depending upon the specific situation. But if the commercial trade efforts of the United States are weak, unimaginative, and sporadic, we shall be beaten in the competitive struggle for export markets and our volume of commercial trade in farm products will decline relatively and perhaps absolutely. This policy choice Americans will make.

A NOTE TO FARMERS

Under the format of this book, the above policy ideas are presented to the city man for his consideration. But these ideas are not secret. Further, and more important, these ideas are not presented as good for the city man and bad for the farmer. They are available for the consideration of the farmer as well as the city man, and in fact I have presented them to farm audiences. These ideas are the best that I can come up with in the middle 1960's for farmers, urban people, and the nation as a whole.

Some farmers may approve of these policy ideas and others may be hurt or angered by them. But however they respond, farmers must recognize that the power to initiate and pass legislation about price and income support and production control has slipped away from them. It has slipped into the hands of the city man as the consequence of developments that were discussed earlier in this chapter and in Chapter 9. Enlightened self-interest, including the need for effective group action by farmers, requires that farmers recognize this political fact, whether they like or dislike my ideas. Seven per cent of the families in the nation, rent by policy and ideological differences, are not going to pass legislation requiring heavy expenditures of public funds for very long. That is a political fact, and wishing will not make it otherwise.

The passage of legislation to deal equitably and effectively with the problem of too many resources producing too much in commercial farming must depend upon good will, understanding of the problems, and a concept of the national interest by the urban consumer and voter. A continuance of the essentially negative attitude of the city man and his congressional representatives toward the commercial farm problem and farm legislation could lead to income disaster for farmers generally, and possibly food supply problems in the long run. The purpose of this book is to try to help the city man understand modern farming and its problems and to present for discussion a set of policy ideas for dealing realistically with those problems.

PART III. RURAL POVERTY

11

The Problem of Poverty

PARTS I and II of this book told a production success story and dealt with its economic implications, both happy and unhappy. Those parts dealt with research and development, farm technological advance, production increases and economic growth, and certain difficult but not depressing social and economic adjustment problems resulting from that development process. But the story changes in Part III to one of failure — economic failure, income failure, social failure, and human failure. The story moves to a description and analysis of a situation in which individual families and communities of families, and their children after them, live out their lives in stark poverty. The story changes from one of chronic overproduction to one of chronic poverty.

In this chapter the problem of poverty in rural America is defined and described and its causes analyzed. The chapter deals with the following questions: What is the poverty problem? How big is it? What are its characteristics? What are its causes? What chains bind millions of rural people to chronic poverty?

The focus of the analysis also changes. In Part II we were concerned exclusively with farmers, their farms, and problems relating to the production and distribution of farm products. Here the analysis is broadened to include the rural community, rural farm people and rural nonfarm people.[1] The analysis is widened for a number of reasons.

First, the causes of underemployment and very low incomes are basically the same for both rural farm and nonfarm people. Second, most

[1] Rural nonfarm people are those living in villages of less than 2,500 population, or in the open country but not farming.

rural nonfarm families falling in the poverty category have close ties with farming; they may be retired or part-time farmers, they may have failed in farming, or they may be part-time or seasonal workers in such agribusinesses as fruit packing, cotton ginning, or a grain elevator. Third, many poverty ridden rural nonfarm families are part-time or seasonal hired farm workers. For these reasons and because, further, the solution to the problem of rural farm poverty cannot be separated from the solution to the problem of rural nonfarm poverty, the focus of this analysis is widened to include the rural community.

THE PROBLEM DEFINED

Families living in poverty are defined as those that cannot, by 1960 standards, afford a decent living in terms of food, clothing, and shelter, and provide for the health and education of their members. The ability to fulfill these needs and requirements depends, of course, on many factors: current income, savings, ability to obtain credit, size of family, age of its members, and the health and educational facilities available in the local community. But in spite of the variety of conditions that affect the needs of a family and its ability to meet them, a simple measure of poverty is required if an understanding of the nature, magnitude, and location of poverty across the nation is to be gained.

For this reason, the Johnson administration in its anti-poverty efforts has determined that families with incomes of $3,000 and below and unrelated individuals with incomes of $1,500 and below fall in the poverty classification. That will be our working definition here: any family receiving a net cash income of $3,000 or less a year is living in poverty.

In the farming business, where local areas and even individual farms are subject to highly variable weather conditions, it is not uncommon for a large, efficient farm to lose money in a particular year. But the problem of poverty in rural America is something more than an occasional family experiencing an occasional very low income. The poverty problem in rural America encompasses millions of families, often comprising whole communities in which families live in a state of deprivation year after year. It is a tenacious thing that has responded haltingly and imperfectly to growth in the general economy and to high levels of economic activity. It is characterized by chronic underemployment, low and irregular incomes, lifetimes of substandard living, and slum communities.

The Problem of Poverty

Dr. William E. Hendrix describes the rural poverty problem well when he says:

We . . . find in farm areas with large concentrations of underemployment small, inadequately equipped and often severely eroded farms; people living in crowded dilapidated houses; farm machinery in poor repair; a high incidence of remedial physical defects; a high level of school dropouts; inadequate community facilities; notable cultural lags; and other conditions all combining to impoverish people and the communities in which they live. These conditions are the incidences of large involuntary underemployment persisting over decades of time. Rural areas with large concentrations of such underemployment are in a situation roughly equivalent to that faced by an urban community with average unemployment per worker of 4 to 5 months per year above the normal levels, a level of unemployment that occurs not once in every 4 to 5 years but annually over decades of time — this without benefits of unemployment compensation.[2]

The central feature of rural poverty is underemployment — involuntary underemployment lasting for decades. Underemployment is the employment of adult men and women irregularly, or in jobs of low productivity, with annual wages below those of comparable workers in other employments. Millions of men and women are "employed" year after year in rural America at odd jobs, irregular and seasonal jobs, and low productivity jobs that yield small and uncertain incomes. This is chronic underemployment, and it leads to a poverty pattern of family and community life — poor schools, poor medical facilities and services, poor library and community services, lack of training for productive jobs, and despair. Once this pattern is established, and a generation or two of families have cycled through it, corrective action becomes exceedingly difficult. Poverty then becomes a hard-core problem not amenable to solution by ordinary social activities and economic development.

THE MAGNITUDE AND LOCATION OF RURAL POVERTY

Nearly half of the poor in the United States live in rural areas. The proportion of families living in poverty is nearly twice as great in rural areas as in urban areas. One out of every three rural families had in 1959 a cash income under $3,000. In short, poverty is commonplace in rural areas.

[2] "Relation of Chronic Low Farm Incomes to Major National Economic Problems," *Journal of Farm Economics*, May 1962, p. 528.

The Problem of Poverty

Table 8. Number of Families (in Thousands)
with Cash Income of under $3,000, U.S., 1959

Residence	Total U.S.	Northeast	North Central	South	West
All families	9,650	1,630	2,451	4,471	1,098
Urban	5,227	1,228	1,245	1,994	760
Rural	4,423	402	1,206	2,477	338
Nonfarm	2,853	330	625	1,647	251
Farm	1,570	72	581	830	87

Source: U.S. Census of Population, 1960.

There were 9.7 million families in the United States in 1959 with cash incomes of less than $3,000. Of this number, 4.4 million lived in rural areas; and of the total number of rural families living in poverty, 2.9 million were nonfarm and 1.6 million were farm (a regional breakdown of these data is shown in Table 8).

Some 17.4 million rural people lived in poverty in 1959 (counting persons living in families and unrelated individuals). Of the total rural poor, 11.3 million were rural nonfarm people and 6.1 million lived on farms. Some 6 million of the total rural poor were under eighteen years of age.

The incidence of poverty is high among hired farm workers' families. Some 56 per cent of all hired farm workers' households were in the poverty category in 1959, which is two and a half times as many as in the households of nonfarm laborers. Poverty is particularly high among nonwhite hired workers' families, most of whom are in the South and in the migratory group; over 80 per cent of these families fall in the poverty category.

Poverty is to be found in all rural areas of the United States (Figure 8). But the incidence of poverty is heaviest in the South; this is particularly true with respect to *farm families* living in poverty (Figure 9). Farm poverty is concentrated along the Coastal Plain of the Carolinas, throughout Appalachia, and up and down the Mississippi delta. Smaller, but nonetheless serious, pockets of both farm and nonfarm poverty are to be found in rural areas across the nation.

Another way of viewing the magnitude of the poverty problem in rural America is in terms of unemployment and underemployment. Very few farm workers suffer total unemployment throughout the year, but many work only seasonally, or irregularly, or at low-productivity farm

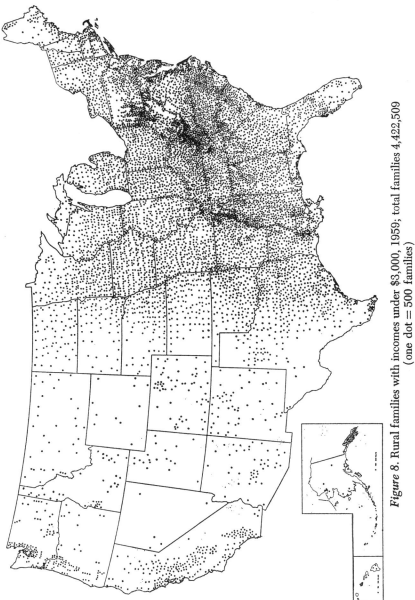

Figure 8. Rural families with incomes under $3,000, 1959; total families 4,422,509 (one dot = 500 families)

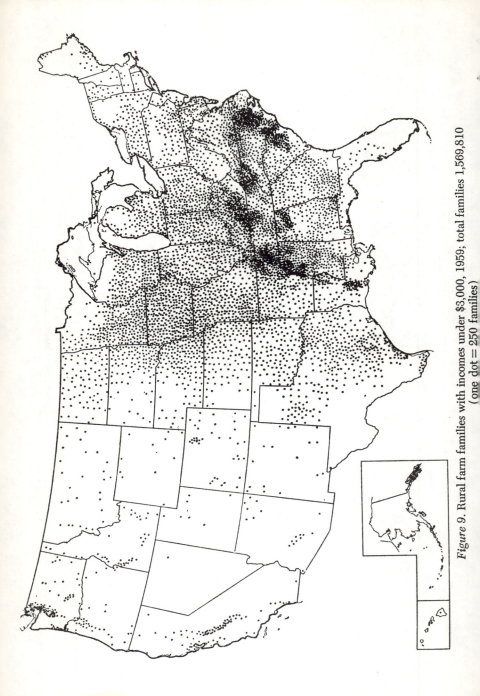

Figure 9. Rural farm families with incomes under $3,000, 1959; total families 1,569,810 (one dot = 250 families)

jobs, and thus suffer that common rural malady, underemployment. When this underemployment is converted to man years of unemployment and added to the small amount of farm unemployment, it turns out that there were about 1.5 million man years of unemployment among farm workers in 1959. And since labor on adequate-sized family farms and larger than family farms tends to be used both efficiently and economically, it must be deduced that underemployment and unemployment among farm workers (which add up to the unemployment of 1.5 million workers) is concentrated on the small, low-production farms and among hired farm workers — in short, is concentrated in the poverty sector.

A comparable estimate of unemployment among rural nonfarm people is about 2.5 million man years. The total underemployment of farm and nonfarm rural workers together with conventional unemployment converts into an estimate of total unemployment equivalent to some 4 million workers per year as of 1959. This estimate compares with a total of 6 million rural families and unrelated individuals living in poverty in 1959. It does not seem improper, then, to surmise that a very high proportion of those 6 million income-earning units suffered complete unemployment, or, more probably, serious underemployment. Underemployment and poverty go together in rural America; they are in fact opposite sides of the same coin.

In Chapter 1 it was argued that the production on farms grossing less than $5,000 a year was so low, and consequently that the net incomes of such farms were so small, that all of them logically fall in the poverty category. There were 665,000 such farms in 1963. It was also argued that the "other farms," part-time and part-retirement farms, with low farm production and low farm incomes, should not really be classed as farms at all. There were 1,321,000 such farms in 1963. The question then to be answered is this: How many of the above families are in the 4.4 million rural families defined in this chapter as living in poverty?

Before attempting a reconciliation of these various figures and estimates, it should be recognized that they come from different sources and are for different years: the data in Chapter 1 came from the farm census as adjusted in the USDA and are for 1963; the data in this chapter came from the population census and are for 1959. We should not expect these income and population data to fit together perfectly, and they don't. But a reasonable reconciliation can be effected.

The Problem of Poverty

Practically all the full-time farms grossing less than $2,499 in 1963 (Table 1, Chapter 1) fall into the poverty classification as defined in this chapter — that is, the total cash income of each of these 202,000 families was less than $3,000. Most, but not all, of the 463,000 farm families grossing between $2,500 and $4,999 fall into the poverty classification; some of these families had enough off-farm income to raise their annual net cash income above $3,000. Thus, something less than the 665,000 farm families in these two groups live in poverty as defined in this chapter.

Who, then, are the 1.6 million farm families described as living in poverty in this chapter? More than a million are part-time farmers, partly retired farmers, and hired farm worker families living on farms, plus some farmers who grossed over $5,000 in 1959, but for one reason or another netted less than $3,000 in that year.

In other words, the total of 1.6 million families described as farm families in this chapter and defined as living in poverty includes nearly all, but not all, of those 665,000 full-time farm operators grossing less than $5,000 in 1963, but it includes a lot more families that somehow get classed as farm families. It includes over 200,000 part-retirement farm families, that many or more part-time farm families, and a large number of hired worker families living on farms. Further it includes more than a few commercial farm families that happened to have a low net income in 1959.

In sum, the estimate of the magnitude of the rural poverty problem presented in this chapter is more inclusive than that in Chapter 1. It includes nearly all those farm families that were placed in the poverty category in Chapter 1, more than a million more farm families of some description, and, of course, the 2.8 million rural nonfarm families.

CHARACTERISTICS OF THE RURAL POOR [3]

The rural poor live under conditions that are alien to the American way of life. They live in substandard and often unsanitary houses, suffer from inadequate diets, go without adequate medical care, and have access to far less education and training than does the rest of the American community. Some 70 per cent of them with incomes of less than $3,000 in 1959 lived in houses so run down that they were classified as

[3] An excellent source of information about the rural poor is the recent publication *Poverty in Rural Areas of the United States*, by Alan R. Bird, Agricultural Economics Report No. 63, USDA, November 1964.

dilapidated. A high percentage lived in houses without such conveniences as central heating, bathroom and toilet facilities, and running water.

Medical services are also scarce in rural communities. The number of physicians and surgeons per 100,000 residents was 52 in rural areas as compared with 161 in urban areas in 1960. The paucity of dentists and professional nurses in rural areas is also striking — 22 dentists per 100,000 residents in rural areas in 1960, compared with 60 in urban areas, and 195 professional nurses per 100,000 residents in rural areas, compared with 387 in urban areas.

Communities whose resources are too meager to provide adequate incomes for their residents are likely to fail also to provide adequate community services. This is particularly true of educational services. Salaries of teachers in rural communities are notoriously low. In the middle 1950's, the salaries of the instructional staff in public elementary and secondary schools in the 101 "most rural counties" in the nation were about 60 per cent of those in the three highest paying states — California, Illinois, and New York. And, of course, the only place that one-teacher, one-room schools can still be found is in rural areas.

The picture is not the one of pastoral beauty — fat cattle grazing in the meadow, painted barns and well-kept fences, and a Sunday dinner of fried chicken — that the reader may have in mind from a visit to grandfather's farm in his youth. For seventeen million people living in rural poverty the picture is one of shabby, unpainted, dilapidated houses, small low-yielding patches and fields interspersed with cut-over timber and brush, and sickness, ignorance, and despair.

Age and Education. Rural families living in poverty have a higher proportion of family heads in the older age brackets than do poor urban families. Some 66 per cent of poor rural families are headed by persons 45 and over, as contrasted with 59 per cent of urban families. Of poor rural farm families, 68 per cent are headed by persons over 45, and of rural nonfarm families, 65 per cent. The important conclusion to be drawn from these estimates is that two thirds of the rural poverty families are headed by persons whose age greatly restricts them from moving either occupationally or geographically.

Vocational mobility, and to some extent geographic mobility, are restricted by educational achievements as well as by age. Seventy-two per cent of all rural poverty families are headed by persons who have

The Problem of Poverty

finished eight years or less of schooling, and this percentage is the same for both rural farm and rural nonfarm poverty families.

The age and educational characteristics of heads of poor rural families are combined and related in Table 9. From this table we observe that about 2.2 million rural *nonfarm* poverty families, or over three fourths of those families, are headed by persons that are either 65 or over or have completed eight years or less of schooling. The situation is

Table 9. Age and Educational Characteristics of the Heads
of Poor Rural Nonfarm and Farm Families, U.S., 1959

Age and Education of Head	Nonfarm	Farm
All heads	2,852,000	1,583,000
25 years and under	198,000	49,000
8th grade or less	69,000	24,500
Beyond 8th grade	129,000	24,500
25–44 years	813,000	452,000
8th grade or less	479,000	237,000
Beyond 8th grade	334,000	215,000
45–64 years	937,000	701,000
8th grade or less	750,000	561,000
Beyond 8th grade	187,000	140,000
65 years and over	904,000	381,000

Source: U.S. Department of Agriculture.

about the same for rural *farm* families living in poverty; about 1.2 million poor farm families, or again somewhat more than three fourths of the families, are headed by persons either 65 or over or with eight years or less of schooling. Poor rural families tend to be headed by persons who are old or poorly educated or both.

Poverty, like wealth, is passed from one generation to the next. Living in the 4.4 million rural poverty families in 1959 were 6 million children under 18. The very poor typically have a smaller proportion of their children ages 14 to 17 enrolled in school than do higher income families, and among those still in school a higher proportion of children from poor families are at least one grade behind the normal grade for their age. These 6 million children represent the opportunity to break the chain of poverty in rural America, but if they are poorly educated and poorly trained they more probably represent the beginnings of millions of new poverty families in the United States.

Boxed-in Families. About one million farm poverty families are boxed in by reason of their age or educational attainment or physical condition. Typically the heads of these families are 65 or older, or have completed 8 years or less of schooling, or are in poor health. Consequently, they have limited geographic or occupational mobility; they are either too old or infirm to move or there is no place for people of their limited skills. Assistance for these families, if it is given, will have to be given to them where they are. They are boxed in.

By the same criteria there are about 1.7 million rural nonfarm boxed-in families, making a total, in rural America, of some 2.7 million poverty-stricken families of which the head lacks the training or the physical capability to take advantage of new jobs in new places, even if they were available. Many of these families are on the welfare rolls or close to it, and it is probably more economical and more humane to provide them with welfare assistance in their local communities than it would be to move them and provide such assistance in strange urban surroundings.

Migrant Farm Workers. Migrant farm workers who were United States citizens totaled 380,000 in 1962, and represented about 10 per cent of the hired farm labor force. About a third to a half were non-white and about 25 per cent women. Most such workers and their families are residents of urban areas, and therefore technically are defined out of the rural poverty problem. But they work in agriculture, and virtually all are poor by any standard; hence it is important to look at them in some detail.

The average migratory worker was employed 120 days in 1962, of which 91 days were at farm work. His total earnings from wage work were about $978; of this total, his earnings from farm work were $679 and from nonfarm work $299. About 70 per cent of all households headed by migrant workers in 1962 had annual incomes of less than $3,000, and thus fall into the poverty classification.

The seasonality of farm production is the basic reason for the existence of migratory workers. The modern commercial farmer, his family, and possibly a regular hired hand or two can operate even a large farm during most of the year. But during cultivation and harvest periods supplementary labor is needed in many crops and production areas to meet those seasonal requirements. The success or failure of a crop may depend upon the timely arrival of migrant workers during periods of peak labor requirements.

From the migrant worker's point of view, the basic reason for following the crops is that his earnings, meager though they may be, are more than they would be if he stayed home. Many of them are farmers who have been forced off the land by advancing technology and who lack the skill and training to take any job except that of a farm laborer. The seasonality of crop production and a supply of poorly trained, landless workers thus conspire to hold a migrant population (men, women, and children) of 600,000 to 700,000 in the worst poverty conditions — in rootless, floating poverty.

This rootless, floating poverty means long periods spent in travel, very often in unsafe vehicles. For the children it means the substitution of work or unsupervised play for regular schooling. And for the family it means continuous exposure to poor housing and other unhealthy conditions. The living conditions of migrant farm workers are something that most Americans can't bear to think about, and therefore they don't. As a consequence, migrant farm workers and their children continue to exist in those unthinkable conditions.

THE CAUSES OF POVERTY [4]

The causes of chronic poverty in rural America are both simple and complex. Basically and simply the cause is too few productive jobs in the total economy. But special extenuating circumstances make the rural poverty problem so tenacious and unresponsive to general economic growth of the economy. Let us consider, therefore, the economic meaning and implications of both the basic cause and the special circumstances.

With rare exceptions, the farm family living in poverty is operating a low-production farm with poor land, too few crop acres, and a plant that is grossly undercapitalized in equipment, livestock, and technology. The direct cause of low income in each case can thus be said to be low, inefficient production. For many years it was accepted doctrine that farmers continued to operate these low-production farms because they were lazy and indolent — because they preferred hunting and fishing to finding a new, more productive job. It was accepted doctrine that much if not most underemployment in farming was voluntary.

[4] The analysis in this section is based on the ideas and conclusions presented by William E. Hendrix in his two important papers, "Income Improvement Prospects in Low-Income Areas," *Journal of Farm Economics*, December 1959, pp. 1065–1075, and "Relation of Chronic Low Farm Incomes to Major National Economic Problems," *Journal of Farm Economics*, May 1962, pp. 522–533.

The Problem of Poverty

But the voluntary theory of underemployment was badly damaged by World War II. Under the forced draft of war mobilization, when war industries needed workers badly and went searching for them, people were sucked off farms. In one year alone, 1942, nearly three million people moved from farm to city. During these years when jobs were available and the underemployed in farming were told about those jobs, they left rural areas in droves to take up those jobs.

Since World War II study after study has shown that farm people take nonfarm jobs as fast as those jobs become available. In fact, whenever a new industry is developed in a low-income rural area, the applicants far exceed the number of new jobs. In sum, all the evidence shows that low-income rural people, both farm and nonfarm, quickly take up new and more remunerative nonfarm jobs when the jobs are there, they are aware of the jobs, and they are qualified or can be trained for the jobs. It isn't lack of incentive that holds the rural people in poverty; it is basically a lack of jobs.

This is not a treatise on employment policy, but the causes of chronic unemployment and underemployment in the national economy would seem to be two. First, the general economy has not grown fast enough since the end of World War II to generate all the jobs needed by the growing labor force. Second, within the rates of economic growth achieved, high wage policies vigorously pursued by organized labor and agreed to by big business and big government, together with restrictions on entry into most trades and high-paying occupations, have resulted in a large surplus of labor relative to the demand for it. There has been a chronic surplus of labor in the general economy at the going wage scales for nearly twenty years.

This is not to suggest that underemployment in farming should be solved by the pursuit of low-wage policies in the nonfarm sector. The happy solution is, of course, a rate of growth in the total economy that generates the number of jobs required to eliminate unemployment and underemployment in both urban and rural areas. But in considering the underemployment-poverty problem in rural America, facts do have to be faced. The facts are that, with the rates of economic growth that have been achieved in the national economy in almost every year since 1945, and the labor policies pursued of high wage rates and restrictions on entry into the better paying trades and occupations, there have been substantial and continuous unemployment and underemployment in the economy that had to come to rest somewhere. And, for reasons now to be considered, rural areas have been especially vulnerable to that underemployment.

These reasons could be detailed into a lengthy list, but they will instead be grouped under three major headings: (1) the farm economy is highly competitive, with no restriction on entry and with flexible labor earnings; (2) the location and personal characteristics of rural people act to discriminate against them in the hiring process; and (3) rural areas are vulnerable to underemployment because of natural population increases and declining labor requirements in farming.

Farming is rapidly becoming the nation's only major industry with competitive characteristics that permit the absorption of large amounts of underemployment. The only real restriction on the entry into farm production is that imposed by capital requirements. But very little capital is required to become a low-production, low-income farmer.

Although there is a heavy *net* migration from farm to city every year, in absolute terms a large number of people (up to 300,000 a year in the early 1960's) enter farming every year from the nonfarm sector.[5] These entrants may be young families with a little capital acquired from some source who want to become farmers. Or they may be families that have previously migrated to the city, don't like it, and decide to give farming another try. Typically, such families pick a marginal area (the northern sections of the Lake States, for example) where the land is poor and cheap in terms of total investment, and thus make a start with inadequate land and capital resources.

They are now in the business of low-production farming which quickly turns out also to be low-income farming. After a few years of low production, low income, growing family, and growing debts, a catastrophe strikes — illness in the family, or an epidemic among their livestock herd — and they starve out. If they are lucky and can find a job back in the city, they leave, and that is the end of that venture in freedom to farm. If they are unlucky they join the landless rural families

[5] Some experts argue that very few nonfarm families enter farming in a real sense; the 300,000 figure, they contend, results from a faulty definition of a farm, and consists mainly of retirees and employed persons who have moved to the country to live and get classified in the census as farmers. This argument may be correct in the main. But it is not completely correct, for I have seen and talked with families from the city that have tried to make a go of low-production farming in northern Minnesota.

living in poverty. In this role they work in the woods or on the roads, drive a school bus, or do other odd jobs to eke out an existence.

The entrant into low-production farming does not always come from the city. He may be, and more often is, a young man with a family, a farm or rural background, and a little capital who is making a start in the world. Because he can't find, or doesn't know of, a productive non-farm job, he takes his limited capital and makes a start in the occupation he knows, farming. Because he and his family know farming and are used to its hardships, they may last longer than the entrant from the city, but whether the time is long or short they will be living in poverty too, because the productive resources at their command are inadequate.

Entry into farming, and particularly into low-production farming, may then occur through back migration from city to farm and from the surplus rural population itself. But new entrants to farming with limited financial resources are doomed from the beginning because they are forced to work with inadequate resources — poor land, too few crop acres, antiquated equipment, and scrubby livestock — hence they are forced to operate low-production farms. As individuals they may work and strive very hard, but their productivity is low; they are *underemployed*. They are underemployed because, working with the inadequate resources at their command, they can produce only one-fourth or one-eighth the product that they could if they were working on an adequate-sized, adequately capitalized family farm. Free entry into farming without adequate capital really means being underemployed on low-production farms and living in poverty.

A second major reason why rural areas are subject to high underemployment is the physical and personal barriers to the employment of rural people. By definition rural people live long distances from the urban and industrial centers where new nonfarm jobs tend to be generated. The new industrial plant in Chicago or Detroit or Pittsburgh is more likely to look for workers among the unemployed in those cities or others nearby than it is to search for the underemployed in the coves of Appalachia or along the Mississippi delta. Thus, distance alone operates to the disadvantage of the rural underemployed; except when a new industry locates in a rural area in quest of an abundant labor supply, the underemployed in rural areas are at the end of the employment line and don't receive offers of employment until all those in nearby places have been hired.

The underemployed in rural areas have other characteristics, already noted, that militate against their being hired. The heads of families, the breadwinners, tend to be poorly educated, poorly trained in technical skills, and too old to learn new skills. Surplus rural labor is thus at a competitive disadvantage with surplus urban labor. A firm or industry looking for new employees, unless it is willing to embark upon a major training program, is more likely to find people with the skills that it requires among the urban unemployed than among the rural underemployed. Consequently, underemployment in rural areas backs up and collects in pockets behind the barriers of physical distance and inferior education and training.

Finally, farming, especially low-income farming, is especially vulnerable to underemployment because of its natural population and therefore labor increases, and its declining labor requirements as the result of technological advances. These conditions make it necessary for a large number of farm workers to move into nonfarm jobs each year to achieve and maintain a farm-nonfarm income equilibrium. Stated differently, there is a flow into the national labor market from two rural sources at all times: from the large natural population increases in rural areas and from workers that have been displaced in farming by new and improved technological processes. And unless there is a continuous outflow from local rural labor markets into the larger urban industrial labor market, the local rural labor markets quickly develop labor surpluses.

For reasons already discussed we know that the outflow of surplus labor from local rural labor markets is slow and halting, and that it encounters formidable barriers to its flow. There is in rural areas a continuous inflow of labor seeking employment, coupled with a faulty outflow of labor into the major labor markets of the nation. This can lead to only one result — surplus labor in rural areas.

To keep alive, surplus labor in rural areas often farms a small patch of land with little or no capital, that is, becomes engaged in low-production farming. In this way the unemployed become the underemployed. But unemployed or underemployed, the cause and the result are the same: the cause is a labor surplus backed up in rural areas because of insufficient jobs in the total economy, and the result is poverty. The result is seventeen million people living in poverty.

SOME CONCLUDING REMARKS

The rural poverty problem is well known and well documented. With improved definitions and more and better data, the estimate of the number of people living in poverty in rural America might increase or decrease by a million. It would be nice to have more facts about the personal characteristics, the farm characteristics, and the living conditions of these unfortunate people. But all that information would not change the magnitude of the problem or its basic coloration.

In terms of the number of people involved this is a larger problem than the commercial farm problem. And in personal tragedy it is a more acute problem. Further, in waste of human resources and the potential production that could result from the wise use of those resources, it far exceeds the economic waste of the excess or surplus of resources in the commercial farm problem. But these have been the forgotten people of the national society. Except for the work and writings of a few rural sociologists and farm economists, and the representations of a few church and charity groups, the rural poor have had no spokesmen. They have simply existed in the backwash of American life.

Major stirrings took place in this poverty area during 1964. Concrete action, with substance to it, was taken to eradicate poverty in the United States. But, although almost one half of the people living in poverty in the United States are in rural areas, it has been difficult to keep this fact and all the other sordid facts of rural poverty before legislators and key people in the administration. Legislators and administrators with urban backgrounds tend to equate poverty with urban slums and ignore the rural poor.

But alert administrators in the Department of Agriculture and the many church and charity groups that have become intimately familiar with the rural poverty problem were ready this time. Hence, the President's anti-poverty program as embodied in the Economic Opportunity Act of 1964 recognized the rural poverty problem and attempted to deal with it comprehensively. The rural poor were not forgotten in 1964. But whether the rural anti-poverty effort has the necessary power and the proper orientation to solve the problem remains to be seen.

12

♠

Policies and Programs: Too Little, Too Late

THE rural poverty problem has been around for a long time, and it remains a hard-core, unsolved problem in the 1960's. It does not remain in this unsatisfactory state, however, because of any lack of knowledge about it. A great deal has been written since World War II describing it, analyzing its causes, and suggesting means of coping with it. The technical literature on the subject since 1950 rivals and possibly exceeds that dealing with the commercial farm problem. And that means there has been a lot of it.

But that knowledge has not caught the interest of the general public or become an integral part of the great debate on farm policy or been converted into policies and programs with the capacity to deal with the intractability of the rural poverty problem. There have been policies and there have been programs for combating rural poverty. But it is a sad story of ineffective policies and programs; it is a record of *too little, too late.*

THE HISTORICAL RECORD

The Great Depression. During the Great Depression almost all farmers were poor, but even then some were poorer than others. To aid poverty-stricken families living on submarginal land the Resettlement Administration was established by presidential order as an independent agency in 1935. It attacked the rural poverty problem by (1) purchasing submarginal farms, consolidating them into economic sized units, and then reselling those farms to qualified farmers; (2) resettling families from whom it had purchased farms; (3) providing loans and

Policies and Programs: Too Little, Too Late

grants to "rehabilitate" farmers who lacked the financial and productive resources to earn decent incomes; and (4) encouraging the formation of debt adjustment committees.

The Resettlement Administration operated for two years, making loans and grants of nearly $300 million to needy farm families. This was one of the first of a long series of programs established to help low-production, low-income farm families.

In 1937 a special committee on farm tenancy, appointed by President Roosevelt, reported on the miserable economic conditions under which many farm tenants, sharecroppers, farm laborers, and families on holdings of inadequate size were living. This report, the first attempt to document the poverty problem in rural America,[1] presented the problem vividly, with pictures and numerical facts.

Perhaps as the result of the report on farm tenancy, but certainly as the result of the social and intellectual ferment of that period, the Bankhead-Jones Farm Tenant Act was passed in 1937. This act created the Farm Security Administration, a permanent agency within the USDA, to provide credit to and attempt to rehabilitate farm families living in poverty. In general, the activities of the Farm Security Administration were similar to those of the Resettlement Administration earlier. It undertook three principal activities: (1) providing loans to tenants to purchase farms; (2) providing rehabilitation loans to farm families that could not otherwise obtain credit on "reasonable terms" to purchase livestock, equipment, and other farm supplies; and (3) establishing a program of submarginal land retirement. This program continued through the late 1930's and World War II, reaching many needy, poverty-stricken farmers. In 1943, for example, rehabilitation loans were made to 232,000 farm families. But the activities of the Farm Security Administration were subject to continuous and widespread criticism, particularly by the more conservative groups in agriculture. Congress, dissatisfied with and suspicious of the "socialistic" tendencies and "unbusinesslike" methods of the Farm Security Administration reorganized it out of existence by legislative action in 1946.

Three generalizations may be made about the programs of the Resettlement and Farm Security administrations. First, for the first time in the history of the United States, programs were designed and put in operation to deal specifically with low-production farms and farm fami-

[1] *Farm Tenancy*, Report of the President's Committee, Washington, D.C., 1937.

lies living in poverty. Second, although in absolute terms a large number of farmers were assisted, the programs of these agencies were inadequate to the task confronting them. Third, the programs of these agencies were farm-production oriented; they sought to eliminate poverty by turning each low-production farm they touched into a productive, adequate-sized unit.

World War II. No new programs or policies were developed during the war to deal with rural poverty, but no other event in modern times has done so much to eliminate rural poverty as World War II. The demands for manpower by the military and war industries, as we have seen, sucked people out of rural areas and into nonfarm jobs during 1941–43. On a net basis, some 6.5 million people migrated from farms to urban areas during that three-year period. Of this total, about 3.8 million left farms in the South, where rural poverty was then and continues to be concentrated.

The war effort did two things: it created jobs, and it created the mechanism for informing farm people about those jobs, for moving them, and for retraining them. The dispossessed in farming — sharecroppers, low-production farmers, hired workers, and migrant workers — left the land by the millions and found more productive and more remunerative jobs in the city. A great war enabled these people to escape grinding poverty. For combating rural poverty, nothing like it ever happened before World War II or after it. World War II brought productive jobs, millions of them, and that is the basic need of the underemployed in rural areas.

The Ferment Following World War II. The years after World War II did not bring any new, novel, or enlarged programs to deal with farm or rural poverty. On the contrary, the Farmers Home Administration Act of 1946, which created the Farmers Home Administration in the place of the Farm Security Administration, retained the more conservative features of the old Farm Security programs, but prohibited ventures into collective or cooperative farming, eliminated farm labor camps, and spelled out more carefully than earlier legislation limitations over loan and operating policies. This was a period of consolidation in government programs that were designed to help low-income, low-production farmers.

But this was also the period when farm economists generally "discovered" the poverty problem in rural America. A task force in the old

Bureau of Agricultural Economics developed a "Conversion Program for the Cotton South" to deal with the interrelated problems of cotton and poverty in the South. Action was recommended along three lines in this conversion program: (1) Cotton would be priced at a level that would enable it to compete freely in foreign and domestic markets. (2) Government payments would be made to cushion the descent of cotton prices to a competitive level; and government payments, credit, and other assistance would be offered to help farm families convert from their existing patterns of operation. (3) Steps would be taken to develop off-farm employment opportunities for those persons underemployed in farming. Under this program, it was argued that at least a million and a half underemployed farm workers, croppers, and operators should be transferred into productive nonfarm farm jobs. The immediate result of this study and these recommendations was to get the Bureau of Agricultural Economics even more deeply into trouble with influential southern congressmen. But the study is indicative of the new thinking about poverty and underemployment in rural areas that was taking shape in that period: a conversion of the rural economy was called for involving a large-scale transfer of the underemployed in farming into more productive nonfarm jobs.

T. W. Schultz, in his influential book, *Agriculture in an Unstable Economy*, also examined the underemployment problem in agriculture To cope with this intractable problem he argued first as to what should not be done:

Do not provide incentives for the return of war workers and members of the armed forces to farms.

Do not under government sponsorship and through the use of government credit increase the number of small, "subsistence farms."

And most important, do not create institutional barriers to the movement of people off farms and into nonfarm employment.

Professor Schultz then argued positively:

Do expand nonfarm industries at a rate three times that of agriculture to avoid chronic underemployment in agriculture.

Do develop a *national outlook* to serve farm labor by supplying information with regard to labor needs and opportunities; such information should in turn be supplemented by a national employment service.

Do greatly increase public grants and aids to rural communities for education, medical services, nutrition, and housing.[2]

[2] McGraw-Hill Book Co., 1945, Chapter IX.

Policies and Programs: Too Little, Too Late

The emphasis in this analysis and in the recommendations is on non-farm jobs — the need to create them and to help rural people to acquire the skills to hold them.

In the late 1940's and early 1950's study after study inquired into the poverty problem in farming and rural areas. These studies probed in depth the characteristics of low-production farming and the people involved, the employment opportunities and requirements in rural areas, the many questions about labor mobility and barriers to mobility, and the problem of skills, training, and education in rural areas. The facts and relationships set forth in these many and varied studies did not add up to a national picture, but they did provide understanding about underemployment and poverty in rural areas where understanding had been nonexistent before.

In 1951 the Joint Committee on the Economic Report issued a pamphlet describing the extent of underemployment among rural families with recommendations for dealing with the problem.[3] This pamphlet put the rural underemployment problem in national perspective and dramatized the magnitude of the problem. It presented estimates showing that there were 2 million farm operator families and 1.5 million nonfarm families underemployed in rural areas in the late 1940's. If these 3.5 million rural families, together with 1.2 million underemployed wage workers whose main activity was farm work, had become fully employed, it would have been equivalent to adding 2.5 million full-time workers to the total labor force.

This study was followed in 1953 by a major study of low-production farms and farming in the United States. In the summary of that report the authors state that:

. . . On the basis of product added per worker, each worker on small-scale farms produced only about half as much as workers on small commercial farms, and only about a fourth as much as workers on large and medium size family farms within the same areas. . . .

Low-production commercial farms were considerably less efficient in use of resources than large and medium commercial farms. The larger farms used greater amounts of capital per farm and per worker, but they used less labor and less capital per unit of output. Apparently this was owing both to the better use of labor and capital items that are not fully divisible and to differences in *kinds* of capital. Limited capital on low-production farms apparently meant that less efficient kinds as well as

[3] *Underemployment of Rural Families*, Joint Committee on the Economic Report, Joint Committee Print, 82nd Congress, 1st Session, February 2, 1951.

lesser amounts of capital were used. In general, the larger farms in all areas studied were more up-to-date in adoption of recent technological innovations. Many more of these farms reported tractors and other kinds of mechanical equipment.

How to increase the productivity of families on low-production farms is a difficult problem. These farms are generally too small to use modern power and machinery effectively and economically. Although substantial gains can usually be made on existing acreages, it is commonly necessary to enlarge the farm as well as to reorganize it. Even if crop and livestock yields on small-scale farms were raised to the yields now found on medium and large farms, production per worker on small-scale farms would still be low — only about half that of workers on medium and large farms.[4]

From the many studies of underemployment and poverty in the post-World War II period several conclusions took firm shape. First, underemployment and the consequent poverty in rural areas constituted a hard-core problem that would not go away with the passage of time, or a good crop, or a prosperous year in the national economy. Second, rural underemployment was not voluntary; poor farm families did not stay on the land because they liked to hunt squirrels; they stayed there because they had no better alternative. Third, commodity programs providing price and income support had little meaning for low-production, low-income farmers because they produced so little for commercial sale. And fourth, a solution to the underemployment-poverty problem in rural America required specially designed programs to meet the needs of families and individuals for education, vocational training, capital, and nonfarm job opportunities.

The Eisenhower Period. In April 1955 President Eisenhower announced a Rural Development Program to combat underemployment and poverty in farming. The main features of this program were outlined in *Development of Agriculture's Human Resources,* which the President transmitted to the Congress.[5] The philosophy of this program was clearly stated in that report:

The approach to the problem of small farmers is here regarded as primarily educational and developmental. There appear to be some di-

[4] Jackson V. McElveen and K. L. Bachman, *Low-Production Farms,* Agricultural Information Bulletin No. 108, Bureau of Agricultural Economics, USDA, June 1953.

[5] *Development of Agriculture's Human Resources, A Report on Problems of Low-Income Farmers,* prepared for the Secretary of Agriculture, USDA, April 1955.

rect aids in the way of credit, improved opportunities for off-farm employment, and the like, which can be offered. But it is considered that whatever is done must be done within the American philosophy that each individual must make his own decisions and set his own goals. Government has responsibility in keeping open the channels of opportunity.[6]

It was recognized in the program recommended to Congress that the problem to be dealt with was a large and difficult one. The report went on to say:

There are nearly a thousand counties in the U.S. where more than one-half of the farmers are mainly dependent on the income from small, poorly paying farms. What they are up against, in innumerable cases, is lack of good land, lack of equipment, lack of credit facilities, and often lack of the management information and skill which might open other opportunities to them. In other cases part or full-time off-farm employment may be their best opportunity.[7]

Underemployment and poverty, under this program, were to be attacked in four ways: (1) by increasing the productivity of low-income, low-production farms; (2) by increasing the opportunities for part-time farming and nonfarm jobs; (3) by increasing the opportunities for education and vocational training; and (4) by achieving a fuller utilization of farm resources in defense production.

Under the plan of operation, the Rural Development Program was to be started in selected pilot counties or areas where local people would be urged to form rural development committees to outline and guide the program. These committees would be assisted by federal and state agencies in whatever ways such agencies were able. Under the program all agencies of the government that had activities at the local or county level were to be considered a part of the over-all Rural Development Program; coordinating responsibility was placed in the Extension Service of the Department of Agriculture.

The Rural Development Program included the following recommended lines of action to aid low-income and part-time farm families:

1. Extension and technical assistance should be made available to community committees to assist in analyzing problems, exploring production alternatives (farm and nonfarm) and developing action programs. Personnel should be added to aid families with limited opportunities through a specially adapted farm and home planning program.

[6] *Ibid.*, p. 1. [7] *Ibid.*, p. 2.

2. Research on more efficient farm production systems (adapted to low-production farms), availability of credit facilities, loaning practices, participation of farm families in improvement programs, and long-term demand and marketing problems should be intensified with respect to low-production farming and depressed rural areas.

3. Private and cooperative leaders should be encouraged to increase their loans to worthy small farmers, expand the amount of intermediate term credit, and gear repayment schedules more carefully to capacity. Government credit services also should be expanded.

4. A proposal for expanding the availability of nonfarm employment information was included in the original statement of the program. This recognized that continued out-migration from agriculture was probable and that it was necessary to find a way to more fully utilize underemployed human resources.

5. Industrialization in low-income areas should be increased through appropriate actions by state and local leaders, surveys of local labor-supply conditions and by making fuller use of the abundant forest products in some areas.

6. Vocational training should be made more useful by obtaining better information about needed rural nonfarm occupational skills, increasing emphasis on those skills, strengthening vocational guidance programs, and establishing several experimental vocational training programs in typical low-income areas.

7. More attention should be given to community and family health practices through educational programs and greater cooperation with health agencies.

To finance the Rural Development Program in its first year, the USDA asked Congress for $2.5 million in direct appropriations and for additional lending authority for the Farmers Home Administration. The Department of Labor asked for $900,000 to provide special employment aid. Congress granted the USDA slightly over $2 million to operate the program and gave it the increased lending authority, but the Department of Labor request was denied.

The accomplishments and achievements of the Rural Development Program of this period have been much debated. The annual reports of the Secretary of Agriculture on the Rural Development Program tell of much activity and much progress. In 1960 it was reported that 210 counties were participating in the program, that 18,000 new full-time or part-time jobs had been created in one year as the result of industrial growth and new business, and that 7,000 low-income, low-production farms had benefited from increased crop production in the previous year.[8] And it is a fact that the input of research resources on low-income farming increased significantly under the Rural Development Program, which in succeeding years has highlighted the dependence of rural people and rural areas on nonfarm development activities, the characteristics of low-production farming, and the failure of commodity price support programs to deal with the problems of low-income farmers.

But in 1960 Professor C. E. Bishop argued before the American Farm Economic Association that

The program has been so poorly organized and given such meager support as to appear that the nation is unconcerned over the welfare of its underemployed citizens. From the assistance given to date it appears as if the Federal and state agencies have told underemployed people in low-income areas (1) that a problem exists in those areas, (2) to determine what the problem is if they can, and (3) to work out a solution if they can. This is hardly to be considered a contribution to the solution of the problem by Federal and state agencies. . . .[9]

In my judgment the Rural Development Program never really moved out of the pilot stage. The federal government invested very little in the program in the way of additional funds; the operating budget was severely limited at all times, and funds for investment in new commercial enterprises and industries were nonexistent. The various agencies of the Department of Agriculture were expected to do rural development work over and above their regularly assigned missions. And with this little outside guidance and technical assistance, local people, poor people, were expected to develop their communities, increase their productivity, and thereby raise their incomes. In some instances creative and exciting development took place, but in general the Rural Development Program barely touched the hard-core underemployment-poverty problem in rural areas.

The Kennedy Period. The Rural Development Program was reorganized in 1961 under the Kennedy administration and given the name Rural Areas Development (RAD). The responsibility for leadership in this area of work, and for coordinating the efforts of the many agencies, was given to an Office of Rural Areas Development in the Department

[8] 5th Annual Report of the Secretary of Agriculture, *Rural Development Program*, USDA, September 1960.
[9] "The Rural Development Program and Underemployment in Agriculture," *Journal of Farm Economics*, December 1960, pp. 1205–1206.

of Agriculture.[10] In this program, as in the Rural Development Program under the Eisenhower administration, it was assumed and expected (and still was, as of January 1965) that local people would provide the leadership and initiative in the development process. The argument for this was that "local leadership has always determined whether a community grows or declines; only in rare instances has a community prospered in spite of itself." Again, as in the earlier program, the Extension Service was expected to provide assistance and leadership in organizing state, area, and county RAD committees and in conducting planning and educational work. And once again, as in the earlier program, the various agencies of the USDA were expected to provide technical assistance to the local RAD committees in addition to their regularly assigned missions.

The goals of the RAD program have been described by Assistant Secretary John A. Baker, under whom the program operates, as follows:

1. to preserve and improve the family farm pattern of American agriculture;

2. to increase the income of people living in rural America — per person and per family — and to eliminate the causes of underemployment;

3. to expand more rapidly job opportunities by stimulating investments in rural America in all the enterprises and services that make up a modern economy — factories, stores, recreational enterprises, crafts, and services of all kinds, and technically trained and other professional people;

4. to develop rapidly but in an orderly way a wide range of outdoor recreational opportunities on privately-owned and public lands — recreational opportunities to serve the needs of a growing population in the cities and towns and rural areas and to provide income and jobs for rural people;

5. to readjust land use, nationwide, to achieve a balance so that each acre and resource are used for purposes to which they are adapted and to meet national needs;

6. to provide appropriate services and adequate financial support for the protection, development, and management of our soil, water, forest, fish and wildlife, and open spaces;

[10] On February 26, 1965, the Office of Rural Areas Development was absorbed by a new agency — the Rural Community Development Service. The mission of this new Service is "to bring the services of all other agencies of the Federal Government into rural areas with increased effectives." Thus, the purpose and plan of operation of the new Service are very similar to those of the Office of Rural Areas Development. The new agency does have the added responsibility to expand the Department of Agriculture's efforts to help rural people make effective use of the new programs provided by the Economic Opportunities Act of 1964.

7. to improve existing rural community facilities and institutions and where needed to build new ones so that people in our rural areas are assured pure water supplies, first-rate schools and hospitals, adequate streets and roads, and other services that are standard in a modern community; and

8. to make continuous and systematic efforts to eliminate the many complex causes of rural poverty.

These aims and purposes cannot be faulted. If they were achieved, poverty would disappear from rural America. The problem begins, and to date has not ended, with the means for implementing the goals. The means have never come up to the goals.

The RAD program does not differ greatly in basic organization or in aims from the Rural Development Program that preceded it. It does not bring any significant increase in budget or resources to bear on the rural poverty problem. It depends on combining or directing the activities of existing agencies in ways that will help to eliminate rural poverty. It is thus not a program in any specific sense, but a mission that gives direction and identity to all USDA programs. RAD is really a planning and coordinating device to bring the existing programs of the USDA to bear on the low-production, underemployment, poverty problem in rural areas.

Fortunately for poor rural families, the total effort to combat poverty in the Kennedy period included more than RAD. Two other programs, the Area Redevelopment Administration and the Accelerated Public Works programs in the Department of Commerce — both with large appropriations, both with money to spend to create jobs — were established to fight unemployment and underemployment and hence poverty. These two programs working with and through RAD have given hope to local leadership and meaning to the local planning process in depressed rural areas by providing funds for needed and desirable development projects. In addition, the Manpower Development and Training Program, administered jointly by the Department of Labor and the Department of Health, Education, and Welfare, has complemented the above programs by providing vocational training service at the community level.

The Area Redevelopment Administration has three tools to assist depressed areas: (1) financial assistance — loans to support job-creating commercial and industrial enterprises, and grants and loans for public facilities; (2) technical assistance to bridge the knowledge gaps which impede economic progress; and (3) retraining programs to fit workers to new jobs. During fiscal 1962–63, 286 loans and grants were made or approved, amounting to $126 million, to finance in whole or part job-creating commercial and industrial enterprises and development projects.

The Accelerated Public Works Program has two principal purposes: (1) to provide immediate useful work for the unemployed in eligible areas; and (2) to help these areas become more conducive to industrial and commercial development through the improvement of their public facilities. The Congress appropriated $850 million in 1962 and 1963 to be used for these purposes. About $150 million of this total was allocated in the first year for direct use in projects of such agencies as the Forest Service and Soil Conservation Service in the USDA, the National Park Service and the bureaus of Indian Affairs and Reclamation and Land Management in the Interior Department, the Army Corps of Engineers, and the Bureau of Public Roads in the Commerce Department — all of which had projects on the shelf and ready to go, many of them in rural areas. It is expected that the whole program of Accelerated Public Works will provide 220,000 man years of employment during its first two and a half years of operation.

The two programs, Area Redevelopment and Accelerated Public Works, provide the fuel to create jobs and put the unemployed and the underemployed to work; they provide funds to support all or part of the building of water and sewer systems, roads, campsites, flood control facilities, hospitals, and commercial and industrial enterprises which contribute to the operating economy of the depressed areas and create jobs in the process. All of the employment provided under these programs is not located in rural areas, but a large part of it is. It is estimated that the total effort in stimulating economic growth in rural areas created between thirty and forty thousand new jobs in 1963–64.[11] Thus, for the first time since the end of World War II an over-all program came into being in 1962–63 which had the power to combat rural poverty with something more than words.

One more point needs to be made about the operation and administration of the Rural Areas Development effort in the USDA and the

[11] M. L. Upchurch, "Progress in Resolving the Problem of Rural Poverty," *Journal of Farm Economics*, May 1964, p. 435.

complementary Area Redevelopment and Accelerated Public Works programs of the Department of Commerce, under the Kennedy administration; they were in the hands of people sympathetic to their objectives — people who believed in using the government's power and purse to fight underemployment and poverty. Secretary Freeman, Assistant Secretary Baker, and other policy-making officials in the USDA believed strongly in such a development program. And they worked hard, first to create an educational, planning, and administrative mechanism to facilitate the development process locally and second to provide the money to implement plans at the local level.

In a speech before the National Advisory Committee on Rural Areas Development in 1964 Secretary Freeman made abundantly clear what the achievement of a parity of opportunity for rural people meant to him, and what the job ahead for the Rural Areas Development Program is.

It means making sure that a rural child, who often does not have as good a chance as a city child for a first-class education, gets an equal chance.

It means establishing economic opportunities in the countryside so that young people who do not want to migrate to the city can make a decent living in their home communities.

It means training and counseling for young people in rural areas so that, if they do migrate to the city, they can compete on equal terms for city jobs.

It means taking steps to see that the proportion of rural youth who go on to college is as high as the proportion of city youth.

It means finding means of providing credit to rural businessmen, insofar as the Government provides or insures credit, on equal terms with that available to urban businessmen.

It means enabling the family who wants to build a house in rural America to obtain mortgage funds on terms as favorable as those available in the cities and their suburbs.

It means bringing rural water supplies, and rural sanitation facilities, up to city standards.

It means establishing services for older people that are as good in small towns and rural communities as they are in larger cities.[12]

Perhaps the most important developments in the long war against poverty in general, and rural poverty in particular, during 1961–64 were first the rediscovery of the poverty problem by the top policy people in

[12] *The Job Ahead for Rural Areas Development*, USDA, November 24, 1964

Policies and Programs: Too Little, Too Late

the Kennedy-Johnson administration, and second the resolution to do something about the problem besides talking about it. Administration leaders discovered the squalor and tragedy of poverty; they learned about the hard-core, intractable characteristics of poverty, and they committed themselves to eradicate it. The Johnson administration, from the President down to the county worker, committed itself to banishing poverty from rural areas as well as urban areas.

ANTI-POVERTY PROGRAMS, NEW STYLE

The Economic Opportunity Act of 1964 signed by President Johnson in August 1964, created the institutional machinery and provided the budget for a widespread attack on rural and urban poverty. The act established in the Executive Office of the President an Office of Economic Opportunity, headed by a director reporting directly to the President. It also authorized a budget of $947 million to be spent on projects to combat poverty in fiscal 1964–65. This was obviously a high-priority effort: it was under the immediate direction of the President, and it has a budget large enough to mount a whole set of large-scale, anti-poverty programs.

The principal programs of this anti-poverty effort include (1) youth programs with a Job Corps, Work-Training Programs, and Work-Study Programs; (2) urban and rural community action programs to deal with human and social problems induced by poverty; (3) special programs to combat poverty in rural areas; (4) a program to assist small businesses; and (5) programs to assist heads of poverty-stricken families to get work experience and vocational training. In sum, this is a major human resource development and rehabilitation effort.

These programs do not supersede or substitute for such existing programs as Rural Areas Development in the USDA, or the Area Redevelopment and Accelerated Public Works programs in the Department of Commerce, or the Manpower Development and Training programs in the Department of Labor. The programs established under the Economic Opportunity Act of 1964 are in addition to the numerous federal programs already in operation in 1964, filling gaps in the arsenal of anti-poverty programs and providing a coordinating responsibility for all anti-poverty programs in the office of the President.

Clearly the new aspect of the Economic Opportunity Act of 1964 is its emphasis on youth programs, and the most concrete aspect of the act is

207

the Job Corps for young men and women. It is predicted that 40,000 young men and women will be enrolled in these camps the first year, and 100,000 the second year. Camps will be located in both rural and urban areas. Corpsmen stationed in rural camps will do needed conservation work on the nation's forests, parks, and natural resources. They will learn skills in surveying, weed and pest control, carpentry, equipment operation and maintenance, cooking, and typing. Young men and women at urban camps will learn to be office-machine operators, shipping, accounting, and file clerks, data-processing machine operators, sales clerks, cooks, machine tool operators, appliance and automotive repairmen, and so on.

The Work-Training Programs and Work-Study Programs are somewhat more vague with respect to purpose and mode of operation. But the budget for all these youth programs is not vague; it is established at $412 million for the first year, or just about half of the total budget for programs under the Economic Opportunity Act.

In the long run this emphasis on training young men and women from poor families in modern skills and occupations, and providing a form of interim employment, may turn out to be the most important anti-poverty program ever devised. Giving economically underprivileged young men and women, ages sixteen to twenty-one, the opportunity to learn a modern trade or train for a productive occupation will help them to break out of the vicious circle of poverty. With this kind of assistance the child raised in poverty, poorly educated and trained, is not chained to poverty throughout his lifetime. And as the children of poor families are trained and placed in productive jobs, poverty generally will gradually disappear.

The budget of $412 million, on an annual basis, is not sufficiently large to support a sustained training program for all the young men and women in need of training, but it is probably as large a sum as can be used effectively the first year or two. After that it will be necessary to expand and regularize these youth training programs if poverty is to be banished in the United States.

How effective the urban and rural community action programs will be remains to be seen. One major purpose of the community action programs is to provide "instruction for individuals who have attained age eighteen and whose inability to read and write the English language constitutes a substantial impairment of their ability to get or retain employment." [13] This particular adult educational program could contribute importantly to the total effort to eradicate poverty, depending, of course, upon the number of illiterate adults reached and what such an educational program leads to in the way of job opportunities.

The range of permissible community activities under this section of the act is very wide, and where the problems are clear-cut or the community is creative in devising programs of action, much good may result. It is also possible, though, that the act's vagueness in setting forth the purposes of community programs may lead to inaction or ill-advised actions. Only time will tell how ready local communities are to initiate programs of direct action to improve and develop the human resource.

One aspect of this section of the act is, however, disappointing. The Office of Economic Opportunity is specifically prohibited from making a grant or a contract of assistance to elementary or secondary education in any school or school system; that is, no funds from this program may be used to improve educational systems in depressed areas suffering from low-quality educational services and inadequate physical facilities.

The special programs of the Economic Opportunity Act to combat poverty in rural areas are both hopeful and disquieting. It is hopeful to see rural poverty, so long ignored, singled out for special attention. It is also hopeful that loans may be made to low-income, low-production farmers to finance nonagricultural enterprises. But it is disquieting to see that the principal mechanism for combating poverty in rural areas remains, under this act, the making of small loans to low-production farmers to enable them to acquire a little more land or pay for equipment, livestock, or other production supplies.

The principal means of attack on rural poverty is once again small loans (up to $2,500 per farmer) to tie the farmer closer to the land or to tide him over for another year or two, when what is needed above all in rural areas are mechanisms to assist low-production, low-income farmers to shift out of farming and into more productive nonfarm enterprises. And no means are provided under the special programs for rural areas for assisting in the difficult and painful human transfer process, although of course the youth programs in another section of the act work in this direction.

[13] Public Law 88-452, 88th Congress, 2nd Session, August 20, 1964, p. 13.

Policies and Programs: Too Little, Too Late

Probably the greatest weakness in the Economic Opportunity Act of 1964 is the absence of programs or activities designed to create new jobs. Almost all of the programs and activities under the act are aimed at education, vocational training, human rehabilitation, job counseling, and the correction of community social problems. The programs under this act concentrate on human development. This is fine, and desirable as far as it goes, but not if the newly trained young men and women and rehabilitated adults cannot find productive jobs at the end of their training or rehabilitation.

As matters stood in 1964–65, the new anti-poverty programs depended upon the normal expansion of the private economy plus the workings of the Area Redevelopment and Accelerated Public Works programs to provide the required new jobs. In the past these sources of job creation have made only a small dent in the hard-core poverty problem. It is possible that training and rehabilitation will convert many unemployable individuals into employable ones, and that the existing level of private and public efforts at economic expansion and job creation will absorb in productive employment the trained and rehabilitated workers from the poverty sector; it is possible, but not probable.

Some four million new jobs are needed within the next few years to fully employ those men and women now underemployed and unemployed in rural America. Probably as many or more new jobs are required to fully employ those persons now unemployed and underemployed in urban areas. It will take a prodigious effort on the part of the private economy to absorb the normal growth in the labor force and create eight to ten million additional new jobs and thereby wipe out underemployment and poverty in America. The funds available for investment in new enterprises and industries by the Area Redevelopment Administration could not begin to create a million new jobs let alone ten million.

The programs envisioned under the Economic Opportunity Act of 1964 take another important step toward eradicating both rural and urban poverty. They recognized the need for, and did something about, training young men and women and rehabilitating adults from poor families and poverty areas. But these programs do not take the next step; they do not undertake the investment necessary to create the jobs that would ensure the employment of the trained and rehabilitated people from poverty backgrounds. The war on poverty thus goes on, but victory is not assured. The Economic Opportunity Act does not launch the programs required to create the new jobs that must be brought into existence if poverty is to be banished from America.

PAST AND PRESENT POLICIES REAPPRAISED

The programs of the 1930's to combat underemployment and poverty in rural America were imaginative, audacious, and they had muscle; they had money to spend in the war against poverty. They were too narrowly oriented in that they conceived the solution to rural poverty in terms of rehabilitating farmers — turning low-production farmers into high-production farmers, and they lacked the funds to fully cope with the size and the persistence of the problem. But they were more effective programs in conception and financing than anything that came before them, or after them for many years.

From the end of World War II through 1960 efforts to fight rural underemployment and poverty were severely limited in financial support and in their scope and orientation. The financial resources available to assist the rural poor came essentially from the Farmers Home Administration and the Rural Electrification Administration. No other agencies in the USDA that were concerned with the rural poverty problem had funds to loan or grant.

The Rural Development Program came along in 1955, but it had no funds to finance development efforts and commercial and industrial enterprises. It was a bootstrap operation: with planning guidance and technical assistance, depressed communities were expected to develop themselves. Relative to the underemployment involved and the number of new jobs needed, the program's funds for financing and supporting economic development in depressed rural areas were pitifully small. It was a classic case of too few resources, too late.

But just as important as the limited financial support was the limited vision of spokesmen for farmers and of administrators and policy leaders in the USDA in looking for solutions to poverty problems in rural America. Except for the scholars whose work we have mentioned, farm spokesmen and farm leaders in this period were seeking the solution to the rural poverty problem in farming itself. The goal of farm spokesmen was, and to an important extent still is, to turn each low-production farm into an adequate-sized, productive unit. The fact that the commercial farm economy was running a surplus of 6 to 9 per cent each year in the 1950's, and that the product of each additional productive farm would aggravate this surplus condition, is irrelevant in this view. The fact that underemployed farm people tumble out of farming whenever productive nonfarm job opportunities are made available to them is ignored in this view. And the fact that the land and other productive resources of several to a dozen low-production farms must be combined to make one productive farm, and that the displaced farmers must find new jobs somewhere, is not discussed in this view.

The facts are clear: the underemployment-poverty problem in rural America cannot be solved in terms of farming itself; the surplus underemployed labor in rural areas must find productive jobs outside farming. Not more than one boy out of every twelve to fifteen raised on a farm can expect to become the operator of a productive, adequate-sized farm, as of the middle 1960's. And of the 1.6 million low-production, low-income farm families in 1960, no more than 200,000 to 300,000 could become operators of adequate-sized farms, even if grants and loans were available to permit them to try. The land base is not available at present price-cost relations to establish 1.6 million adequate-sized units, and the market could not take the product if such a number of productive units did come into being. These are the facts of the situation.

But regardless of these facts, the view has prevailed that the underemployment-poverty problem in rural America could be solved by improved and expanded farming operations, and that view still prevails among many farm spokesmen and leaders. Programs to combat rural underemployment and poverty in the late 1940's and the 1950's looked inward to farming as a solution rather than outward to nonfarm opportunities. While that remained the case there could be no solution to the rural underemployment-poverty problem, even if the investment and programs funds had been there.

Basically a policy for coping with the problem of low-production farming, underemployment, and rural poverty has not emerged that is comparable to the production policies and the price and income support policy for commercial farming. Perhaps the strong orientation of the USDA toward farm production made impossible the development of a policy focusing on nonfarm enterprise and activities in rural areas. In any event, such a policy has not developed. Programs in the USDA for dealing with low-production farming, underemployment, and poverty in rural areas have, over the years, simply borrowed from the on-going programs designed for the commercial sector.

But in the Kennedy years the emphasis and content of programs dealing with rural poverty changed somewhat. As we have observed, investment funds from the Area Redevelopment and the Accelerated Public Works programs began to flow into depressed areas and to create jobs. Policy leaders in the USDA from Secretary Freeman down recognized that rural underemployment could not be eliminated through the conversion of each low-production farm into a productive, adequate-sized unit. That is why Secretary Freeman hammered away at establishing private recreational enterprises in low-production areas — fishing ponds and ski lifts, for example — at the need for improved nonfarm vocational training and education, and at the need for the location of new industries in rural areas. He and his lieutenants knew that the rural poverty problem would only be solved by a flood of new nonfarm jobs. And because they believed, further, that it is preferable to take new industries and new jobs to rural areas and thereby avoid the problem of geographic mobility, they tried to bring about this flood of nonfarm job opportunities in rural areas.

It should be recognized, however, that the policy of developing non-farm job opportunities in rural areas is a matter of taste. It is not essential that job opportunities for rural people be created *in* rural areas. The automobile and modern roads bring most rural people within the reach of urban jobs. The rural underemployed will be sucked out of rural areas to the jobs, if the jobs are available.

In sum, there have been gains in 1961–64 in the formulation of programs to combat rural poverty effectively. But those gains have been modest. The number of new jobs required in the early 1960's to fully employ the rural underemployed was estimated at about four million. But the total number of new jobs created in rural areas by the anti-poverty effort in 1963–64 was thirty to forty thousand, directly, and possibly sixty to eighty thousand jobs if the full multiplier effects of the program's spending are taken into consideration. It is possible to reach the total of four million jobs by adding sixty to eighty thousand new jobs a year, but it would take a long, long time. Rural areas need a flood of new jobs to eradicate poverty; the programs of the early 1960's provided a trickle.

With regard to the need to make the anti-poverty programs for rural

America look outward rather than inward, there is no problem in the office of the Secretary of Agriculture; Secretary Freeman and his policy staff know that the hope of depressed rural areas rests upon new nonfarm enterprises and the productive, remunerative jobs that such enterprises provide. But many farm spokesmen in 1964, and many who man the old-line agencies in the USDA, considered it a sin to move a man out of farming, even if he was starving at it. This means that it has been and will continue to be difficult to work with these farm leaders outside the USDA and old-line administrators inside the USDA to achieve programs whose objective is creating nonfarm jobs and training farm operators, hired workers, and farm youth to fill them. The natural tendency within the USDA and among farm spokesmen and leaders, a tendency that is very strong, is to promote loan programs that rehabilitate farmers as farmers by modestly enlarging their farm enterprise, meanwhile ignoring nonfarm vocational training programs and the development of such nonfarm enterprises as recreation on the land and industrial enterprises in centers of growth adjacent to depressed rural areas.

The conclusion must then be that the national effort to fight rural poverty began to move in an effective way in 1961–64. But it only began. To wipe out rural poverty will require an investment of many billions, not the $300 to $400 million which has been realized. And the grip of agricultural fundamentalism on the anti-poverty programs must be broken.

Now it must be asked — Will the program under the Economic Opportunity Act of 1964, President Johnsons anti-poverty program, continue to combat the hard-core poverty problem in an effective manner? As of January 1965 it appeared that the Johnson administration anti-poverty program for rural areas would continue to make headway on the problem. It recognized and emphasized the need for nonfarm vocational training for rural youth, and it did something about that need. And it provided funds for local communities to begin to take corrective action on some of their more critical social problems arising out of poverty. But it is silent on that all-important issue of job creation and job availability. It lacks the budget, it lacks the investment funds, to mount an all-out attack on poverty.

Finally, the special programs to combat poverty in rural areas under the 1964 act fail to come to grips with the great problem of rural areas, the creation of productive *nonfarm* job opportunities as an alternative to low-production farming. True, provision is made under the act for loans to finance nonfarm enterprises on farms — recreational enterprises, for example. But no *special* program is advanced to create nonfarm job opportunities and assist underemployed rural people to realize those opportunities. The special programs are primarily aimed at assisting low-production farmers to become slightly larger farmers. Agricultural fundamentalism still maintained a firm hold on the anti-poverty programs for rural areas in 1964–65.

13

The City Man and the Problem of Poverty

THERE are over fifteen million people living in poverty in rural areas. Rural nonfarm families living in poverty tend to be scattered across the nation, but rural farm families living in poverty tend to be concentrated in the South. The heads of these families are poorly educated, in poor health, and past middle age, and a large proportion of them are unemployable except at the most unskilled manual labor. The children of these families tend also to be poorly educated and poorly trained, and therefore not prepared to become effective citizens in a democracy and productive workers in a modern economy.

Rural poverty has become a hard-core phenomenon. Poverty begets poverty in a vicious circle. To date, policies and programs designed to cope with this social cancer have been too little, too late. They assist a family here and there, and provide a few new jobs here and there, but they have not come to grips with the hard-core poverty problem — with the millions of men and women who grow up, marry, raise more children, and die in poverty. These millions live out an existence contributing little or nothing to the daily operation of society and the economy, and exert a positive drag on the development of society and the expansion of the economy.

The issue confronting society, and the city man in particular, since he is a member of the dominant group in society, is whether we shall accept the social cancer of chronic poverty in urban and rural areas and live with it, or take corrective action to get rid of it. In one sense the answer has already been given. President Johnson and his administration are committed to banishing poverty from the United States. And an important step in the fulfillment of that commitment has been made, the passage of the Economic Opportunity Act of 1964.

But as we have already observed, the programs resulting from that act alone are not going to solve the problem. Much more will need to be done, first in improving educational services in poverty areas, and second in developing public projects and commercial enterprises that create jobs — millions of jobs. To take these additional corrective actions, which will involve large expenditures of public funds, society as a whole must come to believe in and support them.

In the long run there can be no question of society's answer. It will be "banish poverty from the United States." It must be. A society cannot be great and an economy effective where 20 per cent of the population acts as a drag on the national community. The only real question, then, is time. That being true, let this book stand as plea for getting on with the job now! If the requisite corrective actions are taken by 1970, chronic hard-core poverty can be banished from America in a generation.

Once there is the will to eradicate chronic poverty both urban and rural, the solution is straightforward: *education and jobs, jobs and education, and more education and jobs.* The most desirable means of improving the quality of education and training for rural youth with poverty backgrounds, and assuring their regular participation in formal education at a satisfactory level, may be open to debate. And the most effective way of supporting economic growth and job-creating projects which make available employment opportunities for the underemployed of rural areas may also be open to debate.

No blueprint is in existence which describes the best, the most effective, way of educating and training the children of *every* poor family, rehabilitating *all* the heads of poor families, and creating *all* the jobs required to eliminate unemployment and underemployment in urban and rural areas. There are probably many specific institutional approaches to the social goal of no more poverty. And as in most social actions, conflicts of interest will obviously arise among specific social goals.

But it is also clear that we as a nation cannot talk or wish our way to a solution to this problem. The programs leading to a solution must have the power to educate millions of rural children and young men and women on a par with their urban counterparts, to rehabilitate the heads of some 4.5 million rural families, and to provide some 4 million new productive jobs to fully employ the underemployed in rural areas.[1] This is the magnitude of the problem, and anti-poverty efforts that fall short of these magnitudes are not going to eradicate rural poverty.

FIRST REQUIREMENT: EDUCATION AND TRAINING

Improvement in the quality and quantity of education and training in rural areas with special reference to the needs of the poor must be made at three levels: in formal, general education in primary and secondary schools; in vocational training for young men and women during and after high school; and in vocational and job training for adults.

It is tempting to argue that the need for vocational training for young men and women is the greatest, because of the present almost total lack of nonfarm vocational training in rural areas, and because this is the strategic point at which to break the circle of poverty. But is vocational training more important than general education aimed at developing the whole man? Probably not in a modern literate democratic society. And is vocational training for young men and women more important than comparable training for the head of a family who is unemployed or underemployed? In terms of human decency the answer once again is probably not. Improved services and increased facilities are needed at all three levels, and the need is great in each case.

Concerning the quality of education in primary and secondary schools in rural areas the following data are instructive. The average salary of teachers in counties where the population was 85 per cent rural, with 50 per cent living on farms, in the school year 1955–56 was $2,882; in comparison, the average salary of teachers in urban areas with a population of 25,000 or more was $5,068. It may be argued with logic that the training offered by schools is affected by the quality of the instructional staff, and that the good teachers tend to go where the salaries are good.

Another indicator of the quality of educational service is the average current expenditure per pupil. In 1955–56 in counties that were 85 per cent rural that expenditure was $200, but in school systems in urban areas with a population of 25,000 or more it was $321. The quality of rural education is low, and the situation is made worse by the fact that

[1] A good discussion of rural poverty and ways and means of breaking the cycle is to be found in C. E. Bishop, *Agriculture and Economic Development*, Virginia Polytechnic Institute, Agricultural Experiment Station Bulletin No. 556, July 1964.

218

The City Man and the Problem of Poverty

drop-out rates are much higher in rural than in urban areas. For example, in 1960, only 32 per cent of rural farm white individuals and 7 per cent of rural farm nonwhite individuals had finished four years of high school, whereas 46 per cent of urban white individuals and 25 per cent of urban nonwhite had completed four years of high school.

It is further the case that most rural counties in the nation tend to be the poorest counties on an average per capita basis. These rural counties can least afford high-quality school systems, and in fact they do not afford them. To improve the quality and quantity of educational service in rural areas, some form of federal aid to education seems absolutely necessary. This is not the place to prescribe a formula, but it is the place to point out to the city man that if urban areas are to escape a constant inflow of poorly educated young men and women, then the wealthier urban areas must help to provide a parity of educational services for rural areas.

The need to help depressed rural areas provide a parity of general education service through federal aid could be argued on humanitarian grounds. But it will not be. It will be argued here in terms of enlightened self-interest. If urban areas want an educated labor supply, want to avoid adding young adult delinquents to their own slums, and want an educated, informed rural electorate, then the city man has a vital stake in the improvement of educational services in rural areas.

The critical barrier to the movement of young men and women from an underemployed condition in rural areas to an employed condition in urban areas is their lack of training for nonfarm jobs. There is almost no place in rural areas to learn a nonfarm skill, trade, or vocation. The typical rural high school provides vocational-agricultural training, but little else. Junior colleges that emphasize vocational training are almost nonexistent in rural areas. And who ever heard of a rural trade school?

A place to learn a nonfarm trade or vocation has been the missing link in the farm-to-city migration process for a hundred years. The land-grant university has provided that link at the university level, but no such link has ever been forged at the trade or vocational level. Farm leaders have refused to consider this need, and nonfarm educators have failed to come forward with a vocational training institution to help bridge the farm-to-city gap. With the increased stress on vocational training and skills in the modern commercial and industrial world this lack-of-training barrier has become increasingly formidable.

The three youth programs — Job Corps, Work-Training Program, and Work-Study Program — under the Economic Opportunity Act of 1964 should help to bridge the training gap. It is possible that effective and regularized training programs for both rural and urban young men and women will be developed under the Community Action title of the same act. If a system of vocational training schools could be set up in depressed and poverty areas under the Community Action Programs, a very important battle in the war on poverty would be won. But the vagueness of the objectives under the Community Action Programs title and the complete reliance on local initiative suggest that the development of vocational training schools in poverty areas, particularly rural poverty areas, is likely to be uneven and inadequate.

What might be helpful in meeting the vocational training needs of young men and women with low-income and poverty backgrounds would be the creation of a Presidential Commission to study the whole problem and recommend a course of action to deal with it. Such a commission would dramatize the need for vocational training and contribute to the development of a systematic, nationwide plan of action. A vocational training plan or school here and there helps here and there, but such sporadic actions do not add up to an effective anti-poverty program.

What is needed is a national plan that blankets all poverty areas, urban and rural, covering high schools, junior colleges, and trade schools, which makes vocational training available to every young man and woman who wants it. This is a big order. But it is what is needed. To plan for or consider less is to be willing to live with chronic poverty.

Finally, ways must be found to rehabilitate — to train in needed non-farm occupational skills and to support during the process — underemployed adults in depressed rural areas. Training centers must be set up, vocational training courses organized, counseling service provided, and support for the adult, and usually for his family too, given during the training period. If local leadership is forthcoming, the Community Action Programs under the Economic Opportunity Act should provide an ideal vehicle for making available adult rehabilitation services.

The tragedy of poorly educated, underemployed, poverty-stricken adults and their families is clearly visible in local communities; assuming that the youth programs break the circle of poverty, the training of adults is a one-shot business; and the nature and size of the rehabili-

tation problem vary from community to community. These characteristics of the adult rehabilitation problem make it amenable to corrective
action under the Community Action Programs.

Perhaps more guidance will have to be given local communities by
the Office of Economic Opportunity in rehabilitating adults than is implied in the act, if that rehabilitation is to be effective and general. This
is particularly true in rural areas where community organization is
usually weak and knowledge of nonfarm vocational training is scarce
or nonexistent. But the instrumentality is there in the Community Action Programs of the Economic Opportunity Act of 1964 for dealing
immediately and constructively with the difficult problem of rehabilitating both urban and rural adults living in poverty.

The total education and training task outlined here is a large one.
Children, young men and women, and adults in poverty conditions
must receive education and training on a par with the rest of society.
This means more effective support of primary and secondary education
in low-income rural areas and of special programs that reach and meet
the needs of young men and women and adults. This is the required
first step toward a complete victory over poverty.

SECOND REQUIREMENT: JOB OPPORTUNITIES

The education and training of young people and the rehabilitation of
adults must lead to productive and remunerative jobs; if it does not we
must expect delinquency, crime, and extremist outbursts. The unedu-
cated and the poorly trained may be content to live and die in priva-
tion and squalor, but educated and trained men are more inclined to
turn to direct action, lawful or unlawful, to break out of poverty. Whereas job opportunities are desirable to assist the ignorant and poverty-
stricken, job opportunities are a critical necessity in an educated,
trained, and aspiring society.

No one can say with certainty whether the present and expected private and public development activities will be sufficient to provide the
jobs required to fully employ the unemployed and the underemployed
from poverty backgrounds when they are adequately educated and
trained. It is possible that the developing economy, without additional
special measures, can generate eight to ten million more jobs over and
above the natural growth in the labor force and provide employment to

all those unemployed and underemployed living in poverty, who, we assume, will be trained in the next few years.

It is possible, but again it seems improbable. The performance of the national economy since the end of World War II suggests that special measures will be required to give employment to the newly trained and rehabilitated. The development of automated production processes raises doubts about the ability of the economy to provide work — at least in the conventional private enterprise sector — for everyone who seeks it. Further, modern investment does not always create jobs: increasingly it eliminates them by substituting capital for labor. Special employment measures, outside the market-oriented economy, may therefore need to be undertaken to generate the jobs necessary to fully employ those people now unemployed and underemployed and to absorb the natural increase in the labor force. This means more extensive investment in public works and building construction, and more employment in public services, such as education, public health, and supervised recreational activities.

An opulent society must provide the kinds of goods and services that an opulent society demands and requires if it is to remove pockets of unemployment, underemployment, and poverty. This is the resource-use issue, and the human employment issue, confronting Americans in the 1960's when they talk about eradicating pockets of poverty.

Many job-creating measures should be considered by those directly responsible for eradicating unemployment, underemployment, and poverty. To make perfectly clear the direction of public actions needed to fully employ those who are currently unemployed and underemployed, both urban and rural, some of these measures will be outlined here. But a complete blueprint of a program of action to guarantee sufficient jobs will not be presented. A full treatment of the specifics of such a program belongs in a technical discussion of employment policy.

Acceptance of the following policy position is critical, however. First, the federal government, either by a proclamation from the administration or by congressional action, must commit itself to taking whatever steps are necessary to fully employ the trained and rehabilitated from poverty areas. Second, such actions must be implemented in or adapted to rural areas themselves, so that pockets of underemployment and poverty do not linger there.

Many actions could stimulate investment in or near low-income rural

The City Man and the Problem of Poverty

areas and thus create jobs — first at the construction stage and later at the production or operating stage. The loan and grant authority of the Area Redevelopment Administration could be doubled or quadrupled, thus increasing the volume of investments in public and private rural development projects. Federal aid to primary and secondary educational systems, including aid for improved facilities, would first increase construction in rural areas, and later increase employment in education itself. An aggressive rural housing program, with adequate funds, would expand construction and provide badly needed improved housing in rural areas. The Accelerated Public Works Program could be doubled or quadrupled and made permanent to provide employment and to protect and develop our natural and public resources. A new community facilities and service program, adequately funded, should be set in motion to build needed community facilities — swimming pools, playgrounds and parks, libraries, museums, and community centers — and then employ the trained personnel to operate them.

All the above activities require increased public expenditures and increased local investment, both public and private. But this is how jobs are created. It takes a minimum investment of $5,000 to create one job in most industries. And since it was estimated that some four million new jobs were needed to fully employ the rural underemployed in the early 1960's, a total investment of $20 billion must be made by some persons, firms, or agencies somewhere if four million new jobs are to be created.

All this total investment need not come from public sources. Perhaps half of it could come from private sources, if the public expenditure share is actually made. The public investment may thus be no larger than $10 billion, but it is not likely to be less, if rural poverty is to be eradicated.

It should further be noted that job-creating investment funds are conspicuous by their absence in the Economic Opportunity Act of 1964. That act concentrated on human development; the task of creating jobs was left to someone else or some other instrumentality. The estimate of needed public investment of $10 billion or more is, for all practical purposes, over and above the present anti-poverty effort.

If poverty is to be banished from America, a really large-scale effort is called for. Much talk and few resources will not excise the hard-core cancer of poverty. We know from the record of the past that a major effort, with the investment of billions of dollars to create a flood of jobs, is required. Either we make those expenditures or we live with rural poverty.

Even if the above general approaches — education and employment — were vigorously pursued, it would be a decade or two before rural poverty disappeared. Further, certain aspects of rural poverty are unique, requiring special consideration and treatment. First, there are about 2.7 million poor rural families headed by someone too old and too poorly educated to learn a new skill or trade, and too old and in too poor health to move physically and start anew in the world. These are the boxed-in families in rural America.

The most humane and economical assistance for such families is assistance in place. Public welfare assistance for the sick and handicapped and unskilled manual labor in public works projects in their local communities are the practical answers to the needs of most of these families. This should be done because it is the decent, dignified way to treat a generation that is already lost.

Second, the commercial farm economy does not have room for all the 1.6 million low-production, poverty farms and farm families if each were to be made into an adequate-sized productive farm unit. In fact, there is space for relatively few adequate-sized units in the place of the 1.6 million low-production units. But there is a place for possibly 200,000 to 300,000 rehabilitated, adequate-sized units. Thus, there is need for a program that has the capacity to convert 200,000 to 300,000 of the low-production, low-income units into productive commercial farms.

Such a program would not involve making a loan of $2,500 or less, as is authorized under the Economic Opportunity Act of 1964, to a low-production farmer; in the usual case a loan of such a size would only prolong the agony of living in poverty on a farm. The typical low-production farmer is more likely to need $25,000 to acquire the resources necessary to develop an adequate-sized unit. In sum, there is a need for a rehabilitation program for *some* low-income farmers that includes (1) the development of a farm plan for an adequate-sized production unit, (2) sufficient credit to enable the farmer involved to build up an adequate-sized unit, and (3) management supervision to help him operate profitably.

A program of farmer rehabilitation can be good and effective if properly conceived, bad and ineffective if improperly conceived. An inadequate loan program designed to give the low-production farmer a little credit help really hurts him; it serves to hold him in low-production farming — to hold him in poverty. But a farm rehabilitation program with a vision of adequate-sized units, credit to bring such units into being, and management assistance at key decision points would be a blessing to farmers and to the rural community. It is the latter approach that is needed, rather than the fundamentalist approach which offers a little help to every farmer and economic salvation to none.

It would be possible to dwell at length on the social services in rural areas that are inadequate: employment counseling and information, medical and nursing services, and community and recreational facilities, to name but a few. Certainly it would not be amiss to develop or expand federal programs in each of these areas; in fact the development and expansion of such programs may be the way to bring full employment to rural areas. But the purpose of this chapter is to outline the corrective actions needed to eradicate rural poverty, not to enumerate all the social ills of rural communities. And I believe that the approaches discussed above, if pursued in adequate scope and with vigor, would eradicate hard-core chronic poverty within a decade or two. If this were the case, the many social and economic ills that are the by-products of poverty would also disappear within a decade or two.

A FINAL COMMENT

Poverty is a major social evil in modern America, and rural poverty is a particularly tough and tenacious problem. But rural poverty can be beaten if the will is there. We know the basic solutions to the problem. They are education to raise the capabilities and aspirations of men and women living in poverty and productive employment to provide self-respect and income.

The answer to the problem, as we said, is education and jobs, jobs and education, and more education and jobs. But the answer is not cheap and easy. If it were, it would have been provided long ago,

The City Man and the Problem of Poverty

because the basic elements of the solution have long been known. High public, or social, costs have barred the way to the solution. The problem confronting the average city man is thus the following one: Does he want to live alongside the evil of poverty and pay for it in crime, delinquency, and mob action, or does he want to excise the evil now and pay the bill now in increased public expenditures? The answer is for the city man to make with regard to both urban and rural poverty because he dominates the modern political scene. But one thing is certain: the evil of poverty will not go away of itself; it has become a self-generating cancerous sore in opulent America.

APPENDIX

Appendix Table 1. Average Net Income of Farm Operator Families, by Major Economic Classes, U.S., 1949

Economic Class	Number of Farms		Percentage of Total Farm Products Sold	Average Net Income			
	Total	Percentage of Total		Net Farm Cash	Off-Farm Cash	Total Cash	Total Including Nonmoney (Farm Food and Housing)
Full-Time Farms							
Annual sales							
$20,000 and over	155,000	2.7%	31.5%	$11,316	$1,613	$12,929	$13,994
$10,000–$19,999	342,000	6.0	18.7	5,968	864	6,832	7,601
$5,000–$9,999	739,000	12.9	22.4	3,342	764	4,106	4,956
$2,500–$4,999	944,000	16.5	14.8	1,829	868	2,697	3,453
$50–$2,499	1,185,000	20.7	5.9	765	479	1,244	1,850
Other Farms							
Part-time	1,585,000	27.7	4.2	428	1,917	2,345	2,906
Part-retirement and abnormal	772,000	13.5	2.5	525	857	1,382	1,939
All farms	5,722,000	100.0%	100.0%	$1,744	$1,083	$2,827	$3,492

Source: Economic Research Service, USDA.

Appendix Table 2. Average Net Income of Farm Operator Families, by Major Economic Classes, U.S., 1963

| Economic Class | Number of Farms | | Percentage of Total Farm Products Sold | Average Net Income | | | |
	Total	Percentage of Total		Net Farm Cash	Off-Farm Cash	Total Cash	Total Including Nonmoney (Farm Food and Housing)
Full-Time Farms							
Annual sales							
$20,000 and over	384,000	10.7%	54.5%	$8,792	$2,419	$11,211	$12,599
$10,000–$19,999	594,000	16.6	23.6	5,173	1,589	6,762	7,796
$5,000–$9,999	609,000	17.0	12.6	2,898	1,811	4,709	5,542
$2,500–$4,999	463,000	13.0	4.8	1,605	2,104	3,709	4,441
$50–$2,499	202,000	5.7	.8	757	520	1,277	1,926
Other Farms							
Part-time	903,000	25.3	2.3	189	4,380	4,569	5,299
Part-retirement and abnormal ...	418,000	11.7	1.4	266	1,880	2,146	2,967
All farms	3,573,000	100.0%	100.0%	$2,629	$2,462	$5,091	$5,965

Source: Economic Research Service, USDA.

Appendix Table 3. Average Net Income of Farm Operator Families, by Major Economic Classes, U.S., Projected 1970

| Economic Class | Number of Farms | | Percentage of Total Farm Products Sold | Average Net Income | | | |
	Total	Percentage of Total		Net Farm Cash	Off-Farm Cash	Total Cash	Total Including Nonmoney (Farm Food and Housing)
Full-Time Farms							
Annual sales							
$20,000 and over	522,000	18.3%	67.3%	$9,891	$3,023	$12,914	$14,303
$10,000–$19,999	529,000	18.4	19.5	5,616	2,000	7,616	8,650
$5,000–$9,999	450,000	15.7	8.7	3,191	2,278	5,469	6,302
$2,500–$4,999	117,000	4.1	1.1	1,726	2,641	4,367	5,103
$50–$2,499	50,000	1.7	.2	820	660	1,480	2,140
Other Farms							
Part-time	792,000	27.6	1.9	210	5,508	5,718	6,448
Part-retirement and abnormal	408,000	14.2	1.3	297	2,363	2,660	3,483
All farms	2,868,000	100.0%	100.0%	$3,522	$3,253	$6,775	$7,709

Source: Economic Research Service, USDA.

Appendix Table 4. U.S. Agricultural Exports and Imports Compared with Cash Receipts from Farm Marketings, in Millions of Dollars, 1910–64

Year	Exports	Imports Supplementary	Imports Complementary	Cash Receipts from Farm Marketings	Exports as Percentage of Cash Receipts
1910......	910	°	°	5,780	15.7%
1911......	996	°	°	5,584	17.8
1912......	1,132	°	°	6,008	18.8
1913......	1,139	°	°	6,238	18.3
1914......	997	598	387	6,036	16.5
1915......	1,608	636	452	6,392	25.2
1916......	1,755	830	578	7,746	22.7
1917......	1,981	1,066	752	10,736	18.5
1918......	2,751	1,144	663	13,467	20.4
1919......	4,093	1,565	1,043	14,538	28.2
1920......	3,443	2,157	1,092	12,600	27.3
1921......	2,114	735	584	8,058	26.2
1922......	1,884	834	773	8,575	22.0
1923......	1,820	1,094	934	9,545	19.1
1924......	2,110	984	927	10,225	20.6
1925......	2,136	1,001	1,339	11,021	19.4
1926......	1,817	973	1,443	10,558	17.2
1927......	1,885	996	1,225	10,733	17.6
1928......	1,863	955	1,145	10,991	17.0
1929......	1,693	1,017	1,201	11,312	15.0
1930......	1,201	701	768	9,055	13.3
1931......	821	447	561	6,381	12.9
1932......	662	296	372	4,748	13.9
1933......	694	366	366	5,332	13.0
1934......	733	413	408	6,357	11.5
1935......	747	589	483	7,120	10.5
1936......	709	695	547	8,391	8.4
1937......	797	868	711	8,864	9.0
1938......	828	477	479	7,723	10.7
1939......	655	526	592	7,872	8.3
1940......	517	544	740	8,382	6.2
1941......	669	786	882	11,111	6.0
1942......	1,179	817	454	15,565	7.6
1943......	2,073	1,059	454	19,620	10.6
1944......	2,096	1,229	589	20,536	10.2
1945......	2,254	1,041	668	21,663	10.4
1946......	3,140	1,196	1,101	24,802	12.7
1947......	3,957	1,406	1,354	29,620	13.4
1948......	3,472	1,618	1,531	30,227	11.5
1949......	3,578	1,440	1,453	27,828	12.9

Year	Exports	Imports Supple-mentary	Comple-mentary	Cash Receipts from Farm Marketings	Exports as Percentage of Cash Receipts
1950......2,873		1,804	2,183	28,512	10.1
1951......4,040		2,319	2,847	32,958	12.3
1952......3,431		1,903	2,615	32,632	10.5
1953......2,847		1,803	2,380	31,126	9.1
1954......3,054		1,558	2,403	29,953	10.2
1955......3,199		1,550	2,421	29,556	10.8
1956......4,170		1,549	2,401	30,564	13.6
1957......4,506		1,695	2,257	29,824	15.1
1958......3,855		1,938	1,943	33,405	11.5
1959......3,955		2,015	2,083	33,512	11.8
1960......4,832		1,919	1,905	34,012	14.2
1961......5,024		1,938	1,753	34,923	14.4
1962......5,034		2,128	1,740	36,077	14.0
1963......5,585		2,292	1,719	36,925	15.1
1964†.....6,100		2,100	2,000	36,600	16.7

Source: Exports and imports, 1930–61, *Foreign Agricultural Trade of the United States*, June 1963; cash receipts, *Farm Income Situation*, Economic Research, USDA.
* Not available.
† Partly estimated.

INDEX

Index

237

Index

Index

Labor, farm, *see* Employment, farm

Land: reshaping of future, 37; values, 65–66, 119–23; inelastic, 116, 162; marginal, 165; under RAD program, 203

Land Bank, federal system, 10

Land-grant colleges, 47–49, 162

Lasers, 37–38

Legislation, farm: legislative process, 139–40; and pressure groups, 139–45; and urban congressmen, 157

Liverpool grain market, 106

Livestock: movement of, 4; of future, 13, 35–36, 38–39; farm areas, 16–17, 19; automatic feeding of, 40; vaccination of, 50

Loans, *see* Credit and loan agencies

McCormick, Cyrus, 47

Maine, 86

Malnutrition, protein-calorie, 34

Manpower Development and Training Program, 204, 207

Margarine, 34, 74

Marginal land, 165

Market, domestic: characteristics of, 72; for food, 72–74, 76, 77–82 *passim*, 85–86, 88; elastic demand, 78–80; for fibers, 82–84, 86; for tobacco, 84–85, 86; and surpluses, 88–89, 107

Market, foreign: and surpluses, 88–89; trade trends, 89–94; commercial potential, 94–100; reappraised, 106–9. *See also* Foreign food aid

Market, free: solution to surpluses, 124–26, 137; economists' views on, 134–35

Marketing, farm: in nineteenth century, 3–4; in twentieth century, 7–9

Marketing costs, 7–8

Marketing margins, 69n

Marketing Order concept, 141

Marketing quota, 127, 165

Masucci, Robert H., 120

Meal, protein, 90–91, 94, 97

Meat: consumption of, 68, 69, 72–76, 77, 90; product elasticity, 78–80; exports of, 90–91; imports of, 94; under Common Market, 97; in free market, 125

Medical services, in rural areas, 185

Microcalorimeter, 36

Migrant workers, 143, 187–88

Milk, 68–69, 101: milk-fat solids, 73, 75; inelastic demand for, 79–80; and controls, 141; surplus of, 148

Minnesota, 65, 190n

Missouri, 65

Morrill Act (*1862*), 9

National Farmers Union, 140, 141, 150

National Planning Association, 157, 164

Nematology, 38

Netherlands, 93, 94

New York, 185

Nonfarm supply sector (producer goods), 5–6, 12, 47, 56, 70–71, 142, 157, 197

Nurses, in rural areas, 185

Nutrition, 34, 67, 72–74, 79

Office of Economic Opportunity, 207, 221

Oils, *see* Fats and oils

Output, *see* Production, farm

Overflow market, *see* Market, foreign

Packers and Stockyards Act (*1921*), 10

Pakistan, 98

Pathogens, 38

"Perfect market," 106–7

Pests, *see* Insects and pests

Peterson, Esther, 145

Photography, and farms of future, 33

Phytochrome, 34

Plant Industry, Bureau of, 49

Plant pathology, 48

Plant sports, 53

Plants: of future, 33–34, 38; and research, 53–54, 62, 128

Population, farm, 29, 70, 153, 156

Population growth: and farm output, 27–28, 89, 110–11; and demand for food, 77, 79, 81, 85; and demand for fibers, 83

Pork, 77, 78, 79, 165

Potatoes, 72–76 *passim*, 79, 85–86, 141

Poultry, 13, 73, 75, 79, 91, 165: broilers, 12, 41, 125, 141

Poverty, rural: definition of category, 18, 178–79, 183–84; magnitude of problem, 179–84; characteristics of, 184–88; causes of, 188–93

Programs to combat: in Great Depression, 194–96; in *1940*'s and early *1950*'s, 196–99; under Eisenhower, 199–202; under Kennedy, 202–7; Economic Opportunity Act of *1964*, 207–11; reappraisal of, 211–15

Future program needs: education and training, 218–21; job opportunities, 221–24; special programs, 224–25

President's Committee on Consumer Interests, 145

Index

102, 103, 105, 148, 159, 170–71; needs of, 108–9
Underemployment, rural, 161–62, 177–83 *passim*, 188–92, 198–205, 212
United Arab Republic, 93
United Kingdom, 68, 82, 94
USSR, 68, 91, 94, 99, 100
U.S. Congress, 94, 96, 128, 139, 141, 142, 145, 149–57 *passim*, 167, 195, 197, 201, 205
U.S. Department of Agriculture: Extension Service, 9, 32, 49–50, 52, 200, 203; contribution to agricultural advances, 9–10, 51; early years, 47–49; reorganization of, 49; and poverty programs, 80–81, 193, 211, 212, 213, 214; and farm legislation, 139–40; on desirable levels of reserve stocks, 169–70; Rural Development Program and RAD, 200–6; and *passim*
U.S. Department of Commerce, 204, 205, 206, 207
U.S. Department of Health, Education, and Welfare, 144, 204
U.S. Department of Interior, 144, 205
U.S. Department of Labor, 201, 204, 207
U.S. Supreme Court, 153
University of Chicago, 164

Vaccination, 50
Vegetable oils, *see* Fats and oils
Vegetables, 72, 73, 75
Veterinary therapeutics, experimental, 38

Viruses, 38
Vocational training, 163, 201, 218, 219

Wage rates, 68, 69n, 189
Water: management of, 32–33, 37; desalting of, 37; problem of, 160; RAD program, 204
Weather: of future, 37, 41; and decreased output, 58; and production control, 127; and poverty, 178
Wheat, 16, 34: size, investment, returns of farms, 19; reserve stocks of, 30, 67, 90, 170; of future, 34; yields, 59–60; consumption of, 72; exports of, 90–97 *passim*; and foreign aid, 101, 148; in free market, 125; controls on, 128, 141, 151–52
Wilson, James ("Tama Jim"), 49
Wool, 83–84
Work-Study Programs (*1964*), 207, 208, 220
Work-Training Programs (*1964*), 207, 208, 220
Workers, farm, *see* Employment, farm
World market, *see* Market, foreign
World War I, 27, 28, 49, 106
World War II, 28, 50, 76, 77, 78, 83, 98, 107, 113, 189, 194, 195, 196, 205, 211

Yields: per-acre statistics, 59–60; increased, 61–62, 113; control programs, 119, 126–29, 148
Youth programs, rural (EOA), 209–10, 214